SALLY SCHWEIZER has enjoyed working with the parents of the children in her care, sharing their joys and sorrows. As a state-trained teacher, she has taught mostly under-sevens for thirty years, been a teacher-trainer for the last twenty of those years and an advisor for the last six. Her principal concern regards children's loss of childhood. Having written many articles related to this theme, this is her first book for parents, teachers and carers. Music has been central to her life, along with spending much time outside, being a keen gardener and conservationist in adulthood. She has discovered that music and the outdoors have a healing and wonderful educational quality. Languages, handwork and the arts are her other loves. Sally also enjoys being a mother to her four children and a wife to her husband.

Well, I Wonder

Childhood in the Modern World

A Handbook for Parents, Carers and Teachers

Sally Schweizer

Sophia Books

For Christian, Lars, Mark, Sven and Nina

Sophia Books
Hillside House, The Square
Forest Row, East Sussex
RH18 5ES

Published by Sophia Books 2006
An imprint of Rudolf Steiner Press

A catalogue record for this book is available from the British Library

ISBN-10: 1 85584 124 X
ISBN-13: 9 78185584 124 6

Cover by Andrew Morgan Design featuring a photograph by Jean McKeague.
Author photo by Lars Lange
Typeset by DP Photosetting, Neath, West Glamorgan
Printed and bound in Great Britain by Cromwell Press Limited,
Trowbridge, Wiltshire

CONTENTS

ACKNOWLEDGEMENTS

My warm thanks to all the parents, students, colleagues and other friends who heartened me in my writing. Also most especially to Sevak Gulbekian who had the courage to invite me to write; to my husband Christian for typing and, as well as my children, Mark, Nina, Sven and Lars Lange, for listening and giving sensitive advice; to my sister Roguey Doyle and to my friends Ann Druitt and Ros Faram for their particular support; to my editors Matthew Barton and Pat Cheney for such wise suggestions; to my students in Ireland who gave me the title, 'Well, I Wonder' because that's what I often say; and last, but by no means least, to all the children, especially my own, from whom I have learnt so much.

My grateful thanks to parents, friends and relations, and also the now adult children themselves, who allowed me to use the photographs they and I took of the children. Many of the photographs were taken by me, but I am very grateful to friends and family for kind permission to use theirs as well. (For full credits, please see over.) There are three photos by parents of which I do not know the authors (pp. 48, 175, 178), but I would be glad to know who they are so that they can be acknowledged in a further edition.

Note: 'Parents' is intended to mean both parents and carers throughout the book.

Most names, some occasions and sometimes the sex have been changed to protect identity.

Most of the anecdotes were experienced by me. For the others I am grateful to friends.

ILLUSTRATION CREDITS

Dieter Hoeltz, p. 174
Jürg Jucker, pp. 58, 210
Jean McKeague, p. 147
Hansjürg Lange, pp. 33, 41, 60, 67, 104, 149, 159, 168, 170
Christian Schweizer, pp. 109 130 131, 173
Eva Schweizer, p. 119
Sebastian Welford, p. 69
Sally Schweizer, all other photos

All line drawings by Marije Rowling

PREFACE

It was the dark-green velvet sofa, the one with the round velvet buttons, the one that gave me a funny sensation under my fingernails. That's why I didn't usually sit on it. But that afternoon I had been left there in sole charge of Judith, just 3 years old, while our mothers were in the garden. I was enjoying myself and, feeling rather grown up at nearly 7, decided that when I really *was* grown up, I'd be a kindergarten teacher.

As a teenager, I wandered through dreams of nursing, ballet, air-hostessing... But when I was 18, my mother brought me down to earth by booking me in for interviews at teacher-training colleges. Helping once a week in a kindergarten in my last year of school certainly hadn't made me suggest teaching to her, because although I enjoyed it, the thought of coping with a bunch of children terrified me. However, I ended up three years later in a London infant school with diverse cultures.

Destiny had other plans for me. Later that year I happened to look at an old Unesco magazine with an article about the *Ecole d'Humanité*, ('School of Mankind'), in Switzerland. Founded by the philosopher Paul Geheeb, its ideas on education corresponded with many of my own. I visited, was offered a teaching post, and worked there for several years before returning to England and State infant education.

My last two years as a pupil at school had been spent in Salem School, Germany, founded by the thinker Kurt Hahn. In teacher training I studied Rousseau, Montessori, Froebel, Macmillan, Isaacs, Pestalozzi, Freud and others. My ideas had become quite diverse by the time my first child was born and I came across Rudolf Steiner's work, which had not been on the agenda at college. His philosophy, 'anthroposophy', is derived from Greek: 'anthropos'—human being, 'sophia'—wisdom. Alongside bringing up my four children (for thirteen years as a lone parent until I remarried), I spent twenty-three years as a Steiner Waldorf kindergarten teacher. For the last twenty years I have also been involved in teacher training, some of this during several trips to Russia. In 2000 I became a part-time advisor with my local education authority. Many happy hours have been spent with groups of teachers, sharing good practice, and discussing how to meet government requirements without stressing the child. Since retirement in 2003 I have been an advisor in the Steiner Waldorf movement, and continue teacher training.

The dialogue between different educationalists goes hand-in-hand with my enduring interest in other cultures and races and their languages. I believe that in our time we need to be willing to understand the inner nature of others more than ever before. This embraces compassion and self-restraint, thinking clearly and independently, with good will towards all, but the times we live in militate against this: materialism, commercialism, racism, nationalism, capitalism, egotism. Our young children are so receptive, so eager. This is where I see our hope for the future.

Children can be wonderful educators. Mine have shown me many a right path without realizing it. We have a supportive relationship, the four among themselves and with me. There are things I would have done otherwise, had I known better. But we learn out of experience. Sometimes parents feel guilty, but even if later regretting it, surely we do what we think is right at the time. Perhaps it even *was* right, who knows? I believe it is good if children can be with their own parents as much as possible; although teachers and friends can be their best helpers, can they replace them? Many children are socially confused today, left with carers when they are very young, and/or living with divided or new families. Having others look after one's children is generally expensive, but may it also be at the expense of the children themselves?

'I always wait until I can put my feet up with a cup of coffee before I open your letters,' said a parent. Another said she was keeping them for her little son when grown up. For as long as I can remember, I wrote to all the parents of my kindergarten when I had something I wanted to share, such as thoughts on a forthcoming festival with arrangements and a song sheet, or some problem. Others covered a description of present activities in the class, or the birth of someone's sibling. It might be an invitation to support a family in trouble (anonymous in the letter of course but people invariably did come to offer), or a request for some other help or guidance. When there was a particular event in the world, which I felt was worthy of reflection because of its effect on the children, I touched on that also. Sometimes I wrote a few tips for parents to take or leave as they wished, arising from comments, observations or difficulties. Occasionally the letter was quite long, but when I apologised I was reassured by many kind parents who said they liked my letters and even filed them. On top of that, people said they didn't mind my writing them by hand, it made them 'more personal'. Sometimes I needed to say something to a particular family, which couldn't be said directly, and was able to present it in a general way in letters or at parents' evenings. The extraordinary thing was that almost invariably the very people I wanted to reach came to me and said, 'What you wrote about... I've been thinking...'. One of the Dads, realizing I did this, called them my 'oblique references'. In frequently thinking about the children, their parents and my colleagues, I believe I receive inspiration from an invisible, spiritual source. I often dream ideas and wake with new courage or thoughts, even mundane things such as a child's apron design.

My task was not to educate parents, but to share in the up-bringing of their children. I wanted people to understand why I acted in a certain way and to hear how they felt too. It wasn't always easy, for there were times when a parent definitely did not agree with me. However, we generally engaged with each other in some way. Someone told me how one of the mothers said, 'Sally and I have had our battles, but I respect her now'. That made me feel good, and grateful! I have much reason to be thankful to parents.

In our school we had the freedom to work as we wanted, but as it arose out of a shared philosophy, colleagues were on similar paths of thought. We all had a termly parents' evening. At my own, we had a drink and something good to eat, did an activity of the children's, such as painting, baking or movement with singing, then sat in a circle for a discussion on some theme or other which I introduced or for which I had invited suggestions beforehand. Also I had a voluntary evening in my own home each term, and sometimes in a parent's house too, round a cosy fire. It all helped us to get to know and support each other, and I often felt humbled, heart-warmed and rewarded as a teacher.

This book is an expression of my work. Many people said, 'You must write a book!' I always laughed it off, saying I was not a writer. I joked to my encouraging, trusting friends that if I ever wrote a book, it would be called 'TOO', out of my concern for the overloading and depletion of childhood: Too much, too little, too early, too late, too often, too seldom, too many, too few. But I never believed I would actually be invited to write a book.

Well, here it is, dear reader. I offer it to you in gratitude for all the good people who have accompanied me in my life.

Sally Schweizer

August 2006

CHAPTER 1

GROWING UP

'I can help myself on my own.'

Hands shot into the air:

'When did you get it?' 'How long have you played it?' 'Where did you buy it?' 'How much did your harp cost?' 'Can you change the notes?' 'How old were you when you started to play it?'

Visiting a primary school, I played my small Celtic harp to 200 children aged between 6 and 9, who had listened and watched with interest. This was their response to the head teacher's invitation for questions.

Then I played to 100 children aged 4 and 5. Their head teacher again invited questions.

Their 'questions' came as follows:

'My Daddy plays the guitar.' 'I can play the pipe.' 'I like your harp.' 'I can play the pipe too.' Two children put up their hands but didn't know what to say.

Another: 'It nearly made me cry'.

A dramatic change in the child after age 6 is evident here: towards what I would call the completion of the first stage of childhood. In the next illustration, we can see further stages.

The conductor waited while the Master of Ceremonies described the music of a children's choral concert. During this time, those between 9 and 12 years old watched the conductor, whilst many of about age 13 upwards were looking at their shoes, nudging their neighbours, and self-consciously glancing round the hall. Those younger ones still needed and wanted to be told what to do, but the older ones, at the beginning of puberty, already had a glimpse of true independence and standing alone in adulthood.

Next, we see a whole range of responses at different ages of childhood.

In a dance performance of *The Magic Flute*, the 4- and 5-year-olds were unco-ordinated and couldn't skip, whilst happily gazing up at the older ones and trying to copy them. The 6- to 10-year-olds knew what to do, could skip and were well balanced, but not yet so much at ease as the children of about 11 and 12 who were beautiful to watch: graceful and light. Those from about 13 and 14 were more awkward. The oldest performers at 18 had a particular kind of awareness, controlled and self-assured.

My experience with children has shown me what seems to be archetypal in humanity. Young children stare, astonished and eager to learn. They are enthusiastic, tender, trusting and loving, simply absorbing it all to recreate it in behaviour, play and outlook, coloured by their own individual selves. In their freshness, they see the world very differently from us.

A young mother said to me, 'Childhood is *so* different today even from when *we* were young'. It is outwardly even more different from when *I* was young, when so much that seems to matter today was irrelevant then. We wore pretty dresses to parties and dancing classes, and otherwise didn't bother about what we wore, happy in an old jumper and skirt. Our annual holiday was two or three weeks of invigorating, uncomplicated fun by the sea or a river in England, in a caravan or cottage. If it rained we still went out, especially to swim in a rough sea. Danger and risks were something we didn't know about, we just trusted implicitly in everyone and everything. A British teacher working in India told me recently, 'Children there are still so open, full of innocence and wonder, real chil-dren, not like in the West where they are little adults grown up too soon'. In Russia I found children also relatively innocent. Despite being so much away from their parents, they led a child-orientated, stable, simple, repeti-tive life in kindergarten.

Nina asked, 'Have we come to misunderstand children (through being in such a hurry); so much so that we have forgotten that children's con-sciousness, their minds, are intrinsically different from ours? Is that why we are trying to train their minds to become 'adult' rather than realizing we need to re-learn our way of thinking in order to understand children?' She added, 'What happened to the quality of young life?' Some parents speak of a daily struggle. Yet family life, despite naturally arising difficulties, generally brings joy and laughter. Parents have much of which to be proud, in coping with the most tricky but rewarding job in the world. After all, they are dealing with young *people*, and having to be psychiatrists, nurses, cooks, bankers, cleaners and teachers rolled into one. And life today can make parenthood unnecessarily complicated.

The coming of a child

My doctor congratulated me on the birth of my third son. I modestly said it was the most natural thing in the world. 'What!' he said, 'it is the greatest miracle of all!'

The pregnant mother may temporarily change: she wants perhaps oranges or fish, can't sleep and feels quite vulnerable. Hormones play a role in this, but it could also be the nature of the child asserting itself. So she needs love and reassurance, especially if it is a first child. She may find herself physically and spiritually well, and experience many intuitive feelings. We know about physical dangers to the unborn, such as poor nutrition, German measles, smoking, alcohol and other drugs. Traumas may also have an effect.

The first three years: walking, speaking and thinking

Steps to walking

There is so much to achieve in life, nowhere more than in the first seven years. The first three are the most dynamic of all. After birth, the head, so much heavier proportionately than the rest, needs support until the child is able to hold it up alone. A higher wisdom drives the child to progress through an evolution of movement, preparing for the particularly human quality of being upright: wriggling, squirming, rolling, sitting, up on all fours, crawling, 'going round the furniture', standing without support, and, finally, walking, at around a year. What a moment! The news spreads fast around family and friends. How astonishing to move oneself about the world—and what an exciting nightmare for parents. 'All action and no sense', said a friend of mine. Yet the child is full of senses, sensitive but not yet sensible.

Gurgles to speaking

At first, wishes and needs are expressed mainly through crying, but babies have the potential to speak every language before devoting themselves to their mother tongue. We hear it in gurgles, coos, squeaks and sounds, delighting one and all. 'Ah' is commonly the first sound, simply opening the mouth, in essence the being of the little child: open-mouthed. Children gaze with astonishment and appreciation into the world and take it all in. Softer parts of speech are heard first: vowels and consonants as in 'mama', 'baba', 'lawa', then the harder consonants as in 'dada', 'papa', later 'k' and 'g'. Desires are articulated: 'ats', 'erts', 'eh', 'a'. First words bring surprise and happiness to every family. Listening to what they hear, they practise unconsciously the unique human quality of speech. Every modulation of sound, phrase and dynamic is rehearsed.

Joseph, 16 months: 'Mama; Mama;—Mama; Mama;—Mama? Mama?—Mameh; Mameh'. Then 'Dehdeh', 'behbeh' and 'ain' as in French 'pain', accompanied by his percussion on a baking tray, allegro con great joy. Children create their own language, whilst naming objects and people. After one word come phrases of two or three, until by 2 years old, sentences are formed. 'Blatalas through the hatch patch, says Pussy', said Sebastian.

Individuals vary. Jeremy spoke in sentences at 18 months but his brother only in sounds until 2 years, at which point he suddenly spoke completely and correctly. Marcus kept his eyes mostly closed after birth for two days. He was still very wet at night when almost 4. Suddenly he didn't want nappies and was dry from then on. His brother Freddy, wide-eyed at birth, could stand but still not walk at 18 months. Suddenly, when lifted down from the high-chair, instead of just crawling he walked away. Holding a hand, Elena walked up the stairs, one foot on each step at 21 months, whereas most children achieve this much later.

'Isn't he dry yet?' 'Isn't she walking yet?' 'Isn't he talking yet?' are so unhelpful. There may come a point at which we become concerned, but the majority do learn to walk and talk, then to think, which is the next human faculty to grow.

Threads of thinking and the first awareness of self

'Do you *like* the airport?' asked an excited young mother of her 2-year-old in the cloakroom. 'What's that?' responded the child, pointing to a dripping pipe. 'That's water. Do you like the airport? Is it exciting?' 'Uh... What's that?' repeated the little one. The child had neither interest in nor understanding of an airport, but a dripping pipe was immediate and tangible.

At 2, most children can run and jump, whilst furthering their linguistic prowess. Around 3 comes the 'Why?' which can drive us to distraction. Knowing that it is a bud of thinking can help not to tear at our patience, and recognizing that it is coupled with a first awareness of self can bring great joy to the parent.

Becoming conscious of a first feeling of separation from surroundings happens at about 3. I am different, I am not the same as everything else, or am I? Where am I? I am my own person, or am I? The big moment comes when the child says 'I' to him or herself, and stops using 'me' or his or her own name. Some children say 'I' correctly as early as 18 months, but it doesn't necessarily mean they are more mature. 'You' also becomes a reality. A grandmother told of her small grandchild who called both grandparents 'Ray'; tricky to know which one was meant. Henry, a little older yet still in a unity of mind at 4: 'Everybody's got a different voice from me.' Tony, 3: 'I can help myself on my own.' *I, myself, my, own.*

> Nina, just 3, was having an argument with Sven, about who was biggest. He: 'I'm 5'. She: 'Well, I'm taller than my neck'. What an amazing picture of self, having arrived at the head, where the thinking has just awoken.

Unity and wonder in young childhood

'I'm a little baby poppy', said Wanda, 3, next to a poppy a head taller than herself. On the whole, children still feel at one with the people and objects around them until the age of 6 or 7. There is lively participation in outer impressions, yet the inner life is only just beginning to manifest.

> 'I had a funny dream last night.'
> 'Did you? Tell me about it.'
> 'But you *know*, because you were in it.'

On awakening from sleep this 5-year-old child was as if still dreaming. She didn't realize that the person she dreamt about couldn't *know* what she was dreaming.

Cathy put her dog puppet on her arm and barked. The children said, 'Are you doing it? Is it real?' But they looked at the dog, not Cathy. She barked again. A boy looked at her mouth: 'Aha, caught you! I saw you. But it was the dog who barked', he said.

I know a little man,	*(child's hand open)*
And he lives just here,	*(touch child's palm)*
And when you touch him,	*(tap palm)*
He goes ... pk!	*(jump finger to behind child's ear)* Anon

Children's humour is straightforward, different from adults': maybe with a twinkle of simple magic.

| Yesterday, upon the stair, |
| I met a man who wasn't there. |
| I met him there again today. |
| Oh, how I wish he'd go away!   Anon |

How do you answer the 4-year-old's: 'How do they put music on to CDs?' 'Go and ask your father', was Grandma's nonplussed answer, but would father be able to explain so the child could understand? Do we need to answer all the children's questions straight away? If they seem too difficult, we might leave a space, and they answer themselves. 'Well, I wonder,' encourages a creative response, fitting many an unanswerable question and leaving the child happy as we wonder at the marvel together. In time, the child will find an academic answer, as yet out of reach. I often told stories of a pyjama case which could come alive. A 6-year-old: 'But how can a pyjama case be alive and talk?' Pause, to my questioning look. 'You mean...? Magic?'

My approach to young children is to create an environment helpful for emulation, rather than actively teaching and interacting. Curiosity, investigation, and incentive grow apace if children are left in peace with their door to mystery, discovery and invention open. The child with time to saunter is watching, listening, experimenting, touching. Stillness gives space for awe.

A teacher showed the 4-year-olds some X-ray slides as part of their project on the body. He was asking questions, thinking the children could relate these cloudy pictures to themselves. One said, 'It looks like the sky.' Another said eagerly, 'Those bones are dead'. They could not relate them to the inside of a human being, under the visible skin of a living person, as such an imaginative concept is yet out of reach.

I was travelling with a 4-year-old to Dolphin Corner. Finding it rather tedious, he wanted to know how far it was. 'It's about as far as home', said his mother. 'How far is that?' 'About twenty minutes.' 'How far is that?' His mother, showing her fingers, said, 'This many minutes'. ' How many is that?' I offered: 'It's a little way and a long way, and a long way and a little way, and then we're there'. The child said, 'Oh, yes,' and was happy with my fairy-tale explanation because he found a connection to it. The main thing was: 'And then we're there'.

Children look up to us for enlightenment: Edwin, 8, watching workmen: 'I'd like to do that when I'm older. I'd like to be a real workman when I'm grown up. Do you have to pay to do that?'

But they may be wiser than us: Lucy, 4: 'I'm really growing up now. My Mummy's grown up now.' I: 'Can I grow up any more?' 'Yes.' 'And Julie?' (Practitioner.)[1] 'Yes.' 'And Daddy?' 'Yes.' 'And Mummy?' 'No, she's already grown up.'

A growing sense of purpose, independence and responsibility

Some children aged between 2 and 7 played with a ball. The older ones were organizing each other and trying to carry out a game. The 4- and 5-year-olds wanted to take part but were getting in the way because they didn't understand what to do. The youngest child ran after the ball wherever it went, not interested in the other children, just the ball. He didn't try to take it: there was no purpose to the running other than an impulse to follow the moving ball. Often very young children run with no sense of where to or what for. Their little wobbly legs just go, with no evident purpose other than the sheer joy of it! When people play with a stick, the dog wags its tail eagerly, bounding after but not necessarily picking it up, hoping you'll throw it again. This kind of eager play, which is goal-less, may be equated with that above. In these animals and children, a lot of seemingly purposeless effort is involved. Parents know not only how fast small children can run, but also that the more you run after them, the more *they* run in joyful imitation. Just the little limbs are engaged—in *action: there* is the impulse, and the *purpose* lies in healthy physical development.

[1] 'Practitioner' means anyone who cares for the young child, as is understood in the United Kingdom today; likewise 'setting' denotes a place of care and education for the young.

Under about 3 years of age, children find a connection to the physical world in play. There may be an *element* of thinking in the activity, such as when the child takes things off a shelf and puts them all back, or pulls things out of a box and replaces them. But there can be tremendous effort and concentration in these games. It is this 'mindless' intent which carries little children about: they don't *know* what they are doing. They just get on with it, running after a ball or tottering downhill, focused on the going. Later, children begin to have a focus in play but, for instance seeing leaves blowing about, they run to catch them without thinking. They may rush to get a rolling ball, oblivious of the on-coming car. In early childhood, children *do*, *act*, and *behave*, without reflection, out of their will.

> *From a letter to parents:*
> *Our early years' work focuses on the healthy growth of the body, and on activity, doing things without thinking, with the will. Towards adulthood this will becomes directed consciously by the self. But little ones don't yet have this capacity. For children who have been exposed to many sensations, choices and experiences, the development of the will is more difficult.*

As individual, creative spirits, we have the freedom to make decisions, to act out of morality or immorality. Young people have a developing sense of freedom and awareness of self. Amongst peers taking drugs, they may be able to say: 'You go ahead but I don't want it'. I overheard a young man of about 17 on his mobile, discussing a forthcoming party. 'But I'm not going to get stoned. I've been cutting down massively lately. It's been driving me nuts'. Surely self-esteem, self-discipline, strong will. Freedom does not necessarily mean to do as we like. It begins with simple independence such as dressing and teeth cleaning, progressing through doing homework without being nagged, to being able to take part in a debate and put forward one's own views which aren't just a garbled version of someone else's. Our inner freedom continues to grow throughout life.

'He's very strong-willed', or 'She has strong feelings', say some people whose children scream and shout. Rather than simply having strong feelings or a strong will, are the children still too immature to be fully in control of them? Local newspapers may show classes of small children who are supposed to look excited or happy. Because telling them to do so doesn't necessarily work (because they can't feel what they are supposed to be doing), the adults may have to shout 'hooray' to get the required reaction. Little children in such photos often look unnatural as a result.

Children like to feel grown-up and important. A dire threat in my kindergarten was: 'You can't come to my birthday party', even if ten months away. But you can help them feel important and needed. Andrew, 6, said, 'But I wanted to be next to Philip' (also 6). I said, 'Yes, and you may be next to Philip later. Just now I need you to look after Jamie (5)'. Rebecca, 6, certainly felt grown-up when she said of her friends, twins aged 5, 'Vicky and Clarissa are so cute, I really love them'.

I believe children should be allowed to be independent in physical needs as young as possible. This requires our patience but is worth it. They can feed themselves, at least partially, when they can sit well. They can dress (upside-down and back-to-front style may need tactful readjusting). They can walk increasing distances and play on their own. Washing themselves, cleaning teeth, wiping themselves after going to the loo, and even washing their hair: all these can be done when they are quite young, so long as they are guided, and form a basis for self-esteem. Faced with a new situation, children may find new independence. Simon, 4, had only just met me for the first time. He was hurt, cried loudly, and called 'Mummy!' When he saw me, he pulled himself upright and said bravely, 'It's ok, it's just here—on my heel'.

It is handy to have a door that opens and closes behind you. Yet there is something to be said for closing a door: a finishing, an ending, a conscious

Daily raking of woodchips back under the swings

action, like pushing the chair in when rising from the table. With independence such as this comes growing responsibility. Children are able to do all kinds of little jobs and tasks in their first years. The best is if such activity is self-propelled. It may arise out of a habit coming from repeated action. By age 7 they should run errands correctly with two or three tasks at a time, be co-operative, reliable, and conscientious.

There was a family of two well-travelled boys, three years apart in age, with inconsistent parents. Even aged 4 and 7 they had to have a parent lie down with them (in the parents' bed), until they fell asleep. How can such a child learn independence? Maybe it arose from insecurity, through often being away from home, and having parents who didn't know their own minds. An inconsistency sometimes exists between holding children back and pushing them. They may still be pushed in buggies yet have 'Harry Potter' or the 'Narnia' books read to them. Some, still breast-fed, watch videos. With stories, games and films beyond their years, what is there left for later? We live in an age of instant gratification; 'Buy now, pay later'. There may be payment later, in egotism, or lack of discipline and conscientiousness. I've met many children partially spoon-fed at mealtimes, whose shoes are put on for them and coats done up after they should do it on their own. Where is the balance? Many children are in pushchairs after they should walk, and if they do walk a little way, they soon say, 'Carry me', because their muscles are so underused through lack of movement that they actually *can't* walk far. This undermines their natural activity, weakening effort and stamina.

Being eager to grow up and be independent, young children find it hard to wait unless it is part of a rhythm they are used to. They need whatever it is *now* because they live in the *present*. They don't remember about yesterday and have little concept of 'this afternoon' until around 6 years old. Jane, 6, started to sew a big puppet: 'I've been waiting two years to do this'. She hadn't actually been waiting, because they'd not done large puppets before, but she now began to have a sense of time. So they have to learn not to interrupt. 'Mummy, Mummy!' from a 5 and-a-half-year-old; Mother, loudly and crossly: 'I'm talking! WHAT DO YOU WANT?' If I was busy or talking, giving my hand to little ones enabled them to wait, even without my looking at them. It meant: 'I'm here for you, I will listen in a moment'.

From 3 to around 5, children grow particularly in the imaginative, play realm, and from 5 years the seeds of sociability germinate. Whilst still mainly egoists, young children are capable of loving acts. I had a weeping child on my knee, and Laura, 5, came to put a red blanket round us both. There was a trio of little friends. Nonnie, loving Jack even more than Richard, followed him everywhere. Once a day Jack was away. Nonnie cried. 'But *I'm* here', said Richard, 6, putting his arms round her.

Come on now, think!

Children can orientate themselves through asking questions, but also want our reassuring engagement. An answer which corresponds to their fairy-tale consciousness may leave them content. 'Why does the wind blow?' 'So he has work to do and can blow the leaves into a pile.' 'Why does the water come out of the tap?' 'So we can wash.' Pumps, reservoirs, condensation and the inner workings of pipes are inconceivable to the young child. 'Why are the trees bending over?' We can offer the child our hair to blow into to see. Answers which don't meet the child's stage of consciousness may lead to more unanswerable questions. Jamie, 4: 'You are full of cells. Everyone is full of cells'. Another child: 'What are they?' Jamie: 'They are little round things, like circles, and you are full of them. My Dad told me'. Understanding such things takes many years. Just as you wouldn't necessarily expect a French person to understand English, so you wouldn't expect a child to understand the language of particles and the like. It takes time to learn a language.

Grandma asked her 18-month-old granddaughter, 'How does the pussy cat go?' Melanie stared blankly. 'Go on, how does the pussy go?' Melanie banged her arms up and down: 'No, no, no, no, no!' Granny: 'Miaow!' Melanie copied: 'Miaow!' Granny: 'How does the cow go?' Melanie banged again with 'No, no, no, no, no, no!' 'You know how the cow goes!' Melanie banged her arms hard and shook her head violently to left and right several times. Granny: 'Moo-oo'. Melanie copied once more: 'Moo-oo'. She really needed Granny's example.

Young children may twist round on a chair, arms and all, and in turning back sweep everything floorwards. Their body is used as one whole. Children think in doing; ideas are simple, physical, visible, attainable. Sidney, 4, walked around outside without shoes, showing me her new tights. I said: 'You'll get holes in them'. Immediately she looked under both feet. 'You'll hurt your poor tights.' 'No', she said, 'I've got strong feet'. The tights were all one with the feet.

My kindergarten group used to walk to my house. We waited at the empty road for all the imaginary traffic to pass: the bus—'grrr grrr grrr'; jumbo jet—'whoooosh'; bicycle—'ting-a-ling-a-ling'; sports car—'brrrwhoosh', we said. This, exciting and age-appropriate, stopped the children at the side of the road to see if it was safe to cross. The thinking lay in the activity, not separated from the action; it was 'automatic'.

I showed them my son's paper birds over our stairs. An eagle with a fish had a metre's wingspan. I said it had taken ages, cutting and sticking all that paper. Every comment the children made was connected to their actual experience, not to the words I had spoken. I let them touch them. 'Are they dead?' 'Are they alive?' 'They look dead.' 'Is that eagle old?' 'That fish looks alive', and so on. They knew something was up, but couldn't yet place it.

Basil, 5 and a quarter, knocked Sam's face. I asked whether he knew what he'd done, and rubbed my face in the place where Sam's hurt. He gazed at me, and wonderingly rubbed his face as well, pure body-thinking.

I had struggled to learn a few words of Hebrew for a child of 4, new from Israel. She was in a crèche one afternoon, then asked her mother, 'Why doesn't Mary [the leader] understand me?' 'But Sally doesn't either', said her mother. 'Yes she does, she understands everything.' My body language had been her dictionary, not my miserable vocabulary.

Sandy, 4, having his grandmother's death explained to him, said they must need a lot of sticky tape to keep all those souls in the sky.

Tureg, 4 and a half: 'My next door neighbour's car just got stolen—the red one—all of it!'

These delightful remarks show the child working things out with new thinking ability. Is it detrimental to try to force it, akin to opening a flower bud to see what is inside before the flower is ready to open? 'Come on now, think!' is an encouragement I have often heard. The child doesn't even know what thinking is. Robert, 4, was listening to his parents discussing news reports about television destroying concentration and diminishing thinking capacity below the age of 2. 'Well, that's all right, because I don't have to think any more today.'

Andy, 4, his imagination evolving, was talking to the rocking chair as though it were alive. Jacob, 6 and a half, beginning to think out images in the mind, was frustrated. 'I'm trying to tell him the rocking-chair can't talk. Rocking chairs *can't* talk, can they?' And even here you can see his slight uncertainty in the experience: he wasn't *definite* about the talking—hence the question. While imaginative concepts are slowly forming, experience is still foremost. Giving the child academic tasks in the guise of play is working, I feel, with something unripe. I think many children are required to use their intellectual capacity before they are truly receptive and ready. Those who are allowed to live in wonder and to develop slowly in early childhood may be more able to make livelier and clearer concepts in later life. Concepts now should be concrete, related to action and movement rather than abstractions. Alan, 4, was 'washing' the rocking-horse. Susan, 6, wanted a ride. Alan: 'You can't ride it yet, it's still wet'. Susan wonderingly touched the horse: 'It doesn't *feel* wet'. One could observe how she was struggling with the thought of a dryness being wet, to combine her experience with what she knew must be.

A teacher wanted her 4-year-olds to decide how the outlined happy and sad faces were feeling, then to check out each other's and their own feelings. Most children had little clue and only parroted the teacher. I thought: lovely teacher, lovely children, lovely waste of time. Young children sit still for more than short periods only unnaturally, and are prepared neither for much thought nor expression of emotions. Government guidelines suggest early-years teachers foster children's thinking and feeling; yet at this age these are, to me, slumbering. Children want to please, so they struggle, and thereby, I think, pull energies away from their bodily growth into their mind. It is also difficult to impart knowledge to young children when they are sitting still. At a different school, the children spent half the morning sitting on the floor doing group work. Otherwise they were sitting at tables, having short sessions of guided role-play, or playing in the playground. In the latter, many were tearing around letting off steam and knocking into one another. Their natural energy had been laced up for ages on end, preventing them from practising spatial awareness properly. Many of today's children sit a lot at nursery and school, whilst being required to use unripe cognitive and affective faculties. They ride in the car, sit in front of the TV and aren't allowed enough free rein of their naturally dancing limbs.

A group of 6-year-olds in sunhats were devising a game outside. Typical of this age, they organized each other, making rules and choosing a leader to 'vote'. Jasper said, 'It depends who's got the coolest hat on who's going to vote'. They looked uncertain. Eventually I offered, 'I should think Jamie's got the coolest hat on because it keeps the sun off his neck'. Jamie, deep in contemplation, felt the back of his neck for two minutes, while the others watched in awe, their minds coming to grips with a different concept of 'coolest'.

Around 6 or 7 years, children have a growth spurt; hunger and fatigue are common. The baby face becomes more individually formed, knuckles, knees, waists and the curved back appear. Gaps and big teeth are charming in the still-little mouth. The body takes on adult proportions as limbs lengthen. Hand-to-eye co-ordination begins to refine itself enough for writing and reading. Understanding matures to a new cognition not bound to what is there all around. From birth to 7 children are self-motivated through example, and although imitation doesn't die away till around 9, after 7 they are ready to be motivated from outside by leadership. They can discern themselves as individual human beings, and are aware of purpose and direction. They hop, skip, and stand on one leg (even with eyes shut), and walk along a beam without falling off, balancing from an inner orientation. Their new mental ability enables them to create symmetry, such as a butterfly, and write and read. Janie, 4 and a half, of the building of a block of flats, 'They are getting on with those like anything. They'll be finished by Friday'. But by 6 or 7, children have a sense of space and time and don't need to rely on outer events to make, albeit primitive, concepts.

Memory and co-ordination

A girl of about 2 stood staring, staring, staring at someone playing the harp in the town square. For about ten minutes she seemed motionless while she absorbed sight and sound, until her father stopped chatting and picked her up to take her away. She screamed. He put her down again and she resumed her intense, silent and outwardly motionless activity. But Dad wanted to go and soon picked her up again, to anguished screams. This event found its way into the child's active bodily memory. How important it is to leave children undisturbed where possible, to give them time to learn for themselves.

> At a Christening, the vicar spoke to some 4- and 5-year-olds. 'What do we use water for?' he asked them. The children stared. 'Come on, you know what we use water for!' Silence. 'Don't we use it for washing?' prompted a mother. 'Oh yes, and we have a bath in it!' said a child. 'And what else?' asked the vicar. Blank. 'What about drinking?' he asked. 'My mummy makes orange squash!' They needed something to remind them about water, for they were unable to imagine it apart from what they could actually see. Yet a couple of years later these children would be able to transfer water in their minds from the font to other situations, and so remember what it was used for.

Sometimes parents said to me, 'My child doesn't tell me anything about kindergarten!' If you give a trigger, for example, 'Didn't you bake?' children may suddenly remember that. Memory exists very early, before 3, but in a quite different form, as *recognition*. Latin *recognoscere*, is to 're-know'. The child recognizes faces, people, things. *Habits* may appear to be memory, but are an unconscious remembering. A 'member' is a limb. Therefore to re-member means to return to the body. Lars, 10 months, had a hard-backed animal book. Mum washed the spinach, found a spider in it and showed it to him. He crawled and fetched the book, clonk, clonk, clonk, and offered the spider illustration to her. Even so young, memory is present but in purely experiential form. 'Where did you put your shoes?' to a little child may not bring results, whereas showing the shoe-shelf might. Not having seen Granny for several months, the 5-year-old asked on the phone, 'What do you look like, Granny?' He recognized the voice but could not place her without the visual experience. When asked whether his mother, who was frequently absent, had prepared his packed lunch today, Andy, 6, said: 'No, Jason, but I know what she looks like'.

> Ruth's mother rang to see if she was all right with the baby-sitter. 'Is that Mummy or Daddy?' asked Ruth, 4, stimulated by the voice but still in a unified world.

When co-ordination and spatial orientation matures around 7, a new phenomenon appears: a memory which can now think for itself independently of a reminder. Although thinking is still stimulated by movement and experience, children can remember without a trigger. Anna, almost 7, told me about the napkin rings, which now lived in a basket. 'I can't even remember how we used to put them in front of our places', i.e. being conscious of memory she actually *could* remember.

> Chelsea, 6 (with no access to computers), ran outside in socks. I called her: 'Why did you go out without your shoes?' 'I forgot. My memory wasn't in yet. I forgot to put it in.'

Judgement

> 'He's deciding whether he wants to come', the mother of Manuel, 3 and three quarters, told the kindergarten children who went to ask her anxiously if he was going to come in.

'Would you like to come to this kindergarten?' was a question often asked by the parents at interview. The child has no idea.

'We're letting him decide' (about joining kindergarten, at 4 years old).

'Would you like jam or cheese on your bread?' Such innocent-seeming choice questions draw the child into discriminating between one thing and another, an intellectual capacity that only awakens naturally in adolescence. 'Do you want to put your red trousers on, or your blue ones, or the ones with the tortoises on?' How much easier, and security building, when we say, 'You may put your blue trousers on today'. People say, 'Oh, but she likes to choose'. That may be true, but perhaps because the child is used to choosing. 'Shall we go to Tooley's Theme park or Pinkey's Zoo?' When exposed to much choice, children may lose their ability for awe, becoming judgemental and conceited. If we adults are filled with awe and wonder, we may actually take a backward step, maybe even in silence, to gaze at or listen to whatever has held our rapture. Young children, naturally full of such awe and wonder, dream through the day in their own often silent 'fairytale' world. Yet they may be drawn out of it when being required to use their unripe intellect for choosing, discriminating. Is there not a subtle difference between children selecting what they want to play with out of their different awareness and dreamy volition, and when they have to make a conscious decision? The child has to think when asked: 'Do I want this jam, or that one? Or ham? Actually I want both and all of them.' In a cold winter wind: 'Do you want your bobble hat or the one over the ears?' . . . 'I'll have my baseball cap, I don't want those!' 'This dress looks pretty on you. But maybe that one is nicer. Which do you want?' Mother lifts the baby out of the pushchair at the end of a walk with the parent and child group, and her tired 2-year-old climbs in. She asks, 'Do you want to stay in the pushchair and have a nap or do you want to go inside now?' Of course the child wants to sleep but also to stay with Mummy. 'Would a pizza be better or a salad?' The eyes of a mother lit up when she realized why her 4-year-old did not ever seem to want to choose and became grumpy: she saw that it was actually beyond him. 'I always had to decide for him as he wouldn't, but now I will do it anyway!'

A parent used to tell her child he was beautiful and perfect. He couldn't live up to these expectations, worried about his clothes and looks, talked in a tight squeaky voice and cried easily. Later she realized she was overburdening him through her praising and devoted love. In praising we set one standard against another, which doesn't mean you should never do it. I tended to be sparing with praise. 'What a beautiful picture', leaves the child uncertain if we don't say it next time. You can smile with appreciation and joy and say: 'How the beautiful colours are playing in your picture!', or 'You *have* worked hard'. This takes the emphasis off the child's ability and into the nature of the colours or the effort—a subtle difference. If a child wanted me to look at his new shirt or her new dress, I might say, 'That's special'. I didn't want to over-emphasize the children's clothes because this can lead, especially nowadays, to competition, obsession with clothes, peer pressure, and helpless com-mercial targets. All that children really want is to know that you love them and appreciate their help and work. Sometimes I clasped my hands to my chest or jumped up and down for joy. I did this also when we had all achieved something together: tidied up properly, eaten with one hand or without any elbows on the table (because this is better for posture and helps avoid slovenly eating) or all put our hats on. The children loved that. If a child had done something particularly special, I sometimes gave them a piggy-back to everyone's great amusement.

Cross-curricular, holistic learning, integrating all subjects within one, educates children from the whole rather than the parts, making for a living thinking, feeling, and acting. Literacy and numeracy teaching is successful when the activities are interrelated with an element of all subjects, especially from daily living. When given good models and examples to follow, children lap up knowledge and expertise, assimilating and accommodating it with no effort, each skill building on to and slotting into the previous one. In 'The Shepherd Boy's Flute'[1] by Dan Lindholm, the shepherd boy loses notes, one by one. Hearing this repetitive story, repeated day by day for a week, several children counted the notes on their fingers out of their own initiative. The littlest ones copied the older, incorrectly, but setting a pattern for later mathematical skills.

Moving from the beginning or first stage, to the centre or second stage of childhood

The children in my kindergarten stayed until they were 6 or just 7 years old, after which they went into the school to which we belonged. In this way they could complete what I see as the first stage of childhood, before being

---

[1] In *How the Stars Were Born* (Henry Goulden, 1975).

ready for slightly more formal education, which included arithmetic, writing and reading, but in a pictorial rather than an abstract way. It was exciting to see changes coming about in the children, indicating a new maturity and eagerness.

Six-year-old Jane's mother, whose father had recently died said, 'I wanted to keep my father's pictures.' 'No, your mother's! You haven't got a father', said Jane. But Jonathan, 7, said, 'My grandmother is my Daddy's mother, isn't that funny?' Such an observation signals the phase when children's memory changes from visible to imaginative pictures, which Jane had not yet reached. This brings its own demands and a child may well react by becoming temporarily listless and bored, preferring to be told what to do. Logic now comes as a new cognitive faculty; if so and so . . . then such and such . . . because . . . . This logical thinking leads on to a sense of justice and fairness.

> Joseph, 5.8 years: 'I'm older than you.'
> Jude, 5.6 years: ' I'm glad I'm younger, because you'll die first, so I'll have longer to play.'

The child makes suggestions and offers ideas. 'We could do the sun like this', said Aubrey, 6, offering a new movement for our poem.

For a play I wrote:

> 'But ah, the secret, what a tale we've to spin,
> Tied a sponge round his neck, very well in,
> Soaked the wine up, drank not a drop,
> Dribbled it down all over his chin.'

'Dribbled it down all over his frock', suggested Leonie, 6 and a half. So that's what we then said; after all, it rhymed just as well.

'Let's do that lorry we made yesterday again', said Joseph, 6. Play has purpose through memory; the child thinks out what he is going to do. Before this age, the kindergarten children generally tied our cords and ropes haphazardly, but now they became knotted together in a thoughtful, logical way. Bridges and ball tunnels, requiring imaginative cognition, took shape in the sandpit. The concentration span lengthens, and work can be carried out independently. After 7, friendships are more stable, which also has to do with memory. The 6- to 7-year-old asks questions such as, 'When do you think the end of your life is going to be?' Children are not satisfied with fairy-tale answers any more. They don't want scientific abstractions, but something in between that they can relate to directly. 'I can't tell; but I hope not for a long time yet, because I have a lot of work to do before I'm ready', was an answer that satisfied him.

Children under 7 seem to be all physical: food, movement, play, sleep. As a certain independence from the parents sets in after this age and feelings become more prominent, they may be weepy, feel bruised and hurt. This is the beginning of predominantly emotional development, continuing until puberty. Social life becomes important. Parents may have a hard time keeping up with their children wanting to be with friends and to stay the night. Caring, sharing, and taking turns comes naturally. Hiding, having secrets, making surprises, whispering and giggling appear after about the sixth year. Children of this age eagerly seek leadership and are able to exercise self-control if their will has been nourished. Hyperactivity and aggression are unlikely if the child has developed inner equilibrium. Imaginative, rather than the later academic, thinking prevails. Work and experience are bound up with developing feelings: sad, happy, exciting, moral, and adventurous stories, poetry, pictures and happenings. They want colour, music, rhythm, beauty, clay modelling, and to decorate the meal table, their books, games and drawings. Crafts and handwork are popular; they have become dextrous and expressive, especially if they have exercised their hands in the first years. At about 9 and previously having been full of the joys of spring, children may become cross, obstinate, unhappy or uncooperative for a while; yet with newly found independence, questions and fears arise as another step in self-consciousness appears. All my own children discovered at 9 that Father Christmas was played by us. Then they just enjoyed becoming Father Christmas's (our) helpers.

The third stage, adolescence: head and intellect

Adolescent life is occupied with questions, rebellion, friendships, temptations and debates. What is truth? Rights, freedom, biography, oppression, life, are constant themes of discussion. This phase opens up scientific experimentation, evaluation and judgement, all absent from earlier phases. Concepts become abstract, academic, rather than pictorial. 'Concept' is from Latin *concipere*, 'to conceive or take into oneself'. After 14 the young are becoming independent and conscious thinkers, and learn what duty and service to others means. Adolescents need our companionship, kindness, humour, strength and compassion. We can perhaps remember and identify with those challenging years.

By adulthood a young person will hopefully develop strength of purpose, be sensitive to the environment and others, and able to think clearly, with a lively consciousness of self. I believe that if a feeling of gratitude has been kindled between birth and 7, and love and morality between 7 and 14, then from 14 to 21 the fire of idealism may grow with an attitude of responsibility.

We can find support in talking with friends and teachers, for as parents we can be quite subjective. I recognized that my children could talk to others too. A young man said to me, 'People can have an influence over children who aren't their own, for instance other parents, grandparents, neighbours. Older children may listen to others more than they listen to their parents.'

It is not within the scope of this book to discuss childhood after the earliest years, but in accompanying young children one keeps their future in mind. (See Further Reading, p. 213, for suggested reading on teenagers).

Challenges for adults

There are many aspects of modern life which are absolutely fascinating, spell-binding. The whole of this book fits into a tiny part of a computer memory stick the size of my thumb. My mind boggles at such extraordinariness. The speed at which my computer works with several billion 'flops' per second is *wonderful* and to me totally incomprehensible.

Surely one hallmark of life today is speed, along with instant gratification, bafflement, and extraordinary and wondrous events. Life often proceeds at a frantic pace for many.

A young man on the train held his arm out in a semi-embrace with a charming smile to let an elderly couple pass. Such common courtesies are now the exception. Changes now are rapid and dynamic. There is an epidemic of Attention Deficit Hyperactivity Disorder (ADHD) especially in boys, and tens of thousands are on Ritalin, a drug taken for it. Overweight or fidgety children and antisocial, anarchic behaviour are on the rise. Life today is not easy for parents who usually have their own pressures and worries to cope with anyway. Relaxation may mean a session on a bike at the gym after a day on a chair, rather than a good walk, but tension and stress are widespread. People are emotionally drained because of an overload of sensations, which they can't stomach or absorb, so switch off because they have emotional indigestion. 'I often switch off the news because I can't take it any more. I think it de-sensitizes people', Roberta said to me.

The loss of attractive, friendly, small shops and homogenizing of large ones has led to dull, dead shopping environments, which many children experience. Village schools are disappearing, meaning long bus-trips for quite small children to larger schools. Globally, children are suffering in various ways, but many young parents are attempting to do something about it. A large number of them are seeking something different. Some of those brought up on a diet of Coke and fish fingers want to give their children music lessons and whole foods, and to find a balance between poverty and the misery which affluence can bring. Many adults are very happy, everything goes swimmingly, while others seek a new way forward.

How can parents and educationalists give each other mutual support to enable children to grow into socially conscious, responsible, happy, active and thoughtful adults? Does the modern trend of teaching the 'three Rs' earlier and earlier lead to greater intellectual prowess? Many teachers and parents don't believe so. Recent studies have shown that children who start formal schooling later, for instance in Scandinavia and particularly Finland, are at an advantage. A Unesco survey in 2004 found that children in Finland had the highest reading standards in the world at 11 years old, yet they start school at 7 years. What is the difference between knowledge and wisdom? Can one teach wisdom? A young man said to me he thought you should forget what you have learnt in order to work it out for yourself. 'You should be taught not facts but how to learn, so when you go out into the world, you can 'read' and understand new situations, outside anything you have learnt before. Then, being open to learning from the new you won't be scared of them but embrace them, controlling them from inside yourself. Animals run away if scared, but we can stand above it.'

How can one find the space and courage to manage, not least as it all filters down to the children, who are so eager, astonished and open? Children need time to fulfil each of their developmental stages. Let kids be kids. Life isn't a race. They hitchhike their way with us, asking for conversation as we accompany them on their journey.

CHAPTER 2

REFLECTIONS

'Children need little change—infrequently.'

Reflection through imitation

The kindergarten playground in Estonia was covered with snow. The hundred children were mostly standing around like their teachers. I, visiting, felt chilly, so I shuffled along in a rhythmic way, chanting 'shoo, shoo'. One by one they came to 'shoo, shoo' behind me. More than a hundred shooing people, adults too, were shuffling through the snow all in a line.

When I shuffled through the snow, I could in a sense see the children as a mirror of myself. You may hear parents' voices mirrored in their adult children on the phone, and think them to be a parent.

> What is this phenomenon of copying—this reflection of the environment we see so clearly in the young child? Latin, *reflectere*: 'to cast back'. This is the most important aspect of my approach to early childhood education. Children learn about the world around them by absorbing it profoundly, becoming it, reflecting it.

Mirrors, interesting for young children, are reflecting, self-revealing. The story of Snow White shows this. Yet are they ready to see themselves as separate rather than unified with their environment? (As in 'I am a little baby poppy'.) Young children are mimics of the world, one unified whole. If made self-conscious, they are drawn outside this one-ness, peeping into a future stage of life for which they are not yet ripe. Of course young children see mirrors! However, could one wait till this natural, early lack of self-consciousness recedes of its own accord rather than encouraging their use? A girl of about 8 tried out different lipsticks before a pharmacy mirror. 'I think this one looks quite nice, don't you?' 'Yes, dear.' They were obviously caring parents. Yet why lead her into adolescence already?

Young children often don't realize that reflections or photos of themselves *are* such unless told, because of their unified consciousness. In kindergarten, the children knew that if I had a camera, I wouldn't take pictures if they were looking, so they largely ignored me. Posing doesn't produce natural pictures, but it was also to protect their unselfconsciousness that I did it this way. A few children took on caricatured expressions, even running in front of the camera, 'So you can get a good shot'. Those children typically weren't easy to handle; photography and mirrors were important ingredients of their self-awareness. Parents laughingly commented that their children wouldn't look at the camera any more. Photography and mirrors wake children up to the fact that they are different from everything else, which belongs to the next part of childhood.

> Charlie's aunt and uncle were over from Australia. Naturally they wanted photos of the family but Charlie didn't seem to be co-operating. 'Look this way, Charlie! No, over here. This way. Arms down. Now smile! Smile!' But the little 4-year-old, not understanding, and feeling uncomfortable in the limelight, shrank into himself and folded his arms over his head.

Change and sameness

Parents know how young children resist change. They may shout 'Yeah!' when some excitement is suggested. Yet they may not enjoy it, or, simply copying their experiences, be out of themselves. Change disrupts them; they like their lives to be as secure as possible, wanting the same, the same, the same and the same again. An educational psychologist friend said, 'Children need little change—infrequently'. Martin very happily heard his parents sing the same goodnight song from birth to 6 years old.

> As a student taking someone's infant class, the children would ask me when the teacher was coming back. Much later I realized it was just because the children disliked the disruption, not that they disliked me. Changes are like little shocks, jolting them out of their reverie-like consciousness, waking them into a snippet of premature adulthood.

Travel may involve change. Some children are unhappy or become ill. Even if a favourite soft toy goes too, it is difficult to make the sameness that children crave. However, it is essential for some families to travel, and the solidarity of a stable and secure background will ensure the minimum of disruption, so the upset may be minimal. We took our children to Switzerland every two years to see the family. They seemed to take it in their stride, for which we were thankful.

Being comfortable with sameness, children become aware through difference. Adults in some ways are the same. Do you automatically think when ironing: which bit of the shirt first? Do you think how to sign your name? What if changing it on marriage? We have to push our fingers to write the new year number. This jogging of the muscle or bodily memory requires conscious effort.

I had dolls from other cultures in my group, but it seemed that although they may have noticed them, none of the children, even those with a different skin, were affected by the variations. They were just dolls, to be cuddled and tucked up, fed and taken for a walk, to be remonstrated with and loved. Is it only when we make young children aware of differences between cultures and races that they become conscious of them? Later on they certainly learn about cultural differences, when they see themselves as no longer an entity with their surroundings. Young children, all-embracing, are universal with everything. They show us love of diversity. Through them we can see a way through the horrors that racism brings.

> A black mother told me that her son, aged 7, suddenly announced, 'I'm not white!' Brought up in a reverent, respectful family, he had not noticed his colour until he slipped into a separated consciousness.

Images

Mother waited for her prescription, with her struggling and wriggling boy of about 2 and a half years on her knee. On leaving, she said, 'Come on, monster!' What picture will the child gain of himself?

If we quarrel with our partner but speak in a calm voice, the children pick up our anger because they absorb the unseen as well as the seen, the heard as well as the unheard. Children absorb and recreate the way we speak, move, act, and *are*. What do we want them to imitate? So many influences mould them. Sometimes we may need to find the courage to put our thoughts on our children's well-being before the opinions of others, because we know that our young children are defenceless.

Imitation may be immediate like Melanie's 'Miaow' and 'Moo-oo', and the following:

In the supermarket a mother pushed the trolley. '*Will* you go in front of me!' Her son, about 3, shook his head. 'Go *now!*' she shouted. He pointed to her saying, '*You* go'.

It may be time-delayed:

Jack, 5 and a quarter, came to kindergarten quite aggressive one morning. Nothing helped. I put him on my knee in a corner of the room.

'What's the trouble, Jack?' I found it helpful to have a little conversation with a child. Devoting just a few minutes in a caring atmosphere in peace and quiet was so soothing. He sank into my lap.

'Nothing', he replied.

'I wonder why you hurt Joseph. Did he hurt you?' He shook his head.

'Did someone else hurt you?' Nod. (I knew he was bullied by two other children near home.)

'I wonder who that was.' (I never wanted to pry but merely see if I could help.) 'Mummy.'

'I see.' Pause.

'What happened?' 'I was slow.'

'Oh.' 'Mummy was cross because we didn't hurry up and get ready.'

'What did she say?' 'Hurry up and get dressed.'

'I wonder why you didn't.' 'I didn't want to.'

'How can we help Mummy?' 'Get dressed!'

'Yes, that would be good', I said. 'Maybe you could help lay the table too?' 'Maybe.'

'Oh, good; then everything will be all right. You can always tell me if you are cross; I won't mind. Maybe we can help each other. You can just pull my sleeve and then I'll know.'

Jack felt he had a confidante, which gave him security. He was calm after that. His mother, who didn't have an easy life and with whom I had a good relationship, had an invisible confidante too.

When at about 7 years old children are more ready to stand on their own feet, imitation doesn't stop suddenly; there is a transition period as they copy their surroundings less, until imitating dies away at the next step in self-consciousness around 9 years.

Rory, 8, was turning a roller-type hair-curler round. Suddenly he discovered its purpose. 'Oh, I know, it's a birdcage.' He was still to some degree a part of his whole surroundings.

Children see who doesn't wipe their feet, who puts their feet on train seats or crosses the pedestrian crossing on red. 'That's not *allowed*!' It hurts their innate sense of morality. Supermarkets declare: 'Just grab and go!' What a picture! When does the child begin to copy such influences? How long does the child's innate reverence and love hold sway, or at what point will the child also cross on red?

'Have a cheery disposition', says Mary Poppins. Children 'ask' for goodness around them, cheerfulness, courage and kindness, a sense of right and wrong. Adults who enjoy what they do are special for children to copy. Yet how can we enjoy ourselves when we are dog-tired and everything seems to be going wrong? Or if our partner or spouse has left us? Nevertheless, within each difficulty there is a small miracle for us to recognize. Therein lies the en-*joy*-ment, for our own sake and for our children to imitate. In picking up the pieces, knowing we are there for the children may give us strength.

During a difficult time, my children and I came home to find the windowsills adorned with glorious flower-filled window-boxes, left in secret by dear friends. Tiny things are little miracles, such as the children hanging up the towel or putting their shoes away, even if they happen every day, and can make us so grateful.

An Australian woman we met in a certain country remarked on the muzzles dogs should have there. 'Dogs seem friendly here,' she said. 'They only get horrid if you're horrid to them. It's like a child. If you get angry with it, it will be angry with you.' Argue at the table, and the mealtime sooner or later will be filled with arguments or fear. Be sharp with children, they will be sharp back. Hold out a hand, it will be taken in response. Start tidying up playthings silently, the children may come along too, driven helplessly by their unconscious force of being as though within the other person. Care given to putting shoes away properly is an image for children of caring generally. They want to look after the world into which they've just come, to feel everything is in order. Placing a mat under a vase or a lamp shows trouble taken, which the child absorbs. Life feels good when shoes are changed for different purposes, when everything has its place, when Mum or Dad has cooked a nice meal and presented it prettily, rather than slopping it on to the plates. This feel-good factor is very strengthening. All such phenomena sink deeply into children, treasured for recreation now and leading to a strong, creative and sociable independence in adulthood. These thoughts formed the basis of my work.

Our village school had created a lovely Japanese garden. The head teacher welcomed the visitors to the opening: 'Good afternoon everyone'. Immediately there was a slowly chanted chorus 'Good af-ter-noon, Mis-ter Jones, good af-ter-noon ev-ry-one'. The head hadn't meant that to happen and we all chuckled.

> On a San Francisco street, two teenage girls danced to a ghetto blaster. A child of 3 went right up to them, and copied them almost exactly, untiringly, for the next twenty minutes.

Imitation lives without barrier or thinking. I was taken in Vancouver to watch a beluga whale with her calf through a glass wall. Every flip of the fin, tiny movement, roll, swish of the tail or closing of mother's eye was imitated by the calf to exact perfection, extraordinary and moving to witness. Well, you say, children are not animals! Yes! But the unconscious openness of the animal is akin to that of the young child. The love and interest the child feels is the same as that of the calf towards the mother whale. What is this extraordinary devotion and trust? We were about to

The ghetto blaster dance

take a small boy home from his grandparents after lunch. 'I must clean my teeth first', I said. He responded, 'I have to clean mine too', (which he didn't normally do then), used his grandfather's brush and paste, and said we must do it properly.

Richard, aged 4, got Granny's cotton reels into a tangled muddle. At first he didn't want to put them away when she asked. Then he became a little dog and picked each one up in his mouth to put soggily back in the basket. Unfortunately the place where he put the basket wasn't too well thought out; after all, children live in the present and can't work out the future or anything logical until towards age 6. So they all fell on the floor, and the tangled heap merrily increased under his direction. Again actually unable to cope, he was reluctant to respond to Granny's pleas to pick them up. I began to roll them up. He did the same, not led by thoughts but by my actions and his capacity to follow.

If small children see me around, they call, 'Hallo Sally', right across a field or car-park, but after about 9 years old the greeting is more self-conscious and intimate. One also often meets this lack of self-consciousness in those with a mental disability. In a performance of Snow White, the queen said, 'Now you are no longer the most beautiful, *ha!*' A small child in the audience immediately repeated '*ha!*' to everyone's amusement. Later, the queen said, 'Now you are well and truly *dead*', and a disabled lady repeated '*dead*'. Of course no one laughed at her, but one can see the link. Imitation, the vital thread running throughout all early childhood, is completely unconscious in the children, arising from the lack of awareness of them*selves* that adults have. I used imitation quite consciously as an educational aid. One has to be so careful, realizing how much damage or good one can do as a model. For example, I did a ring game with gestures and movements: 'Will you come and dig with me...?' Alan, a poor imitator, just stood still. I gave him an imaginary spade: 'Alan, you may use *my* spade'. He began to copy me 'digging' and I 'found' another spade. Through my gesture, this child understood that he could 'work' too.

Out of deep interest, children 'hear' with their whole being, then repeat the experience. Adults copy too, but consciously: 'What a good idea, we could use those tiles too. Where did you get them?' Children who are 'awakened' to early self-awareness from the state of being all one with the world, may have difficulty in creativity and sociability, and find it hard to join in the group in a natural, imitative way. They interrupt and move about inharmoniously, copying the images in their minds of what they have

Like father, like son

experienced in the way of competition, pressures, certain books or toys, computer games or various media. Their understanding may lag behind those of their peers, although they seem bright because they can parrot information and knowledge. Such children may find it difficult to hold back, moulded by a frenzied background, or have an unchildlike, unnatural cleverness, their thoughts and tongues running around instead of their limbs, which are inactive or make jerky movements.

Some things accepted as 'normal' in the child's environment may not be wholesome. So the child can be surrounded by experiences to copy which are actually unhelpful, then can't cope, and so protests through unsociable behaviour. When my own children were young, let alone an earlier generation, it was easier to bring them up. Although there was some stimulation about in the way of 'early learning', and some toys and books that left something to be desired, there seemed to be a good deal less pressure in those days.

> *From a letter to parents:*
> *In the young child's eyes everything in the world lives; you will have plenty*
> *of experience of this. Clouds talk to each other, doors sing, leaves play*
> *games on the streets. Children soak up the whole environment like a*
> *sponge. How important it is then to try to surround children with good and*
> *beautiful things, for whatever they drink in has strong forming forces*
> *whether good or less so. A 90-year-old African lady, former nanny, said to*
> *me, 'The most important things in educating young children are first: Love,*
> *and second: Example. Nowadays there is just* more and more, *and more*
> *and more* bad.*'*
>
> *How can we protect children without mollycoddling them? We must*
> *strengthen them! In kindergarten we quite deliberately provide many things*
> *for them to imitate, for instance the way we move across the room, wash up,*

sweep, sit, speak and so on. They watch and imbibe how we handle tricky situations and are grateful for our calm warmth.

People who play, speak and work well together are a wonderful example for children to absorb and recreate. Where there is joy and love, they will feel and give out joy and love down to their toes. My friend Jen's grandson, 21 months, used to toddle about hugging his loved ones.

Very often the mouth in children listening to a story is open, because they are still drinking in the world through the senses, through the whole body. By about 7 years old children are ready to do what the adult *says*. Up till then, they respond truly mainly to what the adult *does*, through the whole imitative being.

> When new awareness appears around the age of 7, and children in many other countries go to school, the mouth closes. At the birthday party of a 5-year-old, all of the 20 children watching someone doing string games sat there with their mouths open, while the adults had theirs closed.

Seeing differently

Little children like to work, be helpful and do as others. The singing game, 'Would you know how doth the farmer . . . go this way and that' progresses with appropriate actions through all the people the child knows, right through to the baby. Being active is second nature, nowhere more than in their play. My children spent hours at the local station with grandpa watching the trains, then spent days playing trains and engine drivers, important and serious 'grown ups'. There is no dividing line between work and play, as anyone who has seen children tirelessly working at their play will know. Sven, 'helping' builders by pushing a barrow about at 5 years, said, 'I like hard work'. There is no discrimination yet, no ability to see how much help it really is: just joy in being amongst people open to it. How many parents are familiar with the child who wants to help but gets under the feet! A child of 5 said to her mother: 'I'll carry anything you want me to carry'. Without responding to this, almost immediately the mother said, 'Oh, for goodness' sake, can't you look where you're going!' It is so easy to close a door, brook resentment and kill initiative even in the youngest child. If a little child is not busy and active, it is a worrying sign. The sick child of course is still and miserable, seemingly lifeless compared to the one whose legs are constantly on the go.

> 'Let's build the house now.'
>
> 'But it's time to tidy up.'
>
> 'Well, if you hadn't spent all that time playing, we could have built the house.'

Children enter right into the moment in scrubbing, singing, smiling, being sour or sweeping. Everything is alive and kicking. Clara, 6, swung her scarf around on her peg and said: 'My scarf keeps telling me I'm 5, but I'm not, I'm 6'. Young children have an all-in-one understanding of life and death. Triplets of 4 years old went to their still sleeping grandparents. 'We can't play with Granny and Grandad yet, they're dead.' The thoughts of young children can make us so embarrassed or make us laugh. Once I came out of the house with some clothes draped over my arm, and a 7-year-old boy asked me: 'Are you selling clothes?'

They have such a capacity for wonder and reverence. Stillness, peace and an awareness of the natural world are an essential part of wonder. Children deeply experience sunlight and darkness, sparkling frosts and fires, muddy puddles. They are intimately linked with the way in which other people think, feel and act. They feel in their whole body what is going on around them. The mood of the people around affects the child's soul as it does that of the adult. Annie expected peace and harmony to reign in kindergarten. Jeremy, with very challenging behaviour arrived. After a couple of days she said: 'He was a bit better today, I expect he'll be all right next week'.

Repetition is imitation of what has gone before

To hear the same story every night for a while is a gift for young children. The same songs again and again (*ad nauseam* for some parents) contribute to their well-being. They love the same toys and familiar old things. It is easy to attract children with novelty and gimmicky entertainment but they really want to re-visit things, to repeat, to do them again, to let them sink into their chest of learning. Children who were used to several stories at bedtime and not much repetition of any, would come new to my kindergarten, and on their second day they would say, 'We had that story yesterday'. On the third, 'Oh, not that story again!' It didn't take long before they began to ask eagerly, 'Are we going to have that story again?' because they actually felt comfortable in its repetition. When leaving their all-at-one consciousness behind at 6 or 7, children begin to want a new story.

Actors repeat lines many times before being word-perfect. Practice makes perfect. The little child learning to stand will get up time and again. The *répétiteur* rehearses with the singers, until the work becomes part of the repertory. Latin *re + petere* means 'to seek again': this is what the child does, until he makes a 'find' and it all sits comfortably. Learning by ear goes into the long-term memory. Chanting and moving to words or music helps children relax and be receptive. In our daily 'ringtime' (a sequence of action songs and poetry, every day the same), group and individual movements, high and low, wide and narrow, loud and quiet, funny and serious, allowed a flowing progression. The children followed without instruction. Each song or poem was generally repeated at least three times. Old singing games and nursery rhymes found their place next to modern ones. I moved, i.e. used body language just before the words, so the child could *see* what the language meant first. A deer might have splayed fingers on its head and done little jumps, whereas big bells might be shown through arms swinging low with a clap of the hands. All songs and poems were accompanied by gestures and movements. The children became good speakers, singers and movers, partly through this daily rhythmic work.

For a play, I made up dancing steps for a 'dancing moonbeam'. Bella, 6, said to Alice, 5 and a half, 'That's really difficult dancing. Can you do it?' After a few days many of the children could do it through the 'picture' of the moonbeam dancing, the repetition and their ability to imitate. If using instruments for such a story (likewise every day), I would fetch one at the appropriate moment, and the children followed suit, just picking up whatever was still there. There was rarely any argument. We had metal instruments such as old telephone bells, tiny cymbals, separated wind chimes played with a chopstick, and tubular bells made of curtain rails tuned to the pentatonic scale, hung on nylon thread and beaten with a drumstick. We also had wooden rattles. It depended on what pure sound picture I wanted to portray for them to 'drink in', so I didn't mix different materials for these young children. There were small bells to hang round the neck on a thin ribbon, for instance to ring for a starry sound. So that we didn't have to hear them at the 'wrong' time in a play, we made a 'secret' by slipping them inside our tops. They were hung as the colours of the rainbow on small hooks from a branch when not being used. In time most children learnt which one went where without instruction when hanging them up afterwards, thereby learning about the rainbow, the prism. The same went for the plain dressing-up tunics, several for each character, which I kept over clothes-horses arranged in colours. Out of their unified consciousness, the children didn't think it was strange to have four children dressed as princesses or bears in a story which actually had only one, in fact they liked to be the same as their friends. It enabled them to be whatever they wanted. Boys took girls' roles and vice versa, because they understood in their own way what they stood for. It became a repetitive rhythm for the children to fold these clothes and put them back in the right colour order. Naturally you can have such clothes and instruments at home too.

The culture of each country in the world is full of song and poetry treasures for children. Many contain repetition. For instance:

> Babies' shoes, Children's shoes, Mummy's shoes, Daddy's shoes, Policemen's shoes, GIANT'S SHOES. GIANT'S SHOES, Policemen's shoes, Daddy's shoes, Mummy's shoes, Children's shoes, Babies' shoes.
>
> Anon

This can be accompanied by increasing and decreasing volume of voice, and widening then contracting arms. Surrounding the child with such repetitions gives security and boundaries, which are the basis of good discipline.

Gratitude

The Seven-Year-Old Wonder Book, by Isobel Wyatt, tells how a fox learns to be grateful to the stars, the trees, the ground beneath his feet, and the little man who saved him from the huntsmen. This was a favourite with the children: they identified with it, being innately full of gratitude and wonder. Every little twig, leaf, feather and squashed pine cone that children brought to kinder-garten was received gratefully and laid down carefully, particularly with the imitative aspect in mind. In many homes I have seen corners for such treasures found and made. This leads to an interest in and respect for one's fellow human beings and the environment. Thinking and a sense of awe make one stand back for a moment. Enthusiasm leads us forward. Our warmth of heart fills the moment with joy. These three together will affect our actions and the quality of respect and understanding for the world and its people. Children, full of wonder, love and enthusiasm, give us hope and courage.

> I was about to post a letter in the box down our road. A small girl who lived next to it watched. 'That's *our* letter box.'
>
> 'I see', I said. 'Please may I use it?'
>
> 'Yes', she sighed, 'Everybody does.'

CHAPTER 3

IMPRESSIONS

'I like roses, they're nature.'

Soaking it all in

Why did Joshua, 4, move his left foot up and down as if beating time to the rhythm of his father's voice whilst listening to the story? Susan's baby, 5 months, drank from her bottle, and the little foot in its soft slipper likewise went up and down. What was it doing? Gilly's little son drank from her breast and his free arm waved gently about. Young babies seem to move at random for a long time. When they begin to focus, the hand tries to follow, and when they drink, it is as if the limbs accompany the milk flowing into the body. Stability is created when little ones drink in a peaceful place. Additionally, it allows them to have one whole experience to absorb. If someone comes into the room or there is a sudden noise, the child may stop drinking and look round. The baby isn't bothered by other children playing happily, as they are equally absorbed.

Robert, almost 3, gazed at the butcher sharpening his knife. He explained how it was done, but the child's attention had already wandered. He was encouraged to watch while a hook was held on by magnetism to the knife, but he wasn't interested and turned to the meat cabinet, despite the adults' saying, 'Is it holding? Look, it is! Yes!' 'Yes', copied Robert, still looking in the meat cabinet, having long forgotten the knife. A moment later, he picked something off a shelf. 'Can I have that?' Children drink in impressions they come across more readily than if we try to impose them. Also, the younger they are, the shorter their attention span.

> 'Why is it so loud?' piped up a young child during a concert. Though it was not especially loud, the situation was too much for her, and she expressed her unease in a sensitively descriptive way.

What memory do we carry of sense impressions in childhood? I remember crunching carrots with soil at the carrot bed, and our coffee-and-tea grocer's shop which was dark brown like the coffee: dark-brown wooden shelves, floor and counter, and glass jars filled with dark-brown coffee beans and tea. Even the smell was brown. I recall flying down the hill on a forbidden fish-cart railway, frozen with fear, and landing in the filthy ditch beyond. We leant on the wind in January, whilst watching wild broken waves shatter the horizon. We puddled about deep in pond-mud collecting gas in a jar for my father to ignite, afterwards snuggling into his lap in his dilapidated half-springless chair. I remember sleeping in our tree house over the pond, safe amongst birds, acorns, fairies and moonlight; the voice of my Godmother, dead these thirty years; nausea on the funfair swings; and that green velvet under my nails.

I walked in soft-soled shoes behind Benjamin, 4, who was sitting poking about with a stick in a muddy puddle with litter and fag ends. He turned and said, 'You're walking a *bit* loud'. He can barely have heard, but I had disturbed his investigation.

> As we have seen, young children, highly sensitive, react very directly through imitation. Their inner life being yet a 'baby', the outer is strong and lively. Every thing we *do* is an experience for them. As what we *say* often goes in one ear and out the other, we might as well see what we can say without speaking, so to speak.

After an adventure in the stream

A child refused to put her slippers on, despite chiding and persuading by her mother. Her teacher put them on the radiator to warm. When they were cosy and snug, she offered them to the child who happily put them on. The outer sense experience and the teacher's inner gesture had won: not the yet undeveloped inner sense of necessity or responsibility.

> At our village pantomime, the scary wolf came in noiselessly. A child of 4 put her hands over her ears and kept her eyes glued to the scene. Once again we see the child's nature of wholeness, one-ness, unable to differentiate.

Since children are so highly sensitive, why does our modern world fill them with impressions which are 'a bit loud', for example, pushchairs facing noise, pollution, traffic and strangers; garish colours; fussy clothing for little adults, and complicated toys? I believe increasing numbers of children are reacting to surrounding 'loudness' by protesting with challenging behaviour and displaying cold feelings, to protect themselves because they can't cope. As they are so flexible and adaptable, they use their coping mechanism to deal with situations, but eventually becoming emotionally closed off does not bode well for the future. We learn to relate to the world and each other through our senses. Therefore it follows that good experiences of the world will mostly lead to good relationships and, later, understanding of our fellow human beings. Is vandalism partly a result of this closing, turning away from what is good and beautiful, or taking revenge on a world which seems too brash or harsh?

Nature and nurture the nursery

> A retired Indian ship's captain said to me: 'Nature is what is your own. Nurture is what you are given after birth'.

What nurtures the child, through imitation and the direct influence of his surroundings? Bruce and Natalie had a dark playroom with curtains permanently drawn, red lamps, huge TV, big cushions and chaos. It looked more like an opium den. Drugs were part of the parents' life, and although loved, their children were neglected. A child's environment matters. What the adults around them wear matters. A childhood friend had a 'day nursery' and a 'night nursery', which intrigued us. But they were no different from our nursery and bedroom. Today they would be 'playroom' and 'bedroom'. The word 'playgroup' sometimes replaces 'nursery', (though the name doesn't mean less care). Yet 'nursery' has a different feel about it, a sense of protection. Nurse—nurture—nursery—nourish, share the same linguistic root. Breast-feeding was once called 'nursing'; the nursing chair where the child was usually fed was a standard piece of baby equipment. Children need care while they are so vulnerable and dependent. The gardener tends the plants of his nursery, nurturing and watching over them so they can flourish. To nurture belongs love: not overpowering and indulging, but unconditional, all-embracing.

Beauty itself is nourishing. It gives rise to joy and happiness, liveliness and a feeling of well-being. Children who have such a feeling move most of the time; we see their inner expression in the way they do. Holding and then letting go of a hand, wiggling a youngster in the air, holding your arms out to receive the child jumping down: such things are confidence building, healthful, joyful, nurturing. Some children are afraid to explore and move around freely; sometimes anxious adults render them fearful.

A parent recalled how she would lie in bed and watch the fire go down. Baking, playing, watching the builders, messing about in puddles, watching the sun going to bed, walking through a bluebell wood in spring sunshine accompanied by birdsong, listening to a favourite nursery rhyme—all such simple but rich, joyful experiences enhance the spiritual and physical health of the child.

Nurturing in the family

Inner, outer and a higher sensitivity

Young children's inner life is neither strong nor under control, yet they understand with their outer sensitivity. A little girlfriend upset Ben: 'She is like a bad apple: all beautiful on the outside and all rotten on the inside.' Their mouths drink in not only blackcurrant juice but also stories and sights and smells. An unusual-looking old lady we knew spoke to my son of 5, who was gazing at her. 'Shut your mouth, child.' He did, but soon opened it again. She shrugged her shoulders at this disobedience, telling me that he looked stupid. I guess she didn't realize about children 'drinking in' sense impressions!

Communication runs deep in the young child. Our whole demeanour 'speaks' to them. One wonders also what else. Our year-old son wanted to get into the dried-fruit cupboard. Standing up, he tried unsuccessfully to turn the large, stiff key. Crawling across the kitchen, he got a bottlebrush, inserted it into the bow (loop) of the key handle, turned it as a lever and opened the cupboard. We were flabbergasted. He'd certainly not seen anyone do such a thing, so it wasn't imitation.

I had bought a harness for my first child before his birth. One day, although he was yet too young to need it, I suddenly thought I'd like to try it. Bringing the pram round a corner, suddenly I found myself in a manhole, clinging to the pram handle, with my baby son hanging out of the pram on his harness. Had he not been in the harness, he would have dropped onto the concrete. The pram had hidden the open hole, the wheels just clearing the sides, myself stepping straight into the abyss. That taught me always to listen if I had a hunch.

When visiting a friend, I wasn't sure where to put the car. Knowing she had a small pond with a thick blanket of duckweed I asked her to keep an eye on my children while I re-parked. She agreed, and the door to the garden was closed. As I was half-way through parking, I had a strong feeling that I had to go, quickly. Abandoning the car, I ran through the house and now open garden door, to see my 2-year-old disappearing into the weed. He was very surprised, as I hauled him out in his cool green 'coat'. No doubt readers will have had such experiences too—earthly life with a spiritual dimension.

Having deep trust in the world, children have an expectation of our having trust in them too. Lars, 21 months, was used to taking all the plates, cups and glasses down off the open shelves, then putting them all back again, never breaking anything. One day someone saw him. 'You don't let him do that, do you? He'll break something!' Lars turned round and dropped a glass. Did he understand the words, or the gesture? Young children are bound to the adults around them by an invisible thread. Some children were making a lot of noise on the other side of the kindergarten room. I was sweeping and sang to myself quite quietly without looking at them, 'I wonder who is making all that noise'. They cannot have *actually* heard me. Almost immediately the noise subsided and a child near to me said, 'Isn't it funny. When you say that they're quiet'.

A child is naturally wondering much of the time: Who is it? Where is it? What and how is it? When is it? Many things that surround children today run the risk of killing this ability to wonder.

Hearing

What a fantastic, delicate, incredible instrument is the ear, with magical, tiny, curly tubes, spirals and hollows. Sound affects speech, so children's language matches that around through imitation. Speech, being a refined motor skill, is closely connected with movement. Actors practise the art of speaking and moving to portray character. You see the connection already in very young children who move to express what they want to say. As the mouth is a sensory organ, what happens when a dummy is in it? A thumb of the child's volition is different. The dummy needs the mouth to be closed to hold it in, and so prevents the child from 'listening' through it and also from speaking properly. A girl of 18 months mumbled something unintelligible through her dummy. Granny said, 'Take that out of your mouth when you want to say something, darling'. The child gabbled on as before, not making the connection.

People need to hear and listen to each other. A new way of such communication is through the mobile phone, both menace and blessing. A father told me he wasn't sure whether he could let his 10-year-old daughter go on an (extremely well-run) camp because she wasn't allowed a mobile phone. How was it before? Do parents really feel their children are safer and better off with a mobile? There is one available for the very young with just four buttons to press.

Many are afraid of silence, blocking out thoughts and emotions with noise of some variety, which may actually make them nervy. An organization called 'Pipe Down' campaigns against piped music in public places. Adults can choose whether to look at junk mail, or at adverts when going up the escalator. Children don't have this 'choice' because they have an intense, universal interest and lack the defence of discrimination. In *hearing,* we adults may also have no choice: forced to hear music in shops, the phone 'queue', restaurants, ring-tones of mobiles, at the hairdresser, in some public toilets and even car-parks. We have become so used to this assault on the ears that many of us don't listen any more. Children hear sirens, alarms, loud bass, phones, domestic appliances, traffic, and poor speech on the media, which may be aggressive or too fast for them to keep up. The decibel level in some amplified performances is too high; at a circus, I felt pain all down my spine. Some fireworks cause pain and temporary deafness, and many have an emphasis on noise rather than visual display!

> A boy of about 3 and a half said to his parents in the station, 'I'm scared, I'm scared'. It *was* scary, big, and noisy, with metal banging on a building site, three mobile phones, the loudspeaker, doors opening and banging shut, people talking and shouting, and three big locomotives, *all at once.*

Parents make huge sacrifices for their children, whilst reaping all the joys connected with their growing up. Before turning on the car radio or CD you can think about the increased volume needed to drown out traffic noise. Do we really want or need the CD? If it is a story, wouldn't it be nicer if I told one myself while driving along, or if we did it all together?

A robust child banged the door shut. I said gently, with my hands to my chest, 'It hurts me inside when that door bangs'. I thanked him when he went to close it gently. Perhaps my sense of hearing stimulated his own. A new, bouncy girl in my group, used to background music, announced at snack time, 'We should have some music on'. 'Yes, we should', added another—so I sang a song, which satisfied them. Music for adults can of course make a nice atmosphere, but I like children to concentrate on their eating. Conversation is enough diversion. Around the home, a quietish vacuum cleaner and mower are helpful, for even these machines may have an effect on the child's behaviour, through imitation, re-creation and general disturbance. Outside, noise is somewhat dispersed compared to within four walls. In many schools, a CD accompanies movement, but there are still some with a real pianist who can respond to the teacher.

Some children are exposed to a waterfall of human and recorded words, filling minds and impeding concentration. Much talking makes them talk more. I find telling children to be quiet less useful than doing something about the environment. Many teachers speak of children's poor listening ability. We need good hearing but we also need to be able to listen. Later this may become a sensitivity to the inmost being of others, surely what humanity needs. Bill, 5, had a scratchy, stressed and tight voice. He was often shouted at and shouted himself, watched videos with cartoon character voices, and was generally frustrated.

Vision

This sense is used intensively in such activities as driving or using the computer. Video games require eyes to move at high speed, and fast changing images on the TV screen don't allow the eye to rest. Soft, light colours can be helpful to the child, also playthings which mimic the gentle organic shapes and surfaces of nature. Many colours in children's books and on the screen are unnatural and quite vivid. If children immerse themselves in simple colours, they gain a relationship to them, which is less possible if they are jumbled up and fast moving. Colours are connected to the emotions, which one recognizes in the way people choose their clothes and decorate their house. Nature abounds with delights to the eye, and where possible natural light is preferable to electric.

Once I started preparing a room for a presentation to pre-school practitioners by building a play house with play-stands and plain materials of different colours. I laid out a 'landscape' of logs, dolls and toys of natural materials on cloths. As people began to arrive, a couple of young women looked in, saw the display, and one said to the other, 'This isn't the right room. This is the art course'. This was an amusing moment, because of course they were in the right place, but I couldn't help feeling a little sad: that a room with lovely colours should be felt to have nothing to do with children, and only 'art'.

On the same occasion, the doorman kindly helped me with my bags, baskets and the branch of twenty-five little bells on ribbons, saying, 'Here come the Morris Dancers!' No doubt my equipment did look unusual. But children *need* beauty. They need both tangible beauty and the beauty within the adults around them. You don't need riches to achieve this. A wild rose from the hedge is beautiful, as is a prettily laid breakfast table, Dad singing a rhyme, or a kindly smile. It doesn't cost anything to choose a gentle, warm colour in preference to a harsh, garish one.

Smell

> 'I like roses, they're nature', said Norman, 5, holding a basket of yellow and pink rose petals. His fingers, eyes and olfactory sense touched the delicate colours. (Three years later I heard him say to a friend, 'Do you like nature?' The other replied, 'Yes, do you?' 'Yes, but I like trains better', said Norman.)

Mum or Dad's scarf or jumper may be an alternative if the child doesn't want to stay with the babysitter or at nursery, for it smells of the parent—delicious and comforting. Letting children rub a little cream with natural fragrance into their hands after washing helps them to feel good and well. Once a coat, which I hadn't seen before, was left behind at kindergarten. Malika, 5, said, 'Let me smell it! ... It's Lydia's!' She was right. Artificial perfumes in cosmetics and cleaning materials may have harmful chemicals in them. Exhausts and some pesticides in food also smell unpleasant. There are plenty of organic foods and natural cosmetics and cleaners to be had. Nature abounds with smells for the child, from the muck heap to freshness after rain, from lavender to a cow in-milk.

Taste

The liveliest impression you can have of a combination of taste and touch is in watching the baby with his first solid food. Taste is of course connected with digestion, an activity involving a great deal of unconscious effort. To prepare for it we should chew properly. In hurrying children when eating, or in giving them toys to play with in order to get them to eat, we may undermine the opportunity for tasting and preparation for a healthy nutritive process. Young children 'taste' their surroundings with their whole body, through skin, mouth, nose, ears and hands. *Tasten* in German means 'to touch'. Children touch and experience their environment through tasting with their body, and drinking milk is almost their first encounter with the world.

Warmth

Love, security and physical warmth make us open up and feel good, and they help anxious children to relax. In contrast, fear is a 'cold' experience, making us close up and unable to move well either inwardly or outwardly. It is advantageous to keep our fears and bad news away from children, as they can't cope with them. Fearful children can be healed through play, because they can relive and overcome experiences and ordeals. Someone asked me: 'Why shouldn't children be scared?' Those over 6 or 7 *want* to be a bit scared, thrilled and animated, and it's fine for them sometimes, as long as they also find the opposite. But younger children can't find any kind of equilibrium because of their open state of consciousness. They don't have the capacity to imagine whether it might come right again, or be real or not. A woman recited a poem about a cat and mouse to a child she'd just met, using scary, scratchy gestures and voice. He shrank back but she continued obliviously, thinking it funny.

Children's way of seeing the world asks for an existence which has under- rather than over-statement, warmth and continuity. Of course they can be exuberant, expectant and excited, yet that is different from being frightened. Life coming and going in waves allows for anticipation and sparkling high spirits.Tony, 5, came to us, pressurized and fearful. He told his mother he liked being in kindergarten: 'It's like snuggling up under a big duvet'. The warmth that he felt came from a peaceful atmosphere, repetition, simple activities and playthings, a rhythmical daily life and the lack of pressure.

Building relationships through touch

Not yet very able with words, young children also use their limbs to express themselves. It is not necessarily from imitation, retaliation or frustration but from testing the end of their own space, through feeling resistance. Those who have too little opportunity to move, frequently push or pull others, roll about, or bang their heads against a wall, simply to experience the existence and boundary of their own bodies. If they have too little experience of touch they may be irritable as if not comfortable in their bodies, or too sensitive to want anyone too close. With natural fabrics and materials, with being outdoors and having plenty of movement, children find stimulation for their sense of touch. Spatial orientation grows when children's fine nerve-endings come into contact with their surroundings, in play, cuddles, food on the tongue, and being out in the elements. The touch sense is supported when children with a tendency to cold hands are allowed to rest them in warm water and feel the rosy glow spreading. How we touch the world has a deep influence on our life, and affects our sense of self, which should lead in adulthood to a sensitivity to and recognition of the nature of others.

Using touch to find relationships

My father used to tuck us in so tightly at bedtime that the mattress formed a boat, gorgeous! Clothes well tucked in support not only the child's good health and feeling of well-being but also the sense of body-awareness. To 'embrace' means to receive and hold in one's arms, to enfold into one's touch. French *embrasser* encompasses *en*—'in', and *bras*—'arm'. German for 'embrace'—*umarmen*, means 'around' and 'arms'. Both touch and sight give a feeling of boundary and depth. In shops you can say to children over about 5, with appropriate gestures, 'We may touch with our eyes instead of our fingers'. A girl of 2 systematically picked up and replaced an object from each of many baskets on the long, low shop shelf, as if she needed to verify what she saw through making contact with her hands. A few years ahead, she would be able to make an imaginative abstraction for herself.

In a reception class, a 4-year-old was upset. Her kind teacher said, 'Come on, let's have a little cuddle, but don't tell any one'. The child recovered on her knee, but what picture is conveyed when a cuddle must be clandestine? Many people regret that so many children are denied the loving touch of a practitioner. Child abuse is more prevalent than once thought, but what a shame it is that because of it so many professional adults may not do what their hearts tell them is the child's right. When I was teaching we were allowed to touch the children when appropriate. Head lice inspections are forbidden in many schools because children may not be touched. At an occasion in our local primary school, the special guest (someone high up in the educational world) led a boy in front of everyone to help her illustrate her story, and laid her hands on the child's head in that wonderful archetypal gesture of caring for the innocence of childhood.

Balance and rhythm

Leading a rhythmical life, with regular meals and bedtimes, not being over-stimulated, and having adults around who have calm and equilibrium, strengthens the sense of balance as much as building with uneven bricks, or walking along an uneven log. A friend told me of children with a plank laid on the floor, running and jumping onto it in turn, arms outstretched, swaying and bending; one could 'see' the skateboard. A boy of 5 was piling up slices of wood, then balancing a large plank against them, which fell down. He repeated it several times. Eventually he succeeded, put a foot on the plank to climb up, but it fell again. He repeated it again and again, increasing determination and inner balance.

Happy and well are those who are allowed to climb, run and jump, and

A leap of happiness

An invitation to balance

also feel inner liveliness and flexibility in the adults around them. Long walks and a rhythmical flow to the day are beneficial. Rhythmical songs and rhymes from a live voice are musical movement—on the knee, in the car or at the kitchen table. Parents sometimes laughingly related how their child copied not only my speech but also my movements. Those who are able to develop a fine sense of balance and movement in childhood will be able to move well later in their limbs, head and heart, enabling a sensibility to grow towards what others have to say, think and bring to society.

Parents have to juggle their lives, performing balancing acts between home, work and the community. To find a golden mean is not easy. I met a wealthy family suffering because of Dad's constant jetlag and absences. They had more than they needed, but considered downgrading because of the effect on the family and the risk to his health. A mother asked what to do while trying to get the supper with children grizzling, and becoming increasingly frazzled herself. I suggested she sit down. 'But then the supper won't get cooked, and what about the children's squabbling?' Yet in imitation of their mother sitting down, the children might well come to her and feel calmed, and she herself receive inspiration as to what to do next. Between the two polar opposites of fretting and letting go, she might find the balance.

Daily, weekly, monthly, yearly rhythms can enhance our lives, nowhere more than as children. Just as meals at regular intervals contribute to good behaviour, so a daily rhythm helps children to be at ease with themselves and their surroundings. Calm becoming chaos followed by chaos resolved into calm contributes to children's happiness: the sink full of washing up then all put back in the cupboard, the toys put away after being all over the floor, the argument resolved peacefully, even the sun shining after the storm. Consciousness of the importance of such contrasts constituted a major part of my work as a teacher.

The lightning and thunder,	
They go and they come.	(Drum feet on floor whilst hurrying to the
But the stars and the stillness	centre of the room and back.)
Are always at home.	(Lift arms upwards and outwards while standing still.)

Children love acting out this poem by George MacDonald. The words live through the movement. Restless or aggressive children found healing in moving to such beautiful poetry. Even the rowdiest boys came to stillness just through copying these simple actions. We all seek balance in our lives: putting our feet up after a long, hard day, longing for sun after long wet spells, or longing for rain after a drought, wearing party clothes and then our old comfortable ones. Alarm clocks have to arouse many from sleep when a balance has not been found between day and night (or events don't even allow for peaceful sleeping). I happily let noise and chaos happen because we could experience peace afterwards. The children, whilst oblivious of chaos at first were grateful for the change, which came about not through emotion, shouting or admonishment but through imitation of my actions. I have sometimes attended social evenings with many skits, and been thankful for the one serious poem in between as my mouth began to hurt from laughing.

Life has many serious moments, kept in balance by light-heartedness and humour. Children have a wonderful way of uplifting us. Emily, 4-years-old, said when Ruby Ring (ring finger, which cannot straighten independently) always 'fell asleep' in a rhyme, 'We'd better buy her an alarm clock'. The humour of the young child is straightforward, different from ours. They don't yet have much cognitive ability for puns and ironies, but Evan, 5, heard the fire-engine go past, winked at me and said, 'It's the ice-cream van'. Sometimes children thought something very funny when I hadn't intended it. Also, to help children needing discipline, I sometimes made a 'cross' face, not being cross inside. They loved that, especially if I responded to their pleas to make more, screwing my face up in all directions. Yet a tiny consciousness 'bell' rang within them and discipline happened as a result. Putting my clothes on inside out or getting in a muddle with my apron or sleeves was another joy for them, as was being a 'dragon', 'breathing fire and smoke'.

A young family was going to the car-park on their way home, as it began to pour with rain. Mother was hysterical. 'We'll all get soaked, run, run, oh, we're so wet, oh, this hateful rain.' The children, copying their mother, were getting hysterical as well. Why not enjoy the adventure and allow children to get soaked to the skin if you can dry them again? This contributes to their sense of balance, just as feeling the balm of a summer sun after a real rain-storm. We often protect our children from extremes of weather by running them everywhere in the car. What are we losing in so doing?

Children like to experience the harmony between kindness and sweetness on the one hand, and strictness and discipline on the other, feeling the reaching forward with the former, and the holding back with the latter. This develops the basis of discrimination and selflessness. We may become unselfish when we have been cared for ourselves with warmth and kindly fairness, translating it into the needs of others. And learning that we need to fit in with others and to do things we would have preferred not to but are actually a duty, may make us stand back and think: what is really the best way forward, how could I have done this better, what is actually the difference between this and that?

An embroidered cushion

If the weeks go by in a steady, stable and safe merry-go-round, children can build on and consolidate knowledge and skills already gained. In a harmo-nious rhythm, good 'automatic' habits form. A balanced, unstressed life will help to form a balanced, unstressed person. Equally, a hyperactive environ-ment may bring about hyperactivity. Harmonious surroundings help to form an invisible 'padding', creating a barrier to protect against a certain amount of less constructive experience. Babies have a protective 'padding' for some time, but if exposed to many strong sensations too often, this 'cushion' will become threadbare, letting a cold wind through the bare patches. Children who are surrounded in daily life by morality, fun, respect and beauty can weave extra threads into this 'padding' to make it firm, embroidering it with stability. Such an invisible cushion creates a feeling of being glad to be alive. One can call it a force of life. Lack of it may lead to pallor, lethargy, a 'thin skin' and disgruntlement. Good walks in the fresh air, nutritious food and enough sleep contribute to this life-force, supporting growth and healing.

> Turn your face to the sun, and the shadows fall behind you. (Maori proverb)

Parents may feel they are limited in what they can do to help their children grow up in the way they want. Yet there is plenty of balance to be found. If you need to go to school by car, you can try leaving it a little way from school, or have a walk when home. It is possible to save time in not being in a hurry with children, for hurrying makes everyone agitated. It may not be possible to reduce pressure put on them at school, but if you can ensure plenty of physical activity and play afterwards, followed by a good meal and quiet bedtime with a story and a song rather than a video, the children are likely to sleep well and long, awakening refreshed, having enlivened their 'cushion'. Would children and babies out in the evening, at a time when they would usually be sleeping, be better off tucked up in their beds? Sometimes children accompany parents in the evening because it is cheaper and easier than getting a babysitter, but maybe parents are making a rod for their own backs by disturbing the child's sleep routine. Some babies are attached to their mother in a sling much of the time, and there again, a balance needs to be found for both parties. Although there are some schools of thought which think this is a very good thing, I believe that babies in a contented home are perfectly happy to be on their own some of the time, relieving the mother for other activities for a little while. There is also the question of the child's soft spine (unless in a flat sling) about which I shall write later.

Finding a way between

We all need to draw breath, whether what we are doing is appealing or appalling. We also need to withdraw from others and be alone, whether adult, child or baby. An artist once told me there should be spaces in a picture—like pauses, like breathing in and out, just as in conversation.

On the way to becoming self-less lie self-esteem and self-assertion. We need the latter, the complement to listening, for survival. Gradually the need for it recedes when we grow in confidence and can make a space for others without having our own thoughts dancing in front of us. Being interested in other people helps one to feel sympathetic and compassionate towards them. It is interesting that technology brings more communication, yet people are not necessarily communicating any better; the breakdown of family life is an example.

Lucy, 24, talked about her unemployment and what this does to people, 'Nothing to work towards, a sense of uselessness, loss, no sense of purpose. There is no rhythm, no routine'. She said it wasn't like a holiday when you could look forward to work afterwards. This sense of loss can be felt in children who lack rhythm and routine in their lives. 'Who is coming to get me today?' 'Where am I going this afternoon?' Children like the sort of

routine my step-grandfather had: the same hairdresser for seventy-five years!
My grandmother wrote of her childhood in the late 1800s. 'On Sundays we
would go to church. After lunch we would scatter. If it was hot, I'd go to the
stack yard and sit on a stack that was in use (so as not to spoil a new one), and
listen to the sleepy clucking of the hens as they pecked in the hot sun. Then
in for tea, a large one of course, after which we all gathered in the porch for
our evening stroll over the fields. We only had cold supper on Sundays. After
we had finished, but while we still sat at table, father would get out the Bible
and read a chapter to us.' Even in a city, a strong routine such as this is
possible. We had to move house when our first child was 5 months old, but
apart from the place being different, everything else was the same—pram,
cradle, feeding times, parents, walks and sleeps. He was just the same happy
baby as before. If the routine is generally strong, the upset from a change will
be minimal.

Rhythm keeps us going

> The choir master consoled his uncertain amateur singers as they practised a gospel
> song. 'You won't come in too late. The rhythm will hold you, so you will come
> in automatically in the right place.' So it is with children; the rhythm their parents
> create holds them securely.

I wore an apron in kindergarten for many activities. If I forgot to take it off
for ringtime or story, the children reminded me. It disturbed them to see it on
at the 'wrong' time. One could well say such details don't matter, but my
experience shows that children actually like even small things to be routinely
observed.

One summer we practised a play of a fairy tale about three girls called
'One Eye, Two Eyes, Three Eyes'. The following Christmas, after a few
days' practice of a different play, we unfolded the dressing up clothes for
it. A boy of 6 asked which one was for 'Three Eyes'. The bodily memory
of the daily dressing up for that previous play overrode the present
experience.

Many years ago I sang a song to signal the start of tidying up. Joël said to his
mother indignantly, 'Sally never asks us to tidy up. She just sings a little song'.
From then onwards, mother also sang a little song to tidy away. It is that
sameness of a routine which brings happiness about, the kind of uncon-
sciousness you see at animals' feeding times. Two horses go to the gate next

to our school path every day just before school is out, hoping for a treat. How do they know? Such habits live deeply within us, and the more you can bring them about in young children, the stronger and healthier they will be, spiced with life.

When you fold your hands or arms, do you put left over right or right over left? Do you feel uncomfortable if you do it the other way? If you fold your hands with the fingers between each other, how do you do it? Does it feel awkward to do it the other way? What makes you do it the same way? It is as if you were asleep, and changing it makes you more conscious of what you are doing. Children are happier when not very conscious of what they are doing, when they live in habits and imaginative play, in their fairy-tale world. They like order, which gives them independence and a feeling of control over their lives. They find joy in learning through the security and stability a rhythm gives them. The word 'habit' derives from Latin *habitare*, 'to inhabit'. 'Habitat' is used to describe homes for wildlife (or a shop for articles for the home). So you can see perhaps how good habits provide a home for a child. A 'habit' is also, of course, a piece of clothing. Habits clothe and protect us.

Kindergarten life constituted alternating times of being in a group together, and being as individuals, like taking a breath in, then exhaling again. In between these activities was a middle moment, like sipping warm, sweet tea after the very hot, very cold, very hot, very cold of a sauna. Not infrequently children would arrive in the morning pale-faced and lethargic or over-active, but return home rosy, bright-eyed and calm. Did this rhythmical structure have something to do with it? Even when we (frequently) spent all morning outside, I kept to the same rhythms. It also made discipline easier as the children responded quickly and unconsciously, even when I sang, 'All my children come to me' when I needed them together at a time that wasn't part of our rhythm. That phrase in itself was a sameness they recognized.

On many holidays with children everyone has a good time, yet taking young children out of their environment can drain them. Special holiday offers may make people go beyond their intentions and means. I feel it is useful to try to stick to the same rhythms when away from home. Strange places, beds, food, people and situations upset children's stability and feeling of well-being. If abroad it may be exacerbated by different climate, language, time-change, or even season, together with a plane ride which doesn't allow time to accommodate the changes so well as a train or boat. So any repetition and rhythms carried over from home can be a great sup-

port. Even little habits such as changing shoes before entering the hotel
room and having a night-light at bedtime give the child reassurance.
Maybe some children who can't afford holidays are better off than those
who travel frequently? Eric was flown around Europe one summer. All he
could remember were the airports and hotel swimming-pools. In contrast,
Stephen, 2 and a half, was watching the stream sparkle by. His mother
wanted to go on but he said, 'Wait till stops'. So they waited. I'm not sure
whether it did.

I repeated my 'ringtime' sequence of seasonal songs and rhymes daily
for about a month. The children seemed to feel well in this space of time,
which is the rhythm, the monthly cycle of the mother, to whom the child
is so attached for the first few years. They learnt them so well (merely out
of imitation), happy to do them again and again. Parents can make the
same kind of repetition at home. Day and night are the most obvious
rhythms of nature: light and darkness. There are all sorts of little habits and
rhythms to keep us going, such as where the butter goes in the fridge or
which clothes we wear to work. When I was a single parent working full-
time and my children were at school, Friday was shopping day, Saturday
cleaning and washing day, Sunday outing day on bikes or on foot, and
Monday dustbin day. Homework and music practice were done after
school, and meal and bedtimes were as regular as possible. It helped us to
have that kind of structure, it was something to hold on to. As the children became teenagers they began to sort their own lives out with paper-
rounds, friends and clubs, but mealtimes and dustbin days stayed the same.
The habits of a structured life contribute to the development of a sense of
purpose, of the will. Children can learn to push their chair in and shut the
door behind them, to put their crayons away and make their beds and
clean their shoes. Do we spoil them if we do these things for them, even
when they are quite young, perhaps even depriving them of an opportunity for learning?

Over-stimulation versus concentration

Jeannie and Howard, 7 and 5, were driven an hour each way to a theme park.
They had to wait at most of the attractions and were tired and grumpy. A
neighbour asked what they had enjoyed most. They both agreed they liked the
slide best. Such a thing stood in the playground near their house.

Many toys which can only be used for one thing, such as a doll's house, shop, lorry or spaceship, are big, making space a problem. Having too many toys is a trouble. Yet a chair with cloths tied round it can be a doll's house, with bits of wood and pine-cones the furniture, and a ribbon the path. An hour later the chair can be a space ship, with ribbons for wires, pine cones as food, wood to be the astronauts and a blue cloth the sky. One may well wonder: does the child need toys with all details, which can only be what they are? Coloured sheep's wool can be rolled into little flowers one moment, then be kindling for a 'bonfire', or turned into a doll, all imaginatively transformable in the child's mind and exciting for the senses. There is little to get lost or muddled, so it all takes up so much less space.

So many things in our environment interrupt our concentration. Check-outs beeping, ice-cream vans, police and other sirens, chain-saws, 'vehicle reversing', and adverts everywhere distract children's attention. Practitioners are guided to interact with their young pupils to further their learning. 'How did you make it? How much did you use? Who helped you? How many more would you need to make another one?' Would *we* like to be asked a whole lot of questions about what we are doing? Or would it actually stop us getting on and thinking about what we are making? Listening to someone on the phone while someone else is trying to talk to you renders you unable to listen to either. Our 9-month-old son sat on my knee for about twenty minutes, watching the birds through the window, deeply absorbed. I held my breath, not daring to disturb this wonder-filled experience.

Lars, 18 months old, spent fifteen minutes in silence trying to replace a cloth, which kept sliding off a shiny table. Eventually he gave up and walked away. What might one have spoiled in doing it with, or even for, him? In a nursery the children had just finished their group counting and were allowed to play for ten minutes. Having only just started this, they then had to finish, and were most frustrated. One Open Day a headmaster visited my kinder-garten and tried to talk to some children who were deeply engaged in their play. 'I don't think much of this education,' he said, 'they can't even hold a proper conversation'. They had been polite and acknowledged his presence but they were absorbed in the game which he had interrupted, and weren't interested in his, to them, irrelevant questions. In fact they were well able to hold a proper conversation at a more appropriate time.

I love music but I don't want it all the time, not even the composers I love most. A shopkeeper friend of mine says people want music, so she has to have it on, but that in the main they neither listen to nor notice it. I wanted to read a book while my car was fixed, but couldn't concentrate because of the garage Muzak. *Live* music is still sometimes played as a background at a meal but the diners can get up and dance, so there is a purpose in it. Children are not spared any of these examples. A class of 4-year-olds had classical music as 'educational' background all morning except for their story and circle time. Where could their listening be directed—to the music, their friends, their teacher, their own small thoughts?

Should children need drugs for hyperactivity? Or may one solution be to do something about the child's sensory perception, to support concentration? I have much experience of children who came to me over-active and with challenging behaviour, and of how, together with their parents' help, a calming, rhythmical, healthy sensory environment changed them. Absorbing too many sense impressions can make children 'numb'. So it is thought they need more stimulation, which leads to more numbing: a vicious circle. The attention span becomes shorter as they can digest their impressions less, smothered by their intake of them. Some are faced with a mixture of sense deprivation and inappropriate sensory bombardment: not enough good impressions and too many unhealthy ones.

Leroy, 6, carpet-sweeping for fifteen minutes, beamed, 'You would never

Time to wait and watch

believe this room was so messy a little while ago'. Such simple, homely and educational activity brings about a sense of harmony and happiness. Children who have been able to reach a fine level of balance and spatial awareness through healthy surroundings and no over-stimulation are guarded against hyperactivity and poor attention and concentration problems. I believe good sensory experience leads later to a sensitivity of perception, an inner sensibility to the outer environment, to going beyond the self, resisting egotistical behaviour. Surrounding children with harshness can only make them hard themselves, closed off from the feelings of others.

> Patricia Clafford said, 'The work will wait while you show the children the rainbow, but the rainbow won't wait while you do the work'.

CHAPTER 4

JOY IN MOVEMENT, WORD AND SONG

'Careful, . . . Careful, . . . **Careful***!'*

Purpose and practice

> A child of two climbed joyfully all around some railings. Then she saw me and
> we looked at each other in delight.

Motivation to grow up and find one's task in the world leads to struggle and
practice, and further to achievement and success, nowhere more so than up to
3 years old. A boy of 15 months was playing in a shallow hole about 50 cm in

'Helping' on a low roof

diameter: going round and round, pushing back and forth, banging his hands on the edge, jumping up and down while holding on, stamping feet alternately very fast. He continued for over a quarter of an hour, almost in silence. Children need in general to achieve each step on their own, with our support and encouragement where necessary. It is tempting to walk the baby across the floor, but why the hurry? In letting her stand and walk in her own time, we allow balance to come naturally. Sitting or leaning the child up before sitting is achieved naturally puts undue pressure from the heavy head on the soft spine and nerves within it. Does having to push children along on a bike or toy car with attached stick mean they are not ready to do it alone? Or is it a subtle undermining of exercise and will? A man pushed his healthy 5-year-old son breathlessly uphill on the boy's bike. Why not let the child push it?

Children may say eagerly, 'I'm going to *really* ride it, all the way, I promise', or 'If you let me take my pram, I *will* push it by myself. You don't have to help me'. But they still need an adult to judge whether they will manage, as they can't know. Maybe we will say, 'We'll take it another day', because otherwise effort and independence are weakened if we end up doing it for them. I believe it is good to let children struggle a bit. They need a

Repeatedly trying to roll the hoop over the rope (his own idea)

challenge, and you can give kind encouragement to do up buttons, empty their plate or push the scooter home. In wanting to help too much, we may spoil our little ones and do *ourselves* physical damage. In crafts, doing up coats, sitting at meals and endless events throughout the day, we find the child's motor skills practised and fine-tuned. You can help the co-ordinating process through letting children move chairs to the right places, lay the table, wash and dry up, clean the floor, put books on the shelf and fold clothes. Children, especially boys, need to push and pull heavy equipment: wheelbarrows, carts, logs, pipes, boards, tables, even beds. It fulfils them and diverts aggression. Tricky self-directed games are devised: Popsy, 5, walked round and round on three stools close together, twisting, turning and balancing, feeling her way. 'It's quite difficult', she said.

All alone, 4-year-old Sydney slid down the snowy slope and round the corner of the shed, cleaned the brake, then trudged back up, dragging the sled behind her. She repeated the whole procedure most of the afternoon until Granny called her in for tea. What wonderful effort and practice of mobility.

The following scene is typical of a young child's ceaseless movement and the adult's lack of it.

First five minutes: Mother sits on a bench in the park. Her child, about 4, picks a dandelion, sits by a tree with it, plays with it, drops it, runs up steps to the slide, slides down, goes to mother then back to the tree, picks up a stick, hits the tree, runs back to mother, runs away again with the stick.

Next five minutes: Mother phones on her mobile while her son walks round and round then backwards along an outdoor table-tennis table, puts the stick on it, lifts the net with it, puts it back on the table, walks round the table again, picks up the stick and puts it down again.

Following five minutes: Mother still phoning while he fetches another stick, goes round and round the table again, puts both sticks on it, lifts the net with them, puts them down again, goes round the table forwards and backwards and leaves the sticks on it.

Last five minutes: He walks a few metres away, picks a daisy, returns to put it on the table, then repeats this *four times*. The fifth time, he throws away the daisy as it obviously isn't up to scratch, picks another and puts that on the table. Picking a bunch of daisies all at once and putting them on the table might seem more rational to an adult, but something much more original is going on here, all in silence. Then mother calls him to go. What is playing in the child's mind, and what drives him to this ceaseless movement?

Mechanics versus muscles

A great deal of physical work today has been replaced by mental work. Before the advent of motorized noisemakers, people paddled or rowed, cut hedges by hand and swept roads with a broom. Now some entertain themselves on water-scooters with expensive, frenzied excitement, smell and buzzing, expending little energy and irritating anglers, other boats and beach lovers. A wholesome childhood with energetic busy-ness may help shield children from the urge for such activity later, making rowing, hiking, climbing and biking interesting and rewarding. We can't turn the clock back, yet seeing leaf-blowers, garden vacuum cleaners and many other unnecessary oil-guzzling, rake- and broom-replacing activities makes one wonder what is happening to people's (including children's) ears, lungs and muscles. Machines at the gym cannot replace fresh air, a pair of shears or a bicycle. When my husband used to bike round a beautiful lake, he often saw someone on an exercise bike outside his house right next to the water.

We are relieved of much effort today and are often grateful for it. However, this may be detrimental to children, who live in activity and may become frustrated. Stir the soup of chopped vegetables? Open a packet!—Close the door? The magic eye does it!—Walk to school? The carburettor is at hand!—Peg out the washing and feel the wind on the cheek? Warm air tumbling round indoors will do the job! Have we though, in saving time, lost time itself? We seem to be so stressed and needy for unnecessary things which complicate our lives in the 'civilized' world. Many find it easier to pop their child in the buggy than let him walk alongside. What effect does that have? The undermining of adult's will power is one thing; that of the child is quite another. As little children live in activity and movement, any deprivation of it weakens their will, basic to all development. 'Come back!' said mother to 3-year-old Martin who wanted to follow Dad down a little slope to the blackberry bush. 'No', said Martin. 'Don't go down there, you'll fall.' 'No' 'You can't go down to Daddy.' What fun it would have been to run down, but his 'No's' were to no avail.

Risk taking

'CAUTION HORSE AND RIDER'. First I saw the horse and rider, then the notice on the rider's back. Cart before the horse? Rider before the cart?

There is a danger in common sense being waylaid by Nanny-State's Health and Safety rules. No one wants children to get hurt, but accidents and risk-taking are part of growing up, learning from experience how to take care, becoming strong and brave. Risk assessments are excellent for making teachers aware of potential problems, but they can restrict us beyond guarding against foolishness. Fear of litigation has gripped many leaders. There is not enough opportunity for many children to extend their physical pluck, which underlies emotional and social courage and free thought. We all need pluck. Disabled children also have the right to experience risk and meet challenges. Risk assessments and environments will be adjusted to their needs, but like children everywhere they should be able to have fun and develop muscles and courage in this way.

What's the difference between risk-taking and actually being dangerous? My children and I were climbing around in a steep mountain stream with dry, smooth rocks between pools. I happened to be standing by a deep pool, when my agile 7-year-old slipped high above. He couldn't swim so I leapt in to rescue him as he flew gracefully down. Were we unwise to play there? A hunch 'told' me to be present at that moment. Being sensible is a virtue, so long as it doesn't wander into fear. Some children are tragically lost in accidents; is there a happy medium? Naturally adventurous, Sven, 5, once climbed from one tree-branch on to another tree, slipped and was left hanging by the end of a sleeve high up. This made him more careful. Depriving children of challenges and chances to make mistakes may make them physically and spiritually weak, leading to risk-taking in an uncontrolled and really dangerous way later. A boy of about 10 on the train observed graffiti all along a wall right next to the (electric) rail. 'How can they do graffiti over *there*!?' he said.

Self-motivation, practice, risk

A mother accompanied her 4-year-old daughter down three small steps which other children had played on many times. 'Careful, ... **care**ful, ... *CARE*ful!' she said, as the child gingerly put one toe down after the other.

'Come off there, you'll drown', said a woman, dragging her 5–year-old off the river wall. Why make him fearful instead of saying, 'Hold my hand, we'll look at the water together'? But Nell, 2 and a half years, refusing the stroller, was allowed to walk over a mile. Copying her sister climbing up and down posts, she picked up interesting objects, lingered, ran, explored sideways and backwards, but always responded to her mother's call if a car came. Lucky, happy girl, out in the fresh air, held by invisible threads to her mother but free to be a child, letting her limbs do what they were born to do. Such experiences are essential for the healthy development of a sense of movement. The same is true of watching or being in things which are moving: swirling water, a pop-up picture book, a boat, a wind-swayed tree, or a moving toy such as the chickens which peck on the board when the ball below is swung round.

Poor diet and a lack of movement are creating overweight youngsters. We can't move properly if cold, but not if fat either. I observed two obese children of about 3, a girl with fat hanging down over her knees who could barely walk, and a boy sitting in a supermarket trolley *amongst* the shopping, eating a whole packet of chocolate drops. Many parents today

Children and water moving in the rain-filled sand pit

are encouraged to be fear-bound, to keep their children indoors and drive them to school. How fearful do we need to be? We certainly need to be fearful of depriving children of movement and play, for this deprivation impinges on their whole development. Traffic has forced an end to the old street games with song, ball and rope, and now the emphasis is on indoor, sedentary activities. If we take trouble to encourage experience, we can help timid children such as Adeola, 6, who after many months dared to jump off a fallen log, or Scott, 5, who finally dared to walk through high grass.

A small child was *racing* downhill next to a busy road in his toy car. Would he have been able to stop? Pedestrians were avoiding him, but suppose he'd wandered into the road? Children are unable to anticipate, and I wondered what his mother was thinking as she ambled down far behind. People sometimes have to swerve to avoid children riding skateboards and roller-blades. One could wonder what their parents are thinking. This is the opposite of the fearful parent: those who are oblivious of their children's activities and safety. Is this foolhardiness? Or do they feel unable to stop their children? There must be a happy medium, being aware and yet not over-protective. Although riding cars, scooters, tricycles and bikes is fun, I suggest young children also spend time on their feet, so they have more all-round physical practice at their own pace, rather than excess speed. Again, a happy medium should be the guide. A boy of 4 was bored by his family's holiday photos, so he pushed his buggy happily round and round the rows of airport benches. Children seize on opportunities for movement; this is a good guide for adults. A huge piece of (strong) modern sculpture marked 'no climbing' was a magnet for many lively youngsters as they waited for the next leg of their journey.

Swimming is a happy thing for children. Most love to be in the water, and if introduced to it carefully are fearless, as they have no concept of potential dangers. It gives all-round muscle exercise and confidence. The child's instinct is to move from dawn to dusk. Young children's bodies are an image of their whole being, malleable and impressionable. Julie at 9 months was developing normally, yet sat by the window with her feet twisted and her legs crumpled up as if they were made of rubber. William, 4, would play all around and up and down the hilly garden with a stream, bridges and old stumps. After his bedtime story and song, he fell asleep immediately. When children are allowed to use their limbs, they grow strong, practising muscle skills and spatial awareness. They are then also healthily tired at the end of the day, so sleep well.

Crawling: a rich experience

Invisible Movement

The inner movement of a young child's soul is not yet very active. For example, unless children are made to feel guilty, truly feeling sorry for what they have done only really begins at about 5 years. Everything we do, think and feel involves movement. Thoughts go round and round in an invisible, living sphere. A 'moving experience' lies within the heart. Thoughtfully changing one's mind, moving on from being stuck, exercising self-restraint, warming to another person, actively practising forgiveness, these are capacities arising out of movement in head and heart, supported by good limb development in the first years, *vital, life-giving*. Movement is the basis of balance, muscle development, speech, creativity and social awareness. In a pre-school, Toby, 6, irritated everyone, using his limbs to demonstrate his seemingly aggressive nature. In allowing my thoughts to revolve around him, I gradually observed that actually he was trying to put things in order, and that he needed protection himself. His practitioner took this on board and he changed into a loveable, popular fellow. Sometimes one finds such a 'key' to a challenging child by allowing warm and welcoming 'heart' thoughts to move around them, picturing the child as a person as big as oneself with a striving spiritual nature beyond the visible one. Children are small only in stature! Occasionally I stood helpless in my kindergarten with a little piece of 'dynamite' or heap of unmovable misery before me, imagining them in their wholeness. Often we were both rewarded by finding a new way of moving forward.

I put an over-active, noisy, challenging boy of 5 next to me in the story corner, not speaking. He wriggled and looked at me quizzically. After a while, copying me, he became still. I said, 'Shall we make a secret?' He liked to play tricks, so this appealed. 'Yes!' 'We could make a prince,' I said. 'Oh, yes'. 'No one else need know, we could do it here.' 'Let's do it now!' he whispered. We sat quietly together stitching a little figure of blue felt with tiny gold crown. He was radiant. Inquisitive children came, but they respected my saying, 'something special', and went away. The prince was to live in the walk-in cupboard, where the children weren't generally allowed to go, on a high shelf which the boy could reach with a chair. I left him free to talk to his prince, or to put him in his pocket for a while if he was bouncy. The other children were curious, but my repeated 'something special' let them trust me and sense his need and so be generous and content. His whole being focused on this upright little prince. His mother said he couldn't wait to come every morning, to go to my cupboard and talk to his prince. He would come out and play in a quiet way. After a few days, I secretly put a circle of red felt underneath the prince. When he saw it, he raced out to tell me his prince had a palace! I quietly put a little star on the 'palace' one day. The transformation in this child was a magical mystery. Here was inner movement, guided surely by spiritual transformation.

Our character is displayed in gesture and speech. We recognize someone approaching long before we discern any details. This is the secret of the silent movie, where words are superfluous and body language says it all. When my father visited, he walked along smoking his pipe, hands clasped behind his back and humming. A week later my 21-month-old son suddenly walked about mouthing the pipe, hands behind his back, humming in his high-pitched voice. And Ryan, just walking, used to grunt when bending down, copying Grandma getting things off a low shelf. How we are, move and think, what we say, feel and do—these are soaked up and recreated by the young child. Once in ringtime I bent down to pick up a thread from the floor. Immediately, several children bent down to pick up imaginary threads. Our words often fall on stony ground, whereas what we *do* may work like a charm.

Training versus free movement

Ballet, gym and martial arts are popular for the young. Dancing teacher Elsie did not like the advent of leotards and exams for children. She thought they stole something from the art and pushed children too much into the trained aspect. 'There is a respectful, beautiful gesture in holding out a little skirt, and dancing flows better in little ones without a uniform and pressure.' When children move in imitation, they remain unconscious of their actions, and their movement is freer and more natural. If taught specific exercises and movements, they have to think about what they are doing, and the amazing element of copying disappears. They become self-conscious, and may even bother about what they have to do. Leotards may help body-awareness and enable movement to be observed, yet I feel the training involved nowadays in most ballet schools, let alone exams, is not ideal for young children. Gym and martial arts certainly support muscle development and control, yet this can also be learnt in free play both indoors and outside. When watching Mozart's *Magic Flute*, (see Chapter 1), I could see that the smaller children were not highly trained because they were unselfconscious and simply imitated the older ones in the group. They were dressed in very simple costumes of gorgeous colours, as birds and animals, which must have been a delight for them. They all looked so happy, and not at all worried and concerned. Who wants to see unnatural, highly-trained small children? Part of the fun is to see them being normal and enjoying themselves.

It is a good idea to let babies lie flat on the floor or lawn on a blanket, away from draughts, and later in a play-pen with two or three toys, from where they can watch the family. Siblings can climb in and out to play. A play-pen is not a prison or place of punishment but one of safety, which can help the parent or carer get on without worrying for a while. Swings and rockers electronically activated with music may seem soothing but

Grandma gives a friendly push

are not a substitute for a friendly hand or voice. Many babies spend much time on their backs or bottoms. It is wise to put them on their tummies for a part of the day as they need to kick backwards, lift their head and push up, stretching neck, spine, arms and shoulders, before rolling over and sitting. When in a sling or rocker they can't practise these skills. Quite a few children don't crawl (important for right/left co-ordination, needed for writing, reading and balance generally). Some push backwards, or do a bottom shuffle. Some paediatricians and therapists advise children with certain learning difficulties to learn to crawl if they didn't do so before. Children have more chance to crawl naturally if earlier movement skills such as kicking, stretching, waving and rolling have been rehearsed. The development of movement is not only that of growing *up*, but also progresses *downwards*: first the head is lifted; arms stretch, hands grasp, then trunk and head are lifted together, the child sits and crawls, and only then do the legs become strong enough to stand.

Through movement one can help children with problems. For instance, a child who is over-active intellectually with an uncontrolled physique can be given plenty of running, jumping, walking and clay or wax modelling. Encouraging climbing, hanging and throwing helps those with weak arms (also often the result of an imbalance of intellectual as opposed to bodily activity). Two girls of about 12 and 10 in a cathedral service fidgeted the entire time. Service sheet, shirts, shoes, hair, skirts, kneelers, jewellery, hair, prayer books. Perhaps they were cold, for they had next to nothing on, or was it sugar or additives in their diet, or were they over-stimulated?

Over the years I experience an increasing number of children who are clumsy, bump into things, fall easily, fidget, rock to and fro, spin round and round or bang their heads on something. These are signs of underdeveloped motor and balance skills, and contribute to increasingly prevalent learning difficulties. If door-bouncers or baby-walkers (exercisers) are used too young, the spine, feet and legs are not ready to support the body. In pushchairs, slings and baby-carriers, the child can't wriggle or kick properly, and the arms are constricted. In the first months, holding up the relatively heavy head over-burdens the soft spine, especially in an upright sling. There are waist-sling seats for those who can already sit up, which have the advantage of the parent's arm around the child. Overuse of slings means that baby may be dragged around everywhere, not left in peace. Little arms and legs float 'touch-lessly' in the air. How much can those in upright slings see the parent's face, whether facing inwards or outwards? Outward-facing slings expose the child to every sensation that comes towards him. I saw a delightful young Dad carrying his sleeping 8-month-old, fast asleep on one arm, managing the shopping and trolley with the other. In a European country I've seen many young parents carrying their babies in their arms, whilst the foreigners had slings or strollers.

Spatial orientation

Rhymes accompanied by movements help children learn body geometry, essential for future thought processes, for instance forwards and backwards, up-down or side-to-side. Balance is nurtured by rocking—in arms, in a cradle, on an adult's knee or in a rocking-chair. Walking along a wall, jumping, climbing, skipping, hanging, rolling, ball-catching and throwing all develop spatial concepts. Lill, 6, in an action game involving 'polishing a sword' (one arm then the other): 'It's difficult for me to polish my right arm, because I'm not left-handed'. It wasn't really, but her cognition and sense of spatial orientation were developing.

Movement of the arms is more conscious than movement of the legs. Of course we don't think about how we pick up a cup of tea, write, or turn the steering-wheel of the car. Yet when beginning to practise hand-to-eye co-ordination such as putting the needle into the fabric where we want it, or drawing a flag at the top of the castle, arm use becomes increasingly deliberate. Learning a drum roll (left left, right right, left left, right right), pulling a church bell-rope in a co-ordinated way in a group, decorating a cake, pricking out seedlings or using a mouse at the computer: all these need consciousness, not possible in the animal world.

Getting about

When I was 14, I went abroad for the first time, the second child in the class to do so. Unthinkable today! Ever more people live in countries away from their family, so they naturally want to visit each other. Holidays with young children may be more advantageous spent in the same country not too far away. Travelling is wonderful for adults and older children. With our mature consciousness we are in control and have concepts of what we want, see and hear, and of where we are, which the little child doesn't. A local paper reviewing a particular event wrote in a positive spirit that a couple 'had travelled two hours by car with their 8-week-old daughter to be there!' It is so easy to pop the little one in the car seat, but she spent a total of four hours crumpled up. Many babies in carriers have their head banging against the sides. In a windy, cold, sunny place, a family was muffled up, but the baby in the carrier had bare head and feet, the sun shining in his eyes.

Not long ago, prams were the usual mode of transport for baby. They lay flat, looking up at sky, birds, trees, clouds, passing houses and faces of loved ones, with plenty of room to kick and play with a rattle. It is a rare but happy thing to see one now. A canopy shielded the eyes from the sun, and there was plenty of room for the shopping underneath and a little seat on top for another child when the walk was too far. With a cat net over it, sleeping in the garden was natural. But it wouldn't go in the car. Ubiquitous convenience for parents can mean long-term inconvenience for children in terms of movement and sense development. The all-comfort scenario of the latest car seats and strollers puts the child into the elderly-in-an-armchair category; some even restrain nearly all the child's movement.

As little shops and village schools disappear, more transport is needed. Reins are rarely seen today because of increased use of stroller and car, but may sometimes be preferable to these if people feel safer with the child in reins. One advantage of them is that they allow the child to walk rather than being pushed along on wheels. Elinor, 2, loved being in hers, and felt safe in the big city that way. She even liked to put them on herself. We did not use them with our children: we just held hands. So long as reins are not used to excess and the child is not dragged along they may serve a purpose. Children enjoy being a 'pony'. 'Faster, faster, faster!' called the little girl, giggling and squealing to her 'rider' Granny who was struggling to keep up. I have seen many children having fun playing with each other using real or play reins.

I had a number of kindergarten children who could only move in the unhealthy way they had experienced from road and screen: jerky, mechanical and stiff, with fidgety or automated gestures. Such children may well need therapeutic education. A movement therapist told me he treats children from as young as 2 up to teenagers, for reasons as varied as not lying flat when a baby, to lolling in front of the computer and TV, and having little or no sport.

What does the defenceless child experience in the *forward-facing* pushchair? Can we imagine ourselves down there, often very close to the ground, and what comes towards us? Legs, noise, dust, exhaust fumes, strangers, traffic, even heavy lorries may be there. Could one find a higher one with the child facing the adult? The child needs to see the adult and be protected from unnecessary, unhealthy sensations. As they are barely moving, children also need extra protection from the cold, including hands, feet and head, and the adult needs to be aware of protecting their heads and faces from the sun. If children are big enough to run about the garden and playground, they don't need a pushchair unless it's really far.

A few observations

Tiny baby in buggy, crooked, arms open and trembling as big lorries pass, completely bemused.

A 5-year-old pushed in buggy on to train, then running about being a nuisance, getting into it again before the train stops, mother struggling to get it off.

A 6-year-old in school uniform on buggy-stand, baby inside, mother having difficulty stretching round her big girl who had probably been sitting a lot already.

A 2-year-old happily walking, screams when made to sit in the buggy.

Mother pants uphill with her children of 18 months and 3 years in twin pushchair; both have bare heads, hands and feet on a cold day.

An 18-month-old in pushchair, imprisoned behind bags of shopping, hood and sides up in the rain, crying piteously, no communication with oblivious mother.

A 5-year-old in December with cold, red nose and hands and white face, on pushchair stand.

But:

Another 5-year-old in December with rosy cheeks, pushing baby brother, laughing with Mum.

Mother hand-in-hand with 2-year-old in supermarket, says, 'Shall we take a basket?' and does so.

Friend takes off own cardigan to wrap chilly little one in buggy.

How important is it for babies and children to see what is coming? When a mother asked her little boy whether he wanted to sit by the window in the train, he replied, 'I want to sit with you, Mummy'. His priority lay not in the view but in the closeness of a loved one.

Speaking and listening, audible movement

'See ya again, please God', said Liam to me, 'Mind yourself now.' This endearing Irish farewell sped me on my way. Communication is essential and life giving. We give children communicative tools from the very beginning, chanting or singing, 'How are you my chick, have you just woken up?' Adults speaking properly and clearly in whole sentences supports speech, as does good articulation, also for babies who learn additionally through lip reading. Manual skills in play and craftwork are connected to small motor skills for speech, which is movement in mouth and larynx. Learning foreign languages enriches the mother tongue and is vital for communication between peoples and cultures. Children understand the gestures in sound and respond accordingly through imitation. Regional dialects and even some languages are becoming homogenized or dying out, losing pictorial expressions as 'a kink in the pots' (strangulated intestine) or 'puddn poke' (long-tailed-tit's nest). Not long ago Fanny, Gay, Dick and Willie were normal names. Great efforts are being made to retain and support the richness and identity of languages, such as Welsh.

Children gradually come to terms with language. 'What's 'doasyou'retold'?' asked a 2-year-old of her mother who was trying to make her replace brushes on the chemist's shelf. Lydia, 6-years-old, said they couldn't buy the house they wanted because there were holes in the roof. Her parents enlightened me. 'Ah, the sale has fallen through!'

Rhyming delights

Action rhymes help body geometry and speech.

Knock at the door	(tap forehead)	
Look in the window	(lift eyelid)	
Lift the latch	('lift' nose)	
Walk inside	(fingers tickle lips)	
Go down in the cellar	(fingers 'walk' down to tummy)	
And eat apples.	(tickle tummy)	Old rhyme

A master I have, and I am his man,
Galloping, dreary dun.
And he'll get a wife as fast as he can,
Galloping, dreary dun.
With a haily, gaily, gambo raily,
Gigg'ling, nigg'ling, galloping galloway,
Draggletail, dreary dun.   Old rhyme

Although young children practise speech, their main movement is in the limbs, so accompanying such rhymes with simple actions made up by parents makes the words become alive and comprehensible. Nursery rhymes are such a rich source. Many rhymes underline communication, such as 'Tommy Thumb' and 'One Misty Moisty Morning'. The younger the child, the less talking and the more action. Yet they can be marvellously descriptive, second only to Shakespeare.

'You painted maypole!' says Hermia to Helena in *A Midsummer Night's Dream.*—'You silly double pig!' said Liam to Louise.

'It's a bit higgely, piggely squiggely', said Rosy, trying to fold a cloth.

'What's "invisible"?' asked Mary. 'It's like . . . like . . . they can't see . . . like air, like the wind', mused Malachi.

My kindergarten group enjoyed watching short, active and humorous parts of *The Tempest* rehearsals by an older class in the open air. Although they didn't understand many words, 'Thou liest' was a favourite for the next few weeks during the daily practice of our fairy tale play of 'One-Eye, Two-Eyes and Three-Eyes': there comes a point when the mother and two sisters speak an untruth. 'Thou liest', the children said sagely to one another. Another phrase from *The Tempest*: 'Let me lick your shoe', was repeated to each other innumerable times. Perhaps they will remember it one day, should they do *The Tempest* themselves. I hope it gave them a taste for Shakespeare!

Language evolves continually. But it is becoming impoverished, with abbreviations, a shrinking vocabulary and poor enunciation. Speech difficulties are increasing. People are talking, talking—through radio, TV, the internet and mobile phones. Some is fill-in chat, and a general emptiness, untruth and unreality is becoming prevalent. The child should have language that is truthful, as a model. Radio and TV abound with fill-the-gap words, and one unrelated item tumbles after another with no space to breathe between. 'It's kind of, sort of, well I mean, you know, as I say . . .'. Visible, tangible, living contact is essential in the vital years of language formation. Children in front of the TV screen cannot practise speaking, for there is no communication. Background radio in the home may render babies unable to hear their family talking. From my work as teacher, advisor and trainer, I am aware of debate and concern about language delays affecting many children, and it is now recognized that spoken language skills have been neglected in favour of more formal literacy skills. The acquisition of speech is vital in early childhood for subsequent linguistic and thinking development. An inability to listen and a tuning out in the emotional realm can arise from bombardment with noise of every variety, leading to unawareness of the environment and spatial problems, and poor concentration and attention span.

Playing with words

A teacher said, 'We made a magnificent soup last week'. Max, 3 years old, 'repeated' quietly and dreamily, 'We were magnificent. [Pause]. We were magnificent. [Pause] We were magnificent'. How children love to play with language and practise without any incentive from anyone. Sartay, who was building in the sandpit and coping with an annoying child, 'I'm trying to make it beautifuller. I'm *trying* to make it beautifuller … I'm trying to make it *beautifuller* … I'm *trying* to make it <u>beautifuller</u>'. 'We saw a mindwill', said Lolly, 4. 'It's willmind', said her sister, 5. Correct speech is generally achieved by 6 or 7, no longer 'buyed', 'merembered' and such like, when the child becomes more aware of what she says. By 6, children can say things like, 'Say you didn't go out and we played together'. 'Yes, pretend I went to bed',—quite advanced grammatical phrases. Lisps should have disappeared by now. Already at 4, grammar is being tried out. 'This is a gooder way.' 'Yes, it's a much better way.' 'Yes, it's a much bettest way.' Words are exciting and important. 'Windscreevers' (windscreen wipers). 'Pig snores' (ripples on the finger tips after a bath). 'Waster paster basket' (waste-paper basket). 'When my brother was born, they had to put him in a conditioner.'

A natural progression is found in listening, followed by singing, then speaking, drawing, writing, then reading. Reading, an academic skill, is the natural progression from writing, an active limb skill, and drawing contains emergent writing. Singing comes before words; you can hear musical sounds already at 3 months. Mark sang the tune correctly (without words) of 'Twinkle, twinkle, little star' before a year old. Some unclear speech and missing consonants can arise from a hearing problem, requiring a second early hearing test, but it often arises through imitation. Being outside in nature opens the child's ear to sounds of every variety. Every year in spring we did action rhymes with bird sounds. The children then noticed woodpeckers, yellowhammers, swallows, different kinds of dove and other birds on our walks. Through activities such as baking accompanied by 'pat-a-cake', children keep the precious listening ability with which they were born. Simple dancing without words encourages listening. Dad can sing a tune and do a twist with his child around the living room. Mum can take her guitar and the children can dance to it, be it ever so simple. Is there really a need for CDs and radios, when the simplest live music is permeated by warmth of heart? In my last years as a teacher we had fun barn dancing regularly in kindergarten, also with parents, very simple of course and mostly in a circle, just accompanied by fiddle and tambourine. Listening and limb skills were strengthened through such rhythmical movement.

We are becoming used to increased volume. Singing with children should be as unaffected and natural as possible, avoiding the loudness of public music. Some is so loud that it actually damages young ears. There are people who think recorded classical music is good for young children, but unless it is for a personal reason, for instance a relative or friend's concert, I beg to differ. It may be too complex in its construction and be treated just as background, definitely no substitute for a live nursery rhyme. We need to work at the singing, chanting, skipping and ball games that used to be played on every street.

A moment for silence can be found in poem or song. This enhances listening quality and self-restraint, and allows the child to 'breathe'. (In music, the rests are sometimes as important as the notes.)

Five little peas in a pea pod pressed; one grew, two grew and so did all the rest.
They grew and they grew and they *grew* and they **grew**,
Till all of a sudden, the pea pod
... (pause as long as you like) ... popped!   Old rhyme

Making up action rhymes for your children is easy and fun once you've tried. They can be a bit local. Here is a selection.

Round and round, we'll be bound, all the way to Harbours Down,
Don't be slow, it's far you know, all the way to Wooders Row
Please mind out, don't get stuck, it's muddy in the River Uck.
Arms swing, legs fling, up the road to Ditchling.

Ears and hands and head and feet, all the way to Holey Street.
Fish and chips and apple pie, you can eat when you get to Lye.
You must use your knife and fork, when you go to lunch in York.
Stretch your legs a few miles more, all the way to Dinmans Tor.

Every parent knows how a hurt knee can be soothed with a hug and a little song. The parent chanting a story can help an unhappy child. Live music has harmony-bringing, therapeutic forces, resounding through the whole child. Latin *re-sonare* means to 'sound again'. Music and words ripple, ring, reverberate and echo through brain, heart, lung and muscle. Not for nothing do our toes twitch and feelings swell on hearing music. Making music at home brings a breath of fresh air to young children. Children of 6 should be able to clap in time. They need a certain physical maturity and consciousness to achieve this step. They should also be able to sing in tune. It has been said that we all have perfect pitch at birth. Repetitive songs, counting rhymes and the worldwide tradition of early lullabies support the child's memory, especially when accompanied by movements. I made a new singing play and told the children I was trying to learn it. 'Don't worry', said Sasha, 6, 'You only have to do it once, then we'll know it and can tell you where you've gone wrong'.

It is advantageous to keep tunes very simple, with gentle dynamics and no great interval leaps. You can make a good tune on just two or three notes. Do songs for little children really need accompaniment, or can they concentrate better on one sound? They practise musicality through repetition of what they hear, and love music-making. Recorded songs and stories for children are generally weak in my opinion, often a-rhythmical, with a confusion of instruments and voices and poor language. They can be helpful for parents who feel uncertain about learning songs and poems or who cannot read music. They can do it quietly on their own when the children are in bed.

The conductor of our local amateur orchestra cares about our sounds even more than the actual notes, making us work at the dynamics, rhythms, ebbs and flows of the music. Somehow the wobbly notes find their way mostly correctly into our music-making. So it should be with our little ones: if we give the ebbs and flows, the sounds and rhythms, this is a basis for everything to fall into place. We can give dynamics in such as the following action rhyme, which can be done with an eye squinting into rounded hands, and a finger popping out, varying the size of the gestures and the pace with the sounds.

In a tiny little house, so very, very quiet, so very, very small,
There lived a tiny mouse, so very, very quiet, so very, very small,
Nobody knew he was there at all,
Till, all of a sudden, ... OUT he popped!

(Fast for Baby mouse:)
In a tiny little house, so very, very quiet, so very, very small,
There lived a tiny mouse, so very, very quiet, so very, very small,
Nobody knew he was there at all,
Till, all of a sudden . . . . OUT he popped!

(Slowly for Grandfather mouse:)
In a tiny little **big** house, so very, very **loud** quiet, so very, very **big** small
There lived a tiny **big** mouse, so very, very **loud** quiet, so very, very **big** small,
Nobody knew he was there at all,
Till, all of a sudden . . . . **OUT** he popped!

(Back to normality:)
In a tiny little house, so very, very quiet, so very, very small,
There lived a tiny mouse, so very, very quiet, so very, very small,
Nobody knew he was there at all,
Till, all of a sudden . . . . OUT he popped!   Old rhyme

Children enjoy knee rhymes well past first childhood. Such verses enliven touch, movement and feel-good factor, through the closeness of another human being, the feeling of one's periphery, and balance in jiggling, joggling, wobbling, falling and coming back to the upright position.

To market, to market, to buy a fat pig.
Home again, home again, jiggety jig.
To market, to market, to buy a fat hog.
Home again, home again, jiggety jog.   Old rhyme

There is so much wisdom in these rhymes! Children can hardly have enough.

Anna Maria, she sat on the fire;
The fire was too hot, she sat on the pot;
The pot was too round, she sat on the ground;
The ground was too flat, she sat on the cat;
The cat ran away with Maria on her back.   Old rhyme

I often did the following with three children on my lap—one (father) on my right knee, one (mother) on my left, plus one (Uncle John) on the lap of my skirt. If I had just one child, I just let him drop to the right, then the left, and then return to the middle.

'Father and mother and Uncle John
Went to market one by one.
Father fell off . . . . . . mother fell off . . . . . .
But Uncle John went on, and on, and on . . . . . . and on . . . . . . and
on . . . . . .' (as long as you want).

Different types of singing game correspond to different ages. 'Ring-a-ring o' roses' is played in a circle, corresponding to the young child's all-in-one consciousness. A child or children in the centre, like 'The farmer's in his dell' is a picture of dawning separateness but still protected by those around. 'In and out the dancing bluebells', where the child goes in and out of the circle, is like the 6- to 7-year-old, peeping into the next stage of childhood and returning to the old one. 'Water, water, wallflower', engages children in turning outwards as a group, one after the other, and then all back in again. In going round the outside of the circle (for example, 'I sent a letter to my love') we see the child able to stand alone, independent of the apron strings.

CHAPTER 5

INSPIRATION AND PLAY

'Let's pretend we're dear little children.'

Creativity is for all

A child complained, 'She's copying me!' I said, 'It's because she thinks yours is so special'. A rosy glow came over her as she pushed her paper a little closer to the other child's.

Aristotle, Mozart, and Picasso were geniuses but parents are geniuses too when imagination is the cradle for inspiration. The architect creating a 'living' space is an artist; so too is the parent who makes a cosy home, neatly fits washing on to a too-small clothesline, or prepares a feast on a tight budget. Thinking how to make extra time to be with the children requires practical, artistic thinking. Directing in the boardroom or at the ship's bridge in a storm, or helping quarrelling children demands flexibility and mobility of imagination. The Indian ship's captain said he wasn't frightened in a gale, 'it

Sticks: an ever-inspiring plaything

just makes me more lively'. Others' creativity can also spur on not only adults, but also children, through their gift of imitation. Experience brings new imagination and ideas. How can I do it better? Imagination brings about new experiences, also in the older child.

You can make a kindergarten or any play-space out of a scruffy room: perhaps sanding an old wooden floor and giving a lick of paint. Treasures can come from visits to jumble sales, asking people to scour their attics, writing to firms for unwanted off-cuts and washing an unwanted but still-decent carpet from a recycling centre. Wood, pine cones, pebbles, shells or feathers are what you can find outdoors. Children collect the same, for their minds can turn any such thing into a multitude of playthings. Our 7-year-old son watched the tractor going round and round the field, then worked round and round the garden for days with his 'plough', a dead branch.

'Let's pretend we're dear little children', said one to another in the sandpit. Variations of this phrase abound, arising from the child's unity with the surroundings. How differently they see and think from us! Other examples of this special consciousness are: 'Let's pretend we're playing', and: 'I don't want to play, I'm doing a puppet show' (on the floor amongst a 'landscape' of playthings from nature). I can't emphasize enough that young children have a completely different kind of understanding from ours. It is so helpful for both ourselves and the child to see this. Healthy children can play all day in their 'other' world, stopping only to eat and sleep. A friend told me he was expected during childhood holidays to appear only for meals—much the same as it was for us when young.

Children 'breathe the world in' through sense impressions, and 'breathe it out' again in imitation and creativity. They have few needs, just love, warmth, shelter, security, food and the freedom to play. Imitating others, Ryan bandaged Granny's imaginary 'owies' (sore places), and Nina spent hours at a table alone, playing travel agents. Play can help children escape from troubles. They identify

Odd-shaped pieces for inspiration

with situations and feel themselves to be managing their own lives. They can relive joys and fears and find healing. In war zones children re-enact horrors and can cope better: they are in charge and strengthened as they play them out.

Play as a tool for learning and practising skills

Children's drive to play and hone their multiple skills tends to be used by adults to further 'learning' of literacy, numeracy and science. Sometimes play is seen as of secondary importance in the anxiety to reach goals and targets, so children are led down a path foreign to them. A bewildered nursery group was to copy a contemporary artist's painting. 'You've all got lots of imagination!' said their teacher. To these young children, words such as 'artist', 'imagination' and 'primary colours' meant nothing.

Truly free play is cross-curricular, weaving through all subjects and skills from emergent writing to learning tolerance. Literal, linguistic, cognitive, communicative faculties are practised in self-directed activity. For instance, pullies and knot-tying promote physical abilities and practical thinking, helping children to orientate themselves in space. Ribbons, string, cords and ropes are invaluable toys, not dangerous if children are guided in their use. The 'house' walls were collapsing. One child held on to the cloths and cords, the other the clothes-horse. 'We'll have to fix it, or we'll have no time to play.' 'Yes, we'll be too late.' What is play? Obviously not the original building, nor the fixing. Left to their own devices with lots of life to play with, the children are naturally faced with problems to solve and will find ways to do it. 'We could try to build a ship.' ' How?' ' We could put a chair here.' ' Oh yes, and we could put another one here and a plank between,' till the ocean liner is complete, with flag, captain, passengers and tickets costing 'twenty hundred seven a hundred thousand'. I could never afford such a trip. But the children have ultimate responsibility and seem to find the necessary coins and notes.

The wooden-brick boats wouldn't go under the wooden-brick-built 'bridge'. 'We could put some bricks under this end.' The bridge was now tilting, but no matter, it was all the better for the (brick) cars to slide down and park in the 'car park' of wooden bricks.

We find early maths in tidying up: categorizing, addition and subtraction into baskets and boxes, and geometry in shape and folding. Gerry, 4, made a triangle of a large cloth. 'I did it all my way, I did it the trangle [sic] way.' Children may be given a pre-built shop and counters to learn arithmetic, but when left to play on their own they will build a shop one day themselves and

Imagination and skills

use buttons or shells to count out the change without any interference from us, simply recreating their own experience.

Mathematics plays a big part in role-play; some roles are bigger than others.

> First child, 5 years old, holding up ten fingers: 'I've got *this* many'.
> Second child, 4, holding up ten fingers: 'I've got more than you!'
> Professor, 5: 'No you haven't, you've got the same, five on each hand. But they have more in countries like Africa and Australia'.
> Third child, 5: 'How many do they have in Australia?'
> Professor: 'Six on each hand'.

'How long is it till we can go to sleep?' 'It's 13 hours to 12 o'clock. It's nearly night-time. Twenty, twenty-one, twenty-two, twenty-three o'clock.' Fine-tuning will come about later.

> Mark and Lars, who had just had a baby sister, were building.
> Mark, 4: 'This is the tower of Bonglingham' (four feet high).
> Lars, 6: ' This is the tower of heaven' (six feet).
> Mark: 'This is the tower of silly' (two inches, great merriment).
> Lars: 'This is the leaning tower of Pisa. The leaning tower is as old as Great Grandma.'
> Mother: 'Oh, quite old then, but not *very* old.'
> Lars: 'Oh, yes, as old as ... as ... as when Great Grandma was in her mother's tummy'.

As cognitive skills develop through play and experience, the correct numeracy will fall into place. Posy, 4, using a long builder's measure: 'Shall we measure this table?' Much furniture followed, with appropriate language: 'Not even long enough', 'six-two metres' . . . .

Sociability

Charlie, 4, struggled to move a basket of wood. Rosy, also 4, came to help. 'We have to pull it together.' It worked, but Charlie with his young memory had forgotten the reason for the move and went to play elsewhere.

Children give us tools for learning too. Through observing their play we can discover some of their needs. For instance, a child who builds the same house to go inside every day may be building reassurance and security or escaping from others, or one who wraps dolly up in endless cloths might be needing protection and love herself.

Lucas, 5, lying on the floor, balancing a squirrel on a log asked, 'Erdal, help me with this'. Erdal did, and one observed balance, sprawling, bending, stretching and curving around. What better way to develop social skills than by being naturally co-operative? Any amount of contrived socializing on the adult's part cannot replace natural knocks and aids. Lulu, 6: 'Do you like my painting?' Helen, 6: 'No'. Lulu: 'I hate yours'. Pause. Lulu: 'I like your painting'. Helen: 'I like yours too'.

Those of different ages play happily together, squabbling too, but this is daily living. I have experienced many children who were previously a bit hard become sociable and rekindle their capacity for imagination.

Creating together

Rose, 7: 'I'm going to be the Daddy'. Sammy, 4: 'I haven't been the Daddy for two weeks'. Philip, 6: 'You can't have two Daddies'. Tureg, 5: 'Why not? You *can* have two Daddies. Why can't we just agree?' Sammy: 'Why couldn't I be the Daddy in another family? I could live over there'.

Letter from a friend: 'Sandy and Thomas play together and make their own fun, which is a tremendous help'.

Freddie, 3, cooked contentedly alone on a stack of shelves. Jack, 6, said, 'Are you playing with that?' meaning the stack of shelves. Freddie, understanding a plate, said, 'No'. As Jack removed the shelves, saying, 'We need it', Freddie cried out, 'Not *all* of it!' Overruled, he swept conkers about crossly. Later, Jack told Freddie, 'We've made a special house' (with the shelves), 'you can come in later, it's not ready yet. It's special'. But Freddie, uninterested, had progressed to higher things.

Older children include younger where they can be useful or want to take part. 'You can be the baby/ dog/ visitor/ patient.' Commonly one hears, 'Who's the boss of this game?' 'Who's the first boss/ second boss?' 'Well, you can be the next boss.'

Cooking in the 'kitchen'

They learn to negotiate, practising co-operation and social balancing acts. Shashma, 6, 'All right then, you *can* come in our game. But you *are* allowed not to play if you want'. Or Holly, 6: 'Don't come in our hospital, you'll get sickness all over you'. To learn to be sociable, 'only' children also really benefit from being able to play with others. Sam put on a star gown for the Christmas play. 'He thinks he's a shepherd', said Dumal, also 5, in a fatherly sort of way. '*I'm* a shepherd.' (He himself had the donkey's ears on.)

The development of play in the growing child

A friend of 58 played on the beach with a little boy. 'How old are you?' she asked. 'I'm not old, *you* are', he replied.

Parties, cards, instruments, puns: adults play too. Advertisements are often based on a play on words. We play with our thoughts, finding the best way forward in social and political situations. The more we play as children, the richer the harvest of effective, moral and philosophical thinking. My thinking was static when I hunted for the square screw-on lid of a square jam jar, but lively when the pushchair axle broke some way from home and I tied it up with string. Phoebe, 6, was constructive: 'If you need a steering wheel, you just take a basket'. Jamie and Alan, 6, were resourceful in language too: 'I'm a collie dog'. 'I'm a bulldozer dog'.

Soon after birth, babies play with their tiny fingers. As the eyes become more focused they grasp a rattle, gurgling with delight at the funny sound; siblings too love to make baby chuckle. In the first years they make discoveries through investigative play. Later on, the child makes a turn around every lamppost, delaying the frustrated parent. Busy mother has to come to an elaborate tea with grass soup and layered cake of wood slices.

To the child below 3 years, objects don't usually represent anything else. The wooden spoon is for stirring, but after 3 it can become a broom, telephone or screwdriver. Now that affective progress is added to investigation, play becomes purposeful and imaginative; creativity is blossoming. The 3- to

Pieces of wood and a cord inspired this play

5-year-old finds inspiration in objects and starts a game. In the 5- to 7-year-old inspiration begins to lead children from within, so they search for what they need. Stamina and will power develop when children become deeply absorbed in play. By 7, children play with pictures in the mind rather than equipment. Examples of the different stages of play:

Lakshmi, 9 months, picked up a water bottle from the restaurant floor, sucked it, then pulled himself up and sucked the side of a chair.

Stephen, 18 months, repeatedly pulled the laundry in and out of the basket.

Susan, 2, held the neighbour's baby, babbling and cooing like mother, giving her a 'drink' from a play cup.

Jennifer, just 3, crouching under a table, was quivering with excitement and peeping out at her mother. 'Catch me! . . . No, don't catch me! . . . Catch me, Mummy!' Shrieks of joy rang round the room when mother got up, but mixed with uncertainty as she got close, then giggles as she hugged her. 'Do it again!' One could see amongst the giggles and sparkles, uncertainty in her new con-sciousness, also that when mother did catch her, she wasn't sure if she wanted to be caught. I am me, or am I? Where am I?

Georgina and Hannah, 3 and a half, were squabbling. I brought them 'food' and asked where the stove was. All troubles forgotten, Georgina said, 'I'm the stove'; 'and I'm the house', said Hannah.

Coran, 4, showed me pine cones. 'These are real ones' (on the table), 'and these' (inspiring his game) 'are pretend ones.'

Children of 5 were cutting up paper to make money, saying some were credit cards.

Marcus, 6, had created a scene with one space for playing and one for going in and out. 'This is where the play hides, because plays hide, you know.' His mind was able to recreate the wings he had experienced in the theatre.

Jenny, 7: 'We can be grown-ups and have a conversation. Let's sit on the bench and discuss our problems'.

Playful talk and action

We need to nurture children's creativity, but can also use our own. Instead of over-reacting to tricky situations, maybe exacerbating the problem, we can call on children's wonderful adaptability. Once my group had aggressive 'tomato guns'. I took a broom (clean!), and talked into it upside-down near my ear. Within a moment there was imitated 'phoning' with every broom and brush in sight. When they had run out, they took whatever else bore some relationship to a phone. Shooting was forgotten and we were peaceful once more.

We can talk to children with their unified world in mind. Jeannie, 6, (from an insecure home) often pinched others. Taking her hands in mine, I talked to them, 'Well, I wonder why you did that? Did Jeannie tell you to? No? Did she say she didn't really like it?' Then I looked at her. 'When you go to bed, you can ask them why they didn't listen to you, and when you wake in the morning you can ask them to be kind again.' Jeannie: 'Yes I will'. Next morning I asked how it went. 'I told them last night but I forgot this morning'. 'Never mind, we can do it now', I said. Such conversations took potential guilt away from the child and nevertheless would achieve their end through consciousness-raising and security given in loving, understanding, playful talk. Children understand this language. To Aidan, who was kicking under the table, I said, 'Please would you ask your feet to sit properly. Did you see them climbing up there?' Aidan spoke seriously to the troublesome feet. I used such playful disciplinary measures with lasting success.

In a fight over a play-stand I said, 'Oh this poor stand is getting rather bruised, I'll look after him for a bit'. The fight stopped and they looked after it themselves. Sometimes I tied myself up in a blanket, put a hat on upside down, got in a tangle with my apron or put a leg into a sleeve if a distraction was needed. The children loved that. Of course it isn't right to distract all the time because children may need to become aware of what they are doing (for example Jeannie's pinching), but you can have fun too. If play isn't happy, you might say, 'If you need a tree/ rabbit/ ball/ bed, let me know', so inspiring them to change course.

A child of 5 had seen the film *Jurassic Park*. He was unable to get it out of his system, and was imitated by others. After a week he was still wild and spent much time bent double on the floor growling with clenched hands. His parents and I were at our wits' end. One day I was chopping apples, and he was still a dinosaur. I asked, 'Can dinosaurs chop apples?' The child, on all fours with head near the ground, slowly nodded. But he couldn't raise himself. In a moment of inspiration, I fetched a book with beautiful illustrations, opening it at a page with a shining prince surrounded by lovely colours, and putting it under his face. After a few minutes his cramp dissolved and he stood up. The other children were released from the spell of the *Jurassic Park* child's play and made a shop. Josy: 'I'm going to be a person now because I'm buying food for the kangaroos'.

How children love a game. They can be 'pedagogical': 'Shall we play the no-talking-game?' (for noisy meals at kindergarten); for elbows on the table—not very good for posture—we might say, 'Does anyone have glue on their elbows?' or 'I'm just going to see whether anyone has elbows on the table', looking first at the children who haven't, and ending up with the child who has by now removed them. At story time, a doll on the knee was allowed. If the children with dolls were fidgeting I said, 'If those dolls are too young to listen they need to go to bed', which pulled them together themselves. Such little games work well in the family too. We would never say such things to an adult or even an older child, but with children in the first stage of childhood it works, because we are meeting their feeling of being all-at-one with their surroundings, before they begin to have physically detached concepts. One day the children were being growly, scratchy leopards and hyenas. Without looking at them, I said quietly to a visitor, 'Those animals are making me a bit nervous. Are they frightening you too?' The room grew quiet as they watched us. 'Maybe they are hungry', I said. Straightaway they found the wooden cotton reels and conkers and 'fed' each other. We had done nothing but appeal to their human natures and given them the opportunity to tame themselves on their own.

Children can relieve awkward situations too. Alexander, 5, was bullied off the rocking-horse by Melanie, 6, who had been making a shop. He watched her, then said, 'I think there are some robbers in your shop'. There weren't, but she scrambled down to see, and carried on playing there, whilst he remounted. I took some 'oil' to George's noisy 'machine'. He responded by 'pouring it in' to make it quieter. Later other children made a noisy machine, and he told them, 'We need a soft drill, not a hard one, a soft one, then we softly hum it. The other one is too noisy'. The deeper one's relationship to the children and the less one speaks unnecessarily, the more one's *doing* will be effective. In order to work in this way, the adult needs trust and confidence. It is demoralizing for all when 'Stop that' and such like lead nowhere except to obstinacy and disharmony, but playful creativity is both easy and healing.

Young children like hiding—under the table, behind the curtain, under your skirt. For them it is a game and a search for security; they want to be found and recognized. They cover their eyes under 5 years old and think you can't see them because they are all one and the same. But they may not like it if *you* hide or shut your eyes, for it is as though you were gone, and it makes them afraid. I never blindfolded children under 7 years old for a game, and I let little ones stay with me for hide and seek.

Endless play

'Know you what it is to be a child? It is to be something very different from the man of today. It is to have a spirit yet streaming from the waters of baptism; it is to believe in love, to believe in loveliness, to believe in belief; it is to be so little that the elves can reach to whisper in your ear; it is to turn pumpkins into coaches, and mice into horses, lowness into loftiness, and nothing into everything, for each child has a fairy godmother in its own soul; it is to live in a nutshell and to count yourself the king of infinite space . . .'   Francis Thompson

My landscape-architect son had designed a playground for a primary school and was helping the children plant a wall of willow. He wound a couple of snippets that needed cutting off into crowns. Soon the children, even the 10-year-olds, were excitedly twisting crowns out of snippets for themselves. After a while with the 5- to 7-year-olds, he said it was time for a tea break, pouring out tea into 'cups' from his imaginary kettle and passing them round. Only about half the children joined in the game. The others couldn't understand what he was doing and asked where the kettle and cups were. Are we giving enough time to play freely as against prescriptively? An old man I met in the Welsh hills echoed this when he said children were losing the art of play and the magic of childhood. Children are not little adults, although much modern pressure would have us think so. What they *are* is *potential* adults. Play lays the ground for us to become flexible, adaptable, independent thinkers, not running with the masses but conceiving individual thoughts and actions. It is vital that unguided play be given *time* in childhood, so children can sail in their imaginations anywhere in the world, and out of it.

> Wallace, 5: 'Your spirit is in your blood'. Denny, 6: 'If it comes out, you die'. Wallace: 'Your spirit is transparent, you can go through it'. Denny: 'Then you have a power vest to swim in the sky'.

Conkers, once part of an essential game, have been branded dangerous. They belonged to essential playthings in kindergarten, as the children knew what they were allowed to do with them and what they were not. As sticks are the first thing children pick up on a walk, I let children have them and taught them how to respect and play with them properly and safely. 'I'm carrying this stick *down*', said Adam, a previously rough boy. Another once-essential game was to push the adult-facing pram off ahead then run to catch it, to the delight of child and pusher.

Observation of children reveals re-creation of experiences, in which, through these powerful forces of imagination and imitation, boundless creativity arises. Creating means making new, and within it is the development of living, original thinking. With simple materials there are limitless possibilities to support children's brimming activity. Through the senses the child absorbs the environment, drawing it into an inner imaginative world. It is so wonderful for the child to be able to imitate an adult involved in some meaningful activity, whether rolling out pastry or laying bricks. Even computers are re-created, such as Arkanie's, of which the keyboard for her 'typing' was a cushion on a chair, and the screen a cushion propped up against the back.

> In the street, a 7-year-old: 'What are we going to do now?' The 5-year-old: 'What are we going to *do*? Play of course'.

From a letter to parents:
If I know of workmen nearby, I take the children to watch, not to learn how to mend a wall or whatever, but so they can take it all in and recreate it in their play. This creative playtime is very precious; within it lie the seeds of their future ability to handle all sorts of situations.

Do you want that on your hips?

The dessert trolley arrived at our table. My friend said out loud to herself, 'Now, Martha, do you really want that on your hips?' This question may crop up when we are confronted with cartoon characters in book, film and toy which can only be described as ugly and intentionally frightening, 'busty' teenage glamour dolls, soft toys with distorted 'electronic' voices, and caricature dolls out of proportion. It seems that the more commerce strives for life-like detail, the less room is allowed for the child's imagination.

'Hurry up with that water, make it snappy', said James, 5, 'Sit down, my lad, sit down'. In this example one can hear an echo of the energetic adult. Once we have understood the way children soak up their surroundings, making everything they see and hear part of themselves, and then recreate them through imitation, maybe we could stop from time to time and ask ourselves, 'Do we want *that* on our child?' It is common to see children working out the images they have received with robot and 'cartoon' talk and unnatural movements. We might brush it off as only a bit of harmless fun, but the observer sees quite clearly how much it works its way into the depths of the child. Wouldn't it be better if that place were reserved for the beautiful, the human and the graceful? My young children and I visited someone who had unfortunately lost a hand. He invited them to see 'some interesting things'. Meanwhile I chatted with his wife, but following up an uneasy hunch, I soon went to join the children. They were sitting white-faced on the floor with a row of hands in front of them while he demonstrated taking them on and off. What was a game for him only frightened my children.

Animals and robots

The majority of girls tend to make social games in which fantasy talk is involved, liking to play families, and animals such as mice, horses, cats and dogs. Many boys tend towards mechanics and reality, preferring to play machines, space ships and animals like snakes and leopards, at times becoming wild and aggressive. Children need to be lifted out of the animal world and back to the human realm when they become unkind, for instance by suggesting to them that someone look after and feed them. (I once saw a colleague saying, 'Let's look for the Mummy Shark'.) Playing with pretend machines can be very imaginative. Animal play is not always so creative. Children easily fall into imitating really wild, aggressive animals rather than the gentle, domestic kind. The books of Beatrix Potter, Jill Barklem and Margaret Tarrant endow their animals with over-ridingly good qualities. The language and illustrations are graceful and meet children in a space where they feel comfortable. However, although these books have an important place in our culture, as do fairy tales such as 'The Three Little Pigs', it is essential to give children pictures and stories of people. Sometimes in kindergarten if I couldn't find a way to divert the children's aggression when they were playing as animals, I had to say, 'Let's put the animals away and play being children and people instead'. Very often the children responded with what appeared to be relief. When Lazlo, 6, was a very threatening lion, I quietly began some handwork (as I knew he liked sewing). 'Can lions sew?' he asked, and the 'lion' soon vanished.

I observed pre-school children at a table of dinosaurs with flashing lights and opening mouths. They tried to fulfil their natural drive of home-play, calling them 'Daddy and Mummy dinosaur', and wanting to give them lunch, but their imaginations found nothing to feed them with except the other dinosaurs themselves, which resulted in their crashing dinosaurs together.

Entertainment

Is it easier to keep children entertained and supervised rather than leave them to their own resources? I believe that on the whole parents don't need to play much with their children, as they are generally happy by themselves. They may be invited to hold the 'baby' or to 'come to tea' or take the 'dog' for a walk as part of the game, from the child's initiative. Some children interrupt others because they have lost the art of play themselves. Then they can be guided and shown how to play by the adult doing it, for instance playing on the floor with a landscape of natural playthings. Theme parks and other entertainment centres usurp the place of free play. They are unhelpful and poorly inspiring to the developing child, and heavy on the purse. Much time spent on scooters and bikes, although fun and physically stretching, is just not the same as freely creative play. Throughout the world, time and space for unguided play are being squeezed out, to the detriment of children's development. Creative children can be so entertaining. Jeffrey's practitioners were tearing their hair at broken heating and a leaking roof. He stood under the leak: 'I'm having a shower'.

> From a letter to parents:
> Freedom of movement and time for play, both essential to the
> development of young children, is becoming restricted. This is one reason

why we ask about extra curricula activities, because they take time away
from play and child-motivated movement. The number of children in our
'civilized' western culture who can play well is dwindling. I often
wonder why they are exposed to dinosaurs, guns, monsters and sharks,
which are foreign to their surroundings. Horridness and sensation are
highly marketable! Most sharks and dinosaurs are and were harmless,
but somehow it is not that on which the consumer marketers concentrate.
These things can have a devastating effect on children's play, mood,
sleep, eating and behaviour. Sometimes of course they learn about them
from older children, but if it is only 'second hand' it does not necessarily
make such an impact. I am so happy when families change things for the
sake of their children.

What is a plaything?

A plaything is something which allows the child's imagination to develop and inspires play, rather than something to be entertained or fascinated by. For example our bobble hat, put over our hand, can become a puppet, 'walking about' on our lap, while we make up a little story. In their minds, the bobble becomes the head and the hat the body. This may inspire watching children to take off their own hats and start their own story. I have made the point that manufactured toys can stifle the imagination by being too detailed. Commerce tends to push what it calls toys on to children, which they can only use as an onlooker, as these toys do everything themselves: there is nothing for the child to do. A grandmother of twelve grandchildren commented to me that children don't need toys; they usually have far too many nowadays and are happy with a cardboard box.

> Many parents have found they have to put a stop to computer games. Robert, 6, told me he didn't like them *Because you have to hurt people to win.* Dumas, 5, watched his brother, 7, on his games console, later explaining to others, *You have to kill to get to the next level.*

A family in a shop had their 3-year-old in a pushchair. They put a large teddy bear, which sang in a deep voice, on to his lap in front of his face. They said, 'Isn't that funny!' He cried and shrank away. Recommended ages given on toys are often astonishing, such as a steering wheel and screen with 'lights, sounds and activities for realistic driving fun' for children from 3 years. I really do think computers have no place in the young child's life, for they demand specific, limited responses in the child instead of encouraging physical, freely imaginative activity. This immobilizes children, who will not have the intellectual capacity to be master of it for many years yet. Children *are* masters of their *own* world. Playing with computers so easily makes them its slave. Electronic games' 'fun' may be hypnotizing.

People are becoming more aware of the inherent ecological problems in the use of plastic, not to mention the 600,000,000 domestic batteries produced annually which are toxic and cause huge dumping problems. We can do our bit towards solving the problem by choosing toys of natural materials. Synthetics in many forms are a very useful part of everyday life now. But I prefer natural materials for children because they are usually warmer and softer, have differentiation of colour and texture, and can usually be mended. Plastic toys left outside crack and fade to become very unattractive. Natural materials may be more expensive than synthetic but the child can benefit from being given fewer toys, and they last longer. I must say that children can get a huge amount of creative fun from the plastic version of the marble run which can actually be put together in any number of ways. There are jug kettles which make bubbling noises. Yet I have watched so many children picking up a piece of wood for a kettle and making their own bubbling and hissing. Which is the more playful? Wood of all shapes and sizes provides hours of entertainment. The less formed the toy, the more work for the child's limbs, heart and brain.

'Why shouldn't they have guns?' a young man asked me. 'It is the most normal thing for boys.' Is there something different about them today? There is a 'gun culture' growing everywhere around us. Certainly parents will want to address this in their own way. 'Bang, bang, you're dead', and the enemy collapses lifeless to the ground, victim of the pointed finger with shouted 'bang'. 'OK, you can be alive again now, get up.' So the dead spring to life and this is all part of living, happy play. But this play is developing in a significantly more unhealthy way with toy weapons of sinister detail. Toy guns, tanks and missiles actually promote more aggressive play, which does not accompany the use of imaginary weapons. Why should children know about them before they are old enough to understand what is going on in the world, unless they are the sorry victims of wars? It is counter–productive to moralize verbally with children on these matters, but one can attempt to channel their exuberance for fighting into knights on horseback, with swords which stay at their side.

Non-representational, inspirational playthings

> Boys of 6 and 4 played cars on a beach, 'brrrrrrming' around, making roads in the sand. For half an hour they crawled, rolled, stretched, kneeled, stood and lay on their sides, driving into imaginary distances. Their cars? Their own and their parents' sandals.

Believing that detailed playthings are impediments makes life easier, for each 'unformed' one can be a myriad of things, replacing twenty or a hundred others. Anton, 6: ' Stop going in and out of my rocket' (chairs with cloth over). James, 5: 'It doesn't *look* like a rocket'. Anton: 'Well, you just don't have any imagination'.

Sometimes children came new to my kindergarten, saw a room full of baskets of cloths, pieces of wood and shells, and said, 'Where are the toys?' They had not been used to transforming objects in their minds to playthings, but they soon found that old bedspreads, blankets, sheets, curtains and tablecloths or dyed muslin and plain cotton make wonderful walls, roofs, floors, fields, rivers, roads, forests. Whether old or newer, children shouldn't just take anything they want without asking. A cupboard, basket or box can be specifically for play-cloths. Natural fabrics help the sense of touch, and plain rather than patterned or pictorial leaves space for fantasy. Such cloths can be draped over chairs, boxes, playpens, benches, tables, or clothes-horses or play-stands. Clothes-pegs keep things together in awkward places, but also help the child to feel himself 'pegged together'. A broom handle hung at both ends from a hook in the ceiling with cloths draped over makes a roof. Into this conjured world can come 'hedges', 'credit cards', 'firemen', 'animals', 'food', 'babies', 'beds'—the list is endless. Everything can become something else, having its place in the child's treasure-trove mind.

Joseph, 6 and a half years, in his 'shop': 'Pigs for sale! Horses for sale!' I: 'Yes, please, I'd like to buy a pig'. 'Four pounds.' I fished about in my pocket for invisible money and handed it over. 'That's no good. I want *pretend* money. Here, you can have this.' He handed me a pine cone to pay for the pig.

> In the hospital waiting room a small boy pulled one large, complicated plastic toy after another out of the large box and spread them on the floor. He didn't know what to do. After a while his father found a teapot in the bottom, then the boy found two plates; at last he could play. He cooked, boiled and baked, then offered

cups of tea to the adults. One lady asked how much it cost; father looked on with embarrassed consternation. She smiled, put her hand in her pocket and said, 'It's only pretend money'.

Simplicity and care in the play space

Playing in a visually quiet room supports the child's powers of fantasy. A couple of nice pictures on plain walls are enough. Because young children don't remember what they have done unless we make a habit of 'forcing' this capability, displaying their work in pre-school can lead to competition and judgement. So we just had very few beautiful pictures or craftwork on the walls. Naturally parents like to hang up their children's pictures at home which is nice, and Granny and Grandpa can admire them.

From a friend: 'I hope Mark will find this bag useful for his toys'. Ideally, toys should have individual places to live, in boxes, drawers, bags, cupboards or baskets, and be put away every day. If possible, try to keep some order in the child's bedroom, for it should be a restful place. Generally, children have far more toys than is necessary. If a child does have a large amount, remember you can gather some up and let them 'go on holiday' to some attic or cupboard space, to let them come out some months later to replace others (by which time the child may have forgotten them anyway). I'm all for simplicity in the child's environment. Do the walls of a classroom, the cupboards and windows have to be covered with pictures, letters and numbers? What with advertising and the media, a child can't escape being bombarded with pictures, especially in the city. Why not give them a play area which allows free space for the child's imaginative pictures? Quality not quantity should guide us.

Tidying up—bore or relief?

Joseph and Daddy were playing with a bucket and tractor. Then Dad walked back up the beach with the bucket. 'Bring your tractor, Joseph.' No response. Joseph, about 2 and a half, ignored him and followed his father, who repeated his request. There was still no response, because Joseph, united in consciousness with his surroundings, did not recognize that *he* was the Joseph. Realizing this, Dad pointed to his son and said, 'Shall we ask that little boy whether he'd like that tractor, because Joseph doesn't want it'. Joseph trotted back to fetch it. Delightful moments such as this demonstrate that the authoritative approach, with orders or instructions for the pre-school child is not always fruitful.

Putting things away can be a satisfying, happy habit. By giving even very young ones a little basket for the cars or dolls' clothes, they can focus on something in the mess while you join in the tidying up. Once, when a teacher visited me, playtime, nearing its end, was getting rowdy. I started folding a cloth as usual at this time, and the whole group, quite ready for a bit of peace, started to tidy up out of imitation and routine. 'How on earth did you do that?!' the visitor asked me. The same place for each thing, and not too much, is already half-way there. The children are led by unconscious repetition and sense of purpose. It helps if the adult is enthusiastic about it and shares in the work as a model. You can appeal to children in class or at home: 'No one came to tidy these. Who will help?' 'I will! I will!' If someone was messing about, you can say: 'Whoever piled these in here may tidy them up. I don't need to know who it is'. Sometimes, when everyone seems tired and there is a seemingly insuperable muddle, a game can change the whole thing round, like the 'tidying-up-game': everyone (even if only one child) shuts their eyes and makes a nest with their hands into which an object which needs tidying away is placed. When they receive something they open their eyes, put it away and come back for more. You might fetch a chair and 'fall asleep' on it: an incentive to do all the tidying in secret with much whispering. When all is done, they 'wake' you and of course you show your delight. Occasionally in kindergarten I couldn't help with tidying, so I said, 'I am too busy to help you now, but shall we play the game where everyone taps me on the shoulder when they put something away?' They became very enthusiastic and busy. Children enjoy a challenge and can be so capable. Although they may love the games, make them the exception not the rule; otherwise they lose their novelty. When children are given time to finish their play and tidying up follows a regular pattern and is part of a rhythmical day, they do it without thinking and are content to do so, for they like order.

Making toys

If toys are individually made rather than mass-produced, they have a life of their own. All adults can make toys if they want, however simple, for creativity helps us to be resourceful. Anyone can use a saw, file and sandpaper, or a needle and thread. It doesn't matter if it 'doesn't look very good',

A 'landscape'

for the love and care that went into it is what counts. Evening classes for wood- or craftwork can be great fun. You can stitch pockets on to clothes for children's little 'collections'. They can work together with parents sanding wood or stitching a doll. These are such satisfying happy activities, lovely for the hands and great for co-ordination and manipulative skills. Leaving the knots of branches creates interest, to become a train funnel, bird-beak, hook, house-porch—whatever. You can chisel or gouge out little spaces to be windows, a doorbell or spots. Texture, shape, colour and smell are important. Inner pictures created with the aid of unformed toys flow in and out of the child's mind, reappearing in magical villages and landscapes. You can spread a couple of cloths on the floor, rumpling them a little, or have a basket, box or little logs underneath, then place a few stones, pine cones and shells there to make a 'landscape': already a picture will spring into the child's mind. I like to emphasize something of the four elements amongst children's playthings, especially, but not only at different times of the year, such as sand, stones and rocks for earth (in winter); water, plants and pieces of wood for the watery element (in spring); birds, bubbles, kites and mobiles for air (in summer); wood for play 'bonfires' and red pressed leaves and cloths for the fiery element (in autumn).

Dressing up—children and furniture

What fun to clip-clop in Mum's high heels or go out in Dad's hat. As with toys, garments can be as adaptable as possible. Bought outfits are expensive and can only be one thing, necessitating several for different characters. Children dressed as cartoon characters may well take on those characteristics, which is not always what the adult has in mind. The best fancy dress for a child is one with which you are happy that your child feels itself that way. Many people prefer their children to be free in their imagination to create anything in their minds from a plain gown. A simple tunic can be anything, and the colour may tell the character. A blue tunic can clothe a sailor, police officer, nurse or any person, with a belt of plaited cord and any hat to round it off. I invented hooded cloaks out of still good adult trousers of nice material, two from each pair. Cut the legs off at the top, stitch each one together there, then undo and hem the inside seams. They were very popular and so easy to put on and also to fold or hang up. We made dolls' sleeping bags out of the ends of old pullover sleeves by stitching up the ends and hemming the cut part, then attaching ribbons to them. Old sheets can be cut up to make tunics (a long rectangle with a hole in the centre for the head, all hemmed), and may be dyed in the washing machine. Unravelled or new wool or cotton yarn can be plaited or twisted to make ropes. These can also make a crown or hold a piece of muslin as a veil on the head. Dyed muslin and pieces of sheeting make landscapes, houses, dressing-up clothes, dolls' bedding, tablecloths or scenery for a puppet show. Clothes-horses and chairs make excellent frames for building. Knotting the corners of the two opposite ends of a cloth together and using these as loops over the tops of two chairs can make a hammock. Children used to make bunk beds by fixing the corners of a cloth to the top corners of two chairs with seats pushed together for the top one, with another bed on the seats and another on the floor. It is amazing what ingenuity they develop when left to their own devices. You can start such games off yourself, of course. You need so little! It is important that everything is kept clean and mended. Cardboard boxes invite wonderful games, and can be made attractive by covering the writing with material or plain paper.

Children need balls to play with, soft knitted or felt at first, then harder ones or beanbags later to practise co-ordination skills. They often make balls in modelling. Babies can have rattles of wood or cane. A cardboard tube from

Preparing a shop using clothes-horses ('play-stands') (note cloth hinges)

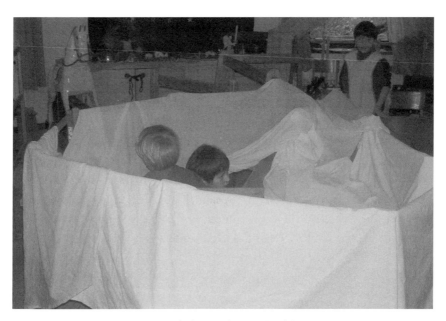

. . . which turned into a 'castle'

Another hinge

a carpet shop makes a great tunnel or funnel. When children stand up they can have toys to push, pull and ride, but you can be choosy regarding shape, colour and material. Toys for riding on may limit free movement, and emphasize speed and leg movements rather than the healthy co-ordination of the whole body. For this reason it can be better to limit the time spent on this sort of activity.

A soft cloth doll in very simple clothes is most appropriate for young children's creativity. A face empty of any features can have any expression, can be happy or sad according to the child's game, whilst a simple tunic (a small version of the rectangle with a hole in it), can become any kind of clothing.

Re: mending, improvising, re-making, and making do

From a letter to parents:
Our hospital week will be from Monday to Thursday 18th to 21st March. We will mend, make new, spring clean, make good. Do come whenever you can, and bring things which need stitching, sticking, repairing—toys, books, clothes. A wonderful time for imitation!

At these events we shared expertise, and the children experienced the reverse of the throwaway age. There are many things to be said for repeatedly reducing, re-using, repairing, recycling, respecting and revering what we have. 'Repair' comes from Latin: *re-parare*: 'put in order again'. The familiarity and love of an old toy deserves such care. By such examples we can help children to learn to take care of the earth's resources.

CHAPTER 6

IMAGINATION IN STORIES AND
THE MEDIA

'Tell it again!'

Listening to a good story

Readers may remember cuddling up on a lap and listening to a loved one's voice repeating a favourite tale. After listening to a story, children may recreate and embellish it in play. As with toys, enough is more! More than one story at a time may sap concentration and is not satisfying; the more stories at once, the more overfed and unsatisfied the child, leading to a desire for another one. What the child really wants is to stay on the lap, so one can sing a song or two or have a little chat. We could tell the tale again at a sitting if it is very short, but once each day should really be enough for a longer story. For a 6- or even 7-year-old one can still tell the same story over several

*Storytime with Mum
(the author)*

days before moving on to another. Repetition leads to familiarity and consolidation. For a mix of ages, care is needed in the choice of story. Older children don't really mind hearing the repetitive ones again (although they may profess to do so). Certain stories for older children can be told with younger ones present, so long as the voice is undramatic. Although the content may go over the little ones' heads, the sounds in the language and warmth in the voice carry their involvement.

A parent read Harry Potter and C.S. Lewis to his children all under 6, because he was so bored with repeatedly telling 'little' stories. However, when he contemplated his children's wish for the same, and 'what is there left for later?' he changed his mind, thinking he could read the others for himself. Some families are able to split the story times between younger and older. A cosy story place such as a large armchair provides the right atmosphere for the children to relax. In our local library parents try to read one story after another to their offspring, but there is so much going on around that concentration isn't really there even for one. After telling or reading the story you can try to leave a few moments for the child to 'unfold' out of the pictures they have in their minds. Children love to hear about people they know (even themselves) and their escapades. 'Once when I was little, I got lost when we were out for a walk . . .' And of course it all comes right in the end. Which stories are appropriate for which age, and which are good value? Some talk down to children, with inartistic, sentimental or aggressive illustrations and bland language. Language is important, including vocabulary and grammar, for it has a formative influence on the young child.

In reading a story to a child over 7, you can inflect your voice and create drama, but below this age it is preferable to use a calm, warm voice, as the child is not ready for such emotion. It is very nice to *tell* stories, either made-up or learnt. Reading it over a few times with the child will help you to know it by heart for another time. Otherwise you can read it several times to yourself and then practise parts of it. Telling the story without a book enables the child to enter into it in a more deeply imaginative way. There is no replacement for human warmth in story telling: you can't be cuddled by a CD or DVD recorder. Many recordings lack good language and music, but however good the speech, it is still no substitute for a live person. The pace is often too quick for children to keep up properly, and there is too much drama and emotion in the presentations. The mixing of music and voices together is also confusing for the young child. Some parents say they listen with their children, but wouldn't it be better to reach their little ones' hearts with their own offerings? 'Oh but he loves his tapes!' Maybe, but we all like things which are not very good for us. Children suck it all in without judgement. Often a child or two in kindergarten would crawl right underneath my story-telling chair and its big red blanket, while the rest sat on chairs or on the floor near me. There they were mousey-quiet and 'good', and felt very safe in their 'harbour' listening to the story.

Children love nature stories. Books such as *The Tomten* and *Milly Molly Mandy* (see Stories, p. 214) are soothing and strengthening for children: they relate directly to the events. From 3 years old, when their fantasy life is growing, you can tell a simple fairy tale such as 'Sweet Porridge' or 'The Three Billy Goats Gruff', for they are human behaviour and character translated into images, a language children can understand. Once upon a time, fairy tales were lifeblood in communities all over the world, a powerful cultural medium. Now the art of story telling is dying. Old tales are often rewritten and thereby lose their original meaning. The modern version of Cinderella, for example, is an amusing story but has moved away from the original tale. There is a profound wisdom in these ancient folk tales. In tribal communities these were stories treasured among the elders, and constituted their lifeblood. They were not stories for children then. Nowadays we might have lost sight of the great wisdom they contain, but although there are those which are beyond the comprehension of young children, many may be serious nourishment for them. It is always better to find a version which is not 'retold by...'. (See Stories, p. 214, for original versions.)

The wonderful thing about fairy tales is that good always overcomes evil, which children want to know. These stories are full of moral teaching without 'moralizing'. If a tale is told in a warm, unemotional, deadpan voice, children should not be frightened by the gruesome bits, for they create their own images. In my experience, if a child does become frightened by a witch or dragon in a story, it is because somewhere they have seen a video or cartoon pictures or someone else's scary image, or heard too dramatic language. Although there are many well-illustrated stories available, it can be better to avoid using too many illustrated books for young children because they create their own pictures while listening. However, occasionally in kindergarten whilst telling the story I showed a book with beautiful and gentle illustrations with soft contours and a fairy tale 'mood'. I turned the pages slowly and at the corners to show the careful use of books. Children learn to tell their own stories if given such a rich background of them.

'Once upon a time, a long, long time ago, when was it, when indeed was it not, there lived . . .
. . . and if they are not dead, they must be living still.'

The same themes are found all over the world, carried down from genera-tion to generation. You have to feel your way into them to see which are suitable for children. If they have more than one main action like 'Snow White' or 'Cinderella', they can be told to 5-year-olds upwards, depend-ing on the complexity of the tale. It is better to tell the tale as a whole and not to split it in two if it is quite long, which limits the age to the over 5-year olds. One thought flows to another, nothing can be missed out. 'Is that a true story?' children sometimes asked. 'Yes', I said, for I believe they are true pictures of life. Often they said, 'I like that story', happy to hear it every day for a week or two. We as adults could get bored, but these are children, for whom also the acquisition of language is cultivated through repetition. I never shied away from words they might not understand at first.

'And they all lived happily ever after.'

Puppet plays

It takes next to nothing to put on a puppet show. For instance, 'The Three Bears' can be presented by three conkers, large, small and medium. An upright toothbrush, wrapped carefully in a handkerchief for a dress, becomes Silverhair (the old English version of Goldilocks), and a scarf, apron or jacket laid over the lap is scenery. The large conker (Father Bear) ambles slowly about the 'apron stage', guided unobtrusively by one's hand. Then, 'Once upon a time, there were three bears, Father Bear, Mother Bear...'. Some children, used to 'finished' images, may take a while to understand but they soon catch on. When this is done lovingly and ser-iously, children imagine all the extras such as fur, bowls and house. The movements tell half the story, the words and the atmosphere the rest. Food for language and imagination for the young child. Food for thought for us adults.

Children can recreate and extend puppet shows in their play. They 'become' the puppets, identifying with them. A child in therapy may speak to a puppet if not a person. It is important that the puppets are moved with dignity, gliding along the 'ground' rather than bounced up and down, or

6-year-olds entertaining their 4 to 6-year-old audience with their made up story

. . . using 2-string puppets

with little jumps or leaps where appropriate for animals. In observing people and animals moving, you can see how to move the puppets. A little movement forward and back is enough to demonstrate a greeting, while a little shivering is enough to demonstrate anger or jealousy. Simple marionettes of dyed pieces of silk without features, held by a thread-loop over the hand, are not too complicated for the children to use as well, or felt dolls without legs, which stand on a table or the floor (see Chapter 7). Occasionally I used puppets with three or four strings, which children over 7 can manip-

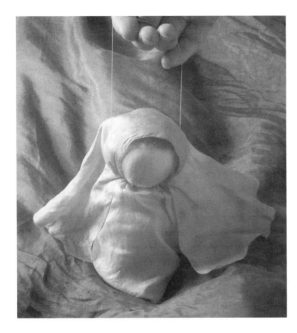

A 2-string (loop) puppet

ulate. A bird or fairy can fly from a thread attached to a finger, and several figures moving together, such as dwarves (on the ground) or ravens flying, can hang in a row from a twig. It is lovely to do a puppet show just for your own children, or for a birthday party. Slow, unemotional speaking and time to think enables even the most nervous person to create wonders. I hope that some readers will now have the courage to do a show if they didn't dare before. As the colour tells the character, each one needs only one or two colours with no details, for otherwise the child's freedom to imagine would be spoiled. A fisherman might be in blue, an old man brown or dark red, a witch clashing reds and greens, a king reddish purple, a prince blue or red and gold, whatever seems appropriate.

Landscapes can be made on plain cloths, perhaps with red for a house, green for a forest and blue for water. Pine cones can be trees, and a piece of wood a bridge, very 'plain' to allow for inner creativity. The adult can be entirely visible, for the child's unity of consciousness needs nothing to be hidden. For children over 7, the adult can be behind a screen. Children love to repeat the show themselves, time and again. If there are two adults around, one can tell the story and the other be the puppeteer, otherwise you need to learn it by heart! I didn't look at the children when I did a puppet play, nor when I told a fairy tale, because I wanted them to dream through the pictures and not be so aware of me, the narrator.

> At a birthday puppet-show, 5-year-old Damin whispered in eager anticipation, 'Let's pretend it's a puppet-show'.

The media

The written and spoken word, and even our own feelings, are all media. The storyteller is the medium between story and listener. The 'wireless' was the medium between myself as a child and the imagined orchestra of tiny black-coated people I believed were playing inside it. Everything young children encounter *lives,* is *real,* whether fingers which talk to each other or the leaves 'which are clapping their hands,' (a 6-year-old). Therefore surely what comes on the screen is 'reality'. I read a notice outside a cinema: 'Please explain to your younger children that the characters in the film are not real'. Well, I wonder, I thought; does the writer have any idea of the consciousness in which those children live? During story time at home, you are there to reassure the child if the story gets a bit frightening. 'Shall we go on?' 'Yes!' 'Ok, come a bit closer then.' Real life can also be frightening, but human closeness helps to counteract it. This is missing when children sit alone in front of the screen or listen to dramatic voices on CDs. There is no compensation for the love and care of a real person, not in lullaby CDs with the baby's name, nor in sentimental videos, let alone the harsh, violent programmes millions of children see every day. I have known some children who were unable to listen quietly to stories because their minds were too full of strong images from the screen. It was only when they got out of the habit of watching that they began to listen happily. A child-minder told me of a child who took several weeks not to be afraid of hearing her tell stories because she was distressed and afraid from having seen disturbing pictures on her videos. The impact of what runs on the screen becomes engraved on the mind. Television is presumably here to stay. Used sensibly it has its place, but millions of people use it to saturation point. Many people switch on the TV when they return home after work, and turn it off when they go to bed. 'I don't look at it much, I just like to have it on.' Nevertheless, everything we hear and see goes into us, and our vitality is needed to digest it. Why do we use it up in this way? Are we depleting children's vitality as second-hand listeners?

Many children are growing up as couch-potatoes fed on a diet of snacks and unhealthy unreality. I experienced long ago what TV can do to children when, as a supply teacher, I had to let them watch their usual programme.

They sat unnaturally still and I wondered where they had 'gone'. At the end, they went wild, shouting and running about. It was not the programme, but the actual medium which had taken them over. Since then I've seen many a child behave abnormally after watching, and then seen the change come about in those children whose parents had the courage to withdraw them from this medium.

'I want you to watch a video, not that mixture of things', says mother to her 4- and 8-year-olds. 'Turn it off. I don't want you watching all those silly adverts.' But she walks away and the children are mesmerized and unable to do as she asks, for that awareness and will power takes years to develop. In Britain, alarming numbers of even very young children watch for hours, zapping before breakfast and falling asleep in front of the screen. This puts children under great stress, allowing them no peace, disabling the development of language, and impressing their minds with images unworthy of human life. 'She never watches TV except at her cousin's; she watches quite a lot of videos but never TV', said Cheryl's mother, as her hyperactive daughter climbed all over a visitor and kicked a cat. 'Was it a nice film?' asked Jane of her young children who had been watching a man drowning. She had no idea what they were seeing, and was just relieved that they were out of the way and quiet for a bit.

The imitative, sensitive consciousness of the child is suited to real life rather than electronic media which, I remain convinced, have a negative effect on our young people. Absorbing the distorted sounds, sights and movements of the media stultifies healthy growth of the child's senses. In adverts and cartoons, violence is offered for amusement. Pushing someone over is considered hilarious. Supposedly friends, the big-bully child shows how to eat up the weaker one's favourite food, with not the tiniest return of fairness. That's life, you can say, but do we want to start our children off with such images, when they have an innate feeling of fairness? Some say aggression is needed to get by in this world, but so many get by without it, so why teach it? The media create value judgements, for instance that sexy, rough, skinny, rich and muscley are best. Anorexia and violence may well be offshoots of these images. Restlessness, lack of concentration and learning problems, along with obesity and diabetes are on the rise in children, and in adults there is a growing awareness of the dangers inherent in poor diet, aggressive advertising, TV and computer screens. Many parents are concerned but don't know what to do, yet some find a creative way round it. It is possible just to reduce it, then replace it with another activity such as an adventurous, exciting walk, sawing wood, cooking or free play. Other parents disconnected the TV plug behind the cupboard so that their children thought it would not work. Children are so full of life that they will gradually find alternatives in play. It is wonderful if adults can make a little extra time for their children.

The electronic media are fascinating and unbelievably tempting to children. However, I believe that deep down they would rather be playing, chatting, having adventures outside, busy with life. Many parents find they want to put a limit on the use of the computer, including games. It helps if different families get together over this. Computers are surely here to stay, and will contribute in a most valuable way to society if we remain their masters and do not become their slaves.

> Donald, a 4-year-old, told his mother to throw the television down the bottom of the garden. But she didn't, unfortunately.

'She has poor mouse control', was in the report of a 4-year-old. Co-ordinating the connection between mouse and screen is not a *natural* function for the young child's stage of cognition. However, it is possible of course to work on children from an early age to advance their development artificially. In this way one can get amazing results, but always at the expense of their vitality and future development.

In real life there is a chance of redemption and hope when things have gone wrong. With many computer games this is not the case. Imaginary adventures lead players to hurt others. They may take on the character, movement and speech of the one they are playing, tending to transfer the aggression to real situations. Frightened children may retreat into nervous, hysterical laughter, which is often misinterpreted by adults as enjoyment. It is difficult for children to return to the real world after watching any screen, as they have been in a kind of trance. People sometimes talk of 'rubbish', but you throw real rubbish away, whereas the effects of the screen remain.

> One way of weaning children from the computer is to use an alarm clock for a time limit, but as with all things, it is no good setting rules you cannot keep. The challenge then is to practise being firm. In this respect I should advise starting when the children are very young! The child's trust in the adult makes it easy at this age. Even Julie, 6, asked placidly, 'Is it going to be like this every day?' as one major routine in her day was changed.

Many films and computer games teach disregard of life, disrespect of others' pain, and shunning of compassion. Many programmes may be designed to be sweet and harmless, but they are often insipid and weak, not giving children much worthiness to emulate, and include babyish language and unnatural movements. Children need good images to look up to, not gimmicks. Nobody likes being talked down to. We have to be aware of creating confusion in the minds and hearts of the young because they conflict with moral values learnt from respectful adults. Parents have already become uneasy about advertising on children's programmes, especially junk food. We now have no real censorship in films. For instance, PG and U films are often quite unsuitable for young children, and one sees quite violent U trailers for PG and A films. So the task of protecting children from unsuitable material is taken out of the government's hands and put firmly in the parents' court, which is really good.

The Indian ship's captain talked about responsibility. He remarked on how many people pass the buck and shy away from the consequences of their actions. From his Hindu religion he believed that, 'There is a God for each and every one of us, yet there are a great number of negative influences of which we have to be aware. We have a responsibility about what we put into the child's environment, and being a parent is a job, a career, the life's work of father or mother. Responsibility goes with the job'.

CHAPTER 7

BUSY-NESS

'Did God sew my hair on?'

Girls do Mum's things and Boys do Dad's

I had a male assistant for my last three teaching years, which was fantastic in the way it turned the kindergarten into a 'family'. If any men reading this are thinking about taking up early years' education, please go and sign up now before you turn this page, then get a female assistant when you are qualified! I've had many excellent women helpers, and although we can do lots of boys' things, it is not the same as having a male aura around.

Many boys are behind girls in school readiness. They may show physical readiness in body proportions and strength, but their cognitive and affective ability tends to lag behind for a while. Boys need men to copy, heavy things to carry, to tumble about and climb. Small boys can spend many blissful hours around old cars or machinery watching and 'helping' an adult. This makes them feel useful, knowledgeable and important. Although some girls may enjoy such activity too, my experience over many years has been that girls may feel knowledgable and important in other ways, for instance looking after a smaller child or baby. Things may well change as they grow older, as there is much crossing over of interests nowadays, with women pilots and men working as early childhood practitioners for example.

On the train to London I met a lad of about 8 in the guard's van. We both had bikes and I wanted to put mine behind his as it was bigger and he might not be travelling far. I: 'Are you going a long way?' Boy: 'Yes, I am'. Pause. Boy: 'I'm going by train'. I: 'Yes, I see. How nice. Are you going to London?' (30 miles) Boy: 'No.' Pause. 'I'm going to . . . [thinking] Wingfield' (3 miles).

A patient walked out with his intravenous drip and small son of about 5 to a mountain-rescue helicopter standing on the hospital pad. They wandered around it a long time, looking, gazing. Then they walked over to the second (empty) pad, looked, chatted, wandered about, then returned to the helicopter, drip obediently alongside, examining, looking, sharing a mutual interest.

Giving children of all ages the opportunity to see into typical activities of the opposite sex enlivens understanding for each other. As a single parent, I tried to be a bit of a father as well, so I had a go at DIY and bike adventures, whereas I prefer to sew, garden and be a homemaker. Small boys adore workshops, old sheds and barns, especially if an adult is working there. They need copious pockets to accommodate bent nails, sticks, string and treasures of sticky obscurity. They are particularly interested in *objects* and how *things* work. The sewing machine is quiet but visible, fascinating to them if not quite comprehensible. Later on, bigger boys relish chemical experiments, demonstrations of electro-magnetism and such like. A friend described her granddaughter of 3 as already feeling empathy, whereas her grandson Mauro, 15 months, was particularly interested in machines. He knew where the key to the tractor was hidden between two beams in the shed, and would say: 'Eh, eh, eh?' to Grandpa, pointing to the key. So much for unisex. Naturally empathy and machines can be combined in one person!

For girls, it's more *social* life and how *people* work that is of prime importance. Their large pockets are full of necklaces, dolly's nappies, secret letters and pretty leaves. Of course there is a crossover of male and female interests. Girls happily watch machinery working or a carpenter in a workshop, or playing with all the little metal bits that belong to a sewing machine. Every day for weeks, Louis, 6, burst through the kindergarten door: 'Can I do my doll?' and stitched it a vast wardrobe, whereas Julie, also 6, went straight to her rasping and filing at the workbench.

On my home visits I was often given cake or other goodies, usually baked by the children. Occasionally the boys did the baking, but on the whole it was the girls, although Ivor made me gifts of wonderful bottles of lavender water and salad sauces. Girls love domestic activities, and are happy when Mum finds time for them so they can share these important, life-giving tasks. As I said before, young people's interests may change as they grow up beyond early childhood, and an education which allows both sexes to experience all activities is to be welcomed.

Children are always doing

Young children are naturally self-motivated. Out of their eagerness for learning, both sexes usually do every activity offered, whether manual or artistic. Sometimes instances such as this happen: 4-year-old Tyler, who so much wanted but was not allowed to make or play with dolls, was told, 'Boys don't play with dolls. They are for girls'. It is always helpful for children to use their hands, especially today when we need to balance the sedentary demands of academic work and modern technology. William, 4, helped his parents dig when they put in a new septic system; when he wasn't digging, he was climbing up and sliding down the mountains of earth created, all this in pouring rain. Washing machines and sewing machines, cars and chain-saws have become an indispensable part of life, but children experience real hands-on activity if they see us write, sew and wash by hand, pick apples or use a hand-saw. If children's need for physical activity is not adequately met, challenging behaviour may well be the result. It is healthy for a child to be physically tired as a result of much activity. This is a different fatigue from that suffered by young children struggling with the hand-eye co-ordination required by the demands of reading and writing.

Automation has put our hands and feet to bed. Instead of being posted at the letterbox, in a couple of seconds our e-mail letter has flown into the receiver's inbox. The knife, scrubber and grater have been made semi-redundant by convenience salads and vegetables, and we press a button to cook ready-meals in the microwave, wash the dishes and warm our rooms. Cars and pushchairs have stolen the children's footsteps. The washing dances in the dryer while the wind and sun mourn the loss of their rightful activity. Alongside all this we are losing the art of improvisation, of making do. How many still knit for their families or make wooden toys for their children, let alone find time to do it? There is something special about the jumper or toy made by a loving relation. There are many people now who cannot knit, sew or make a simple wooden toy (but who would like to learn how). Individually inspired creativity becomes progressively squeezed off the agenda, in a growing anxiety that children will not be literate early enough. Padded plastic books for 2- and 3-year-olds to be read in the bath and home spelling practice books for 6-year-olds grace our shops. Many young children have a book bag with reading matter to take home every day, but very few take home a little piece of handwork.

Inspiring creativity in the young finds its way into every corner of humanity in the future. Manual activity serves the academic, as threads of thinking are tied together by finger work; imagination infuses both. Originality, fostered by creativity in childhood, brings inspirational solutions to the trickiest problems, whether replacing bits of plumbing, counselling the bereaved, or studying the non-sexual reproduction of amoeba. Wholeness of activity in childhood is essential for wholeness of growth. Given plenty of time and space, children can enter *fully* into their work, and leave it feeling fulfilled. They may need encouragement if they are not used to it, but their natural urge to imitate in work and play will soon overcome diffidence when given the opportunity. Children who continue to avoid certain activities may be giving us a clue to particular learning needs, or the possibility that the activity has not been introduced or handled in the best way.

Adults at work create curiosity, interest and enthusiasm in the children. I must have heard, 'Can I do it too?' thousands of times. Jeremy, 2 and a half, liked to climb up a ladder with a paint brush, accompanying this by saying, 'I'm a man!' If a work project takes a long period to complete, such as laying a garden path, this offers the child a picture of endurance and stamina, showing that work has meaning and is a process from beginning to end, inspiring confidence and happiness. In play and work, children show remarkable levels of inventiveness. There is beauty in the quality of the activity. We must bear in mind that it is quite usual for young children not to recognize their handwork, to which they have applied such conscientious devotion, when seeing it next day. It is the *work,* the *process,* the *devotion to the task*, which matter now, not the result. After the age of 6, a child may suddenly not be happy with what has been achieved and want to alter it, but in the case of younger children, dissatisfaction is likely to arise out of a culture of praise, comparison or judgement.

> *From a letter to parents:*
> *There are so many things that we can do as teachers and parents both to help the child's development and spot potential difficulties which are so easy to let slip. For instance, if we dress or undress a child, including shoes, we don't give him/her enough chance to learn co-ordination, strengthen initiative or be independent, and we also can't observe if the child is actually unable to do it. Young children, as you know, want to be active themselves, and we should let them where possible.*

At what age can children start trying to dress themselves? They will usually show us by demonstrating trying to pull on a sock or hat, or attempting to take off a coat. If we can find the time and patience to leave them in peace to try it out on their own, their ability will grow well. Extra-curricular activities such as skating, craft club, riding and sailing can be encouraged from 7 upwards, so long as they don't take too much time from the child's need for play and scope for imitation and manual activity. It is all a question of balance and the demands of common sense and safety. It is likely that more opportunity for imaginative play and creative outlets in childhood would reduce the amount of vandalism that exists today.

In the kitchen

Cooking lies at the heart of every family, so anything a parent or carer can do to let children help is wonderful. Bread making is particularly special, involving hands, nose, eyes, tongue and oven warmth.

> Charlotte, 5, used to baking, saw a rather large lady: 'She must have eaten a lot of margarine—oh, no, she's had some yeast and then she's risen'.

With the addition of olive oil, you can make pizzas and foccacia bread, which children love to decorate. Kneading the dough gives an opportunity for messy hands, which magically become clean with more flour.

Smell, touch, warmth, sociability, movement . . . and taste in baking

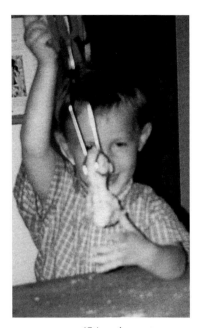

'Scissors'

Little rolls, big loaves, snails, all shapes can be modelled. When two children were visiting me, the 7-year-old made a hedgehog by snipping prickles along the back of a roll of dough with scissors. Her brother, 3, a bit young for such a tricky job, wanted to do it too. So I gave him barbecue tongs for 'scissors' and he was blissful. Scissors can also snip 'ears of corn' on long small rolls. Nuts, raisins and seeds make nice decorations. 'I've made a man with chickenpox', said Alexis. Singing a song with an activity as a kind of sea-shanty helps things go with a swing. Most people know: 'Pat-a-cake, pat-a-cake, baker's man...' and some know: 'Mix a pancake, stir a pancake, pop it in the pan; fry a pancake, toss a pancake, catch it if you can'. Otherwise sing your own made-up ones. So long as the adult is sharing the activity, children can be trusted with knives for chopping fruit and vegetables. They like to stir in a big bowl or saucepan, and even make their own cakes. In these days of prepared food and microwaves, spending time to cook is worth every minute, saves a lot of pennies, and gives children confidence, dexterity and joy. Salads, pies, fresh fruit muesli, soups, biscuits, steamed vegetables: all are lovely things to make. Aprons, washed hands, cleaning and washing up belong to it all, and children shouldn't be spoilt by parents doing it. Nadia, 2 and a half years, took chocolates out of the fridge and screamed when they were taken away, but this was short-lived when her mother said, 'You can dry up'. She gave her a towel and china bowl, and Nadia was happy again. It is heart-warming to see such trust in a parent. Even little ones can help lay the table, and by 4 or 5 years old they like to do it on their own. I know many children who are a real help at home. They *want* to help, and must not be squashed by our thinking they can't do it. It's good if some dishes are washed with the children by hand, even if you have a dishwasher, not least because putting hands into warm water supports visual, tactile and warmth senses. A mild, plant-based detergent will be kinder on the hands.

A 'sea-shanty' accompaniment:

Sing a song of washing up,
Water hot as hot,
Cups and saucers,
Plates and spoons,
Dishes such a lot.
Work the dishmop round and round
Rinse them clean as clean
Polish with a clean, dry cloth,
How busy we have been!   Elizabeth Gould

If it is possible to buy a hand-mill for flour grinding, this is a marvellous activity for children. The rhythmical turning requires some effort but is popular. Organic grain is freely available nowadays. 'You mustn't put your fingers in there. In real true life you mustn't', said Lamumba, when turning the kindergarten mill. Children enjoy grating carrots, apples, nuts and cheese. (You can sharpen graters with sandpaper.) They can also dry (organic, unwaxed) orange and lemon peel in the oven till crisp, and then crush it with a rolling pin. It will smell delicious and give a wonderful flavour to cakes and puddings. You can of course use finely chopped fresh peel. Making biscuits needs a certain amount of adult interaction to show children how to grease tins, put the cutters to the edge of the pastry and not handle it more than necessary. Rolling the dough and placing shapes on the tray develops small motor skills. Gingerbread houses are wonderful to make, especially in winter. Good gingerbread recipes are easy to find, and everyone can have lots of fun decorating. To avoid the roof collapsing, make sure not to cover it with icing or it will sag from the moisture.

One can buy children's prepared dessert mixes, slush and milk-shake makers, with several 'colourways' and charts and refills and batteries and sprinkles and a large bill. Making all these in a simple way at home avoids the colouring and other additives. A nice present for a child is a recipe including the ingredients and a wooden spoon. A special gift for a sick person or their family is to cook for them, then deliver it in a basket, perhaps with a little bunch of flowers and a home-made card on top. Children can be involved in all of this.

Housework or play?

What is child-initiated? It is so easy to overwhelm children in an enthusiasm, or anxiety, to get them to learn. A mother whose son was about to start

THE DEVELOPMENT OF CHILDREN'S DRAWINGS
(see Chapter 7)

Around 2 years children draw circles and spirals . . .

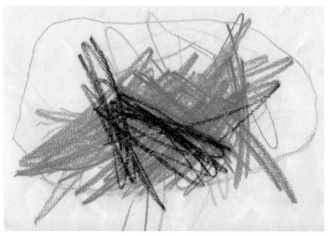

. . . and horizontal and vertical lines appear.

Somewhere around 3 years, 'rays' are often drawn.

A cross is typical of the 3-year-old.

Between 3 and 4, horizontal and vertical lines may become more ordered.

Around 5 years, 'ladder' images begin to appear.

Another 'ladder' image in a representation by a 5-year-old.

After 4 or 5, children love to draw rainbows.

Around 5 or 6 years, rows of objects may appear as the teeth begin to fall out.

Another row of objects.

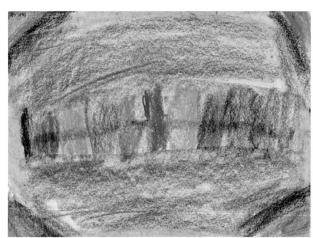

More rows, maybe even teeth! from a 6-year-old.

Rows, with diagonals appearing, typical of 6 year olds.

By 6, the child may become quite able in representational drawing.

Diagonals of a 6-year-old.

Sky and earth represented at 6.

Sky and earth, with people and objects on the ground, by a 6-year-old.

Symmetry begins to appear. A 6-year-old.

Sky and earth meet.

A joyful 6-year-old.

The child can put details into the work.

Emergent writing.

Symmetry may appear around 6 years.

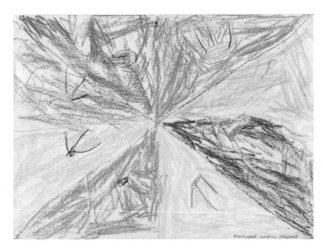

Diagonals, symmetry and emergent writing by a 6-year-old soon going to school.

A watercolour painting by a 5-year-old.

private school at 3 and a quarter said, 'They are so receptive at this age; we may as well pump as much as we can into them while we are able'. Yet young children are so anxious themselves to be part of this world, to grow up and find their own task and be needed in society, that actually all we need to do is offer them the opportunities appropriate to their age and they will take them eagerly, through their powers of imitation and self-motivation.

So long as children haven't been spoilt by seeing sweeping treated as a chore, it can be a really favourite activity. Using a broom, brush and dustpan, sweeping right into the corners, then emptying it all involves large and small physical skills. Working with others to make a beautiful, clean, ordered place for everyone creates fun and social skills. Such activities actually enliven artistic ability. Intelligence is well applied in working out where and what to sweep. If I started sweeping, children would fetch a brush and dustpan out of imitation. I had only to pick up a broom, when I would hear, 'Where are you going?' The following conversation was typical: 'I'm going to sweep the path outside'. 'Can I come too?' 'Me too.' 'Oh, I'd be glad of your help.' Self-motivated activity brings real satisfaction. Sweeping outside can also involve wheelbarrows, rakes, and mat beating. Our asphalt path was on a slope outside, and the children so

Sweeping right into awkward places

Movement, joy and skills

enjoyed turning the mats upside down, jumping on them, and sliding down, doing a good job of cleaning as they went. Jumping on them in the snow is the best cleaner of all. Feather dusters are fun for children. You might have to check that they, along with cloth dusters, get shaken *outside* rather than *inside* the door. If children are allowed to help and receive appreciation, they become remarkably capable in all types of cleaning: sweeping, dusting, mopping, scrubbing, cleaning windows, polishing, brushing and beating mats all can be enjoyed if done with a happy adult.

There are generally a few clothes, including dolls' clothes, that are better washed by hand, and children should be able to help. They enjoy passing pegs or even hanging up clothes on their own. It's so good for children to experience clothes flapping in the breeze and to smell their special freshness when dry. They can help with folding and putting away some washing. 'I'm folding mine into a posh triangle', said Mike, 5. By the time children are 8, they can iron some simple things. I used to do the ironing in the kindergarten, and gave the children things to 'iron' when they wanted. They made themselves an 'ironing board' of a plank and stools, and an 'iron' of a smooth block of wood.

Happy domesticity

A song to accompany household work:

'Twas on a Monday morning
That I beheld my darling,
She looked so sweet and charming
In every high degree.
She looked so sweet and charming
A-washing of her linen, oh!
Dashing away with the smoothing iron,
Dashing away with the smoothing iron,
She stole my heart away.

Every day has its own flavour:

'Twas on a Tuesday morning . . .   a-hanging . . .
'Twas on a Wednesday morning . . .   a-drying . . .
'Twas on a Thursday morning . . .   an-ironing . . .
'Twas on a Friday morning . . .   a-mending . . .
'Twas on a Saturday morning . . .   a-folding . . .
'Twas on a Sunday morning . . .   a-wearing . . .   Old rhyme

These once universal domestic activities, part of children's lives, have largely been dropped from our culture along with all the benefits that went with them: feeling useful, developing motor skills, feeling joy and pride in achievement, playing at being adults in a healthy way, and learning how to take care. That is not to say that children today don't learn these things otherwise, but rich opportunities can be provided simply in learning from daily living.

Whenever I visit a setting as part of my advisory work, I learn something new. 'Lifelong Learning' is such a good expression. In a kindergarten recently I observed two very happy, smiley 6-year-old boys rubbing the week's napkins on a washboard, while a 3-year-old grated a lump of soap on a small grater to provide them continuously with soapflakes. The teacher told me she melted down the little pieces of left-over hand soap with a little water in a saucepan, and when it was cooled to a stiff jelly consistency, they formed balls with it. Wonderful!

When the cleaning is all done, it is lovely to celebrate by arranging flowers with the children. Bought flowers can fill the gap for those without a garden. It is good to have flowers that are in season, such as chrysanthemums in autumn, cyclamen in December, daffodils in spring and roses in summer. A vase of wild flowers is so pretty (make sure not to pick those which are rare or protected); they can be collected on walks with the children. Bulbs can be potted in bulb fibre in autumn (peat-free if possible), then left in the dark till they sprout. How exciting to watch the flowers emerge!

The workshop

Domestic activities are necessities of life and tremendous tools for learning. Woodwork is a popular activity too. Even 2- and 3-year-olds enjoy rubbing sandpaper over a piece of wood, for as many minutes as their concentration lasts. Sandpaper stuck to a large wooden block can be clamped onto a work-bench or table, so flat wood can be sanded back and forth across it. Penelope, a hyperactive 5-year-old, was sanding too fast, but she gradually slowed down to match, through imitation, my own slower rhythm and song. Rasps and files should be pushed forward then *lifted* back rather than pulled, so that they don't get blunt too quickly; this in itself helps to make a rhythmic swish rather than a hectic scrub. It is not necessary to make any particular thing: children just enjoy the activity, the

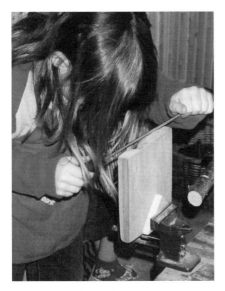

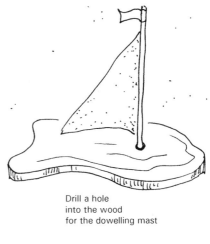

Drill a hole
into the wood
for the dowelling mast

Filing with intensity   *Boat*

busy-ness of the work and the smell of the wood. Older children may want to make something, for instance a small boat with mast and stitched sail, which might need a little guidance. At home, children over 5 might be allowed a mallet and chisel under your eagle eye. Arbitrary nailing is noisy and the randomness doesn't give a good image, especially in these days of vandalism. It is so much better when there is a particular purpose. Things can be put together by drilling then screwing or using dowelling. Children like to handle saws, and if shown slow, rhythmical movements, can do it properly. Rubbing the saw edge with soap makes for smoother cutting. For play, you can saw up thick and thin logs fallen in the woods, and ask in the local woodyard for off-cuts. These can be filed, sanded and waxed with beeswax polish. When they get dirty, waxing them again removes the dirt. If such logs are sliced in half, you 'discover' boats, beds, a (wheel-less) train or a tractor. They are especially attractive if the bark is left on. Wheels aren't really necessary; imagination makes up for their absence. (I found an old Indian saying to be so true: 'When the wheels come in, the peace goes out'.) Large hooks and eyes become the links between engine and carriages, or tractor and trailer. The colours in the wood don't need to be covered up with paint. A round slice of wood attached to each end of such a half piece of wood makes a cradle; your own originality will find other objects, the simpler the better. Short lengths of log or half-log make 'stilts', with string loops attached by staples to each side to hold on to. Swords are good to make for boys who want them. They can take a nice long time to prepare, cut, rasp, file and sand into a blunt point. Finishing them off by polishing with wax or a golden crayon makes them 'strong' and special. If not swung about but tucked into a belt, they guard a shining, brave knight.

We are woodmen, sawing trees, sawing, sawing, sawing trees.
We don't care about wind or weather,
We keep sawing all together,
We are woodmen sawing trees, sawing, sawing, sawing trees.

Old rhyme

Gerry, a new child, was crying. I needed to stay at the workbench with other children, so I started filing a piece of wood in a rhythmical tempo with my hands over his, singing all the while. He soon settled down and went on by himself.

Modelling*

Most children enjoy getting their hands messy with natural materials such as bread-dough, mud, sand, clay and real plasticine, which is made of clay and linseed oil. The cold nature of clay makes it unsuitable for some children who may lose warmth and grow pale as a result. My favourite modelling material is prepared beeswax, which smells, feels and looks gorgeous. Making it soft in the palms requires effort, but soon the hands become warm. It is quite expensive, but it lasts for years if children wash their hands first, don't mix the colours and avoid putting it on the table, which would make it cold and hard again and pick up any fluff. If flattened again while still warm, it is ready for next time: it is difficult to soften when in a lump, although it can be put in a warm place. The waxiness can be rubbed into the hands afterwards, which is good for the skin.

Colouring pictures

Another fun activity for children is to fill a blank space with colour. One or two colourings done carefully are worth twenty rushed off. The paper

---

* For the tools and materials mentioned in the rest of this chapter, see the Resources, p. 217.

shouldn't be too large: A4 is about right for over 3-year-olds, or it could be A5 for little ones. Just a few chunky crayons are enough. Good quality file paper can be placed on a thicker piece of paper as an underlay and protection for the table. If crayon marks appear on the table they can be removed with a piece of unwashed fleece (also found on barbed wire where there are sheep) or beeswax polish. This is also a way of cleaning crayons. The colours of felt tips lack nuance, and for this reason I prefer the warm, rich colours of beeswax crayons and the graded way they are able to cover the paper. Coloured pencils are more suitable for older children who need to draw the detail not so possible with wax crayons. There are beeswax block crayons on the market, which make wonderful broad sweeps of colour when used on their end or side edge, almost like painting. Beeswax stick crayons are also available.

Colouring with these crayons can make wonders appear. Drawing on the first side of the paper and holding it up to the light will show up the colours and whatever has been drawn. Colouring the other side and holding it up likewise makes both pictures shine through the paper at once. A little story can accompany this revelation, such as one about a shepherd and his flock. You show the first side *away* from the window: 'Once there was a shepherd . . . One day he could not find all his sheep . . . He hunted high and low . . .' and so the story is embellished and continues until the sheep are found, and the paper held up to the window, revealing the shepherd on the front and the lost sheep which were drawn on the back of the paper. Such magic, and so simple. Children love to look at their own work in the window in this way.

If an adult draws with the children sometimes, demonstrating generous, sweeping movements with the crayon and filling up the whole paper with colour, then the children will be led through imitation into movements which engage the whole upper body, rather than careful lines which make demands only on the head and finger-ends. If children want a second drawing, they can just turn the page over, but often the energy is spent on the first. When a child crumples up the paper and throws it away, it may be done in imitation of older children, or may indicate that praise or competition exist at home, for young ones are naturally happy with what they have done.

Children's drawings

If children are left to draw naturally, without being taught how to form such things as people, birds, hearts and cats, then archetypal shapes appear which can be seen as illustrations of how children grow downwards as they develop (see Plate section). The child under 3 years old has a proportionately large, round head, and her consciousness feels itself as a whole revolving entity of everything in her surroundings. So she draws circles and spirals. Horizontal and vertical lines also appear in the scribble, indicating the beginnings of a sense of orientation in space. Around 3 years, when she can confidently say 'I', she may draw a head with body, possibly with arms and hands (maybe projecting straight out of the head) and feet. A cross may appear, as a picture of the self, often contained within a circle—like standing within a house or the world. As the child reaches outwards with a little self-awareness at 3, flowers and suns (circles with rays) may appear. At 4 we see the house with windows, and illustrations become more colourful. Between 3 and 5 the developing chest, the 'affective' or 'feelings' area, is depicted with ladder shapes (ribs), sometimes presented as trees. Rainbows come as children develop more awareness of themselves in the world. Drawings are even more representational after 5 years old, when play becomes purposeful and social, and the need for much play equipment begins to diminish. As the limbs lengthen, as co-ordination increases, and the chest and face take on more shape, then objects are drawn in the correct place rather than haphazardly. Sky and ground appear (separately), as spatial awareness increases and children begin to feel no longer completely at one with their environment. The tree finds its way on to the ground, as do the houses, flowers and people, instead of floating above it. Now we see symmetry and diagonals such as in flags, roofs, mountains, showing an awareness of space in three dimensions. Lots of details are drawn: petals, smoke, stars, battlements, and hair with ribbons. It is quite wonderful to observe how rows of objects appear when the child's teeth begin to fall out, almost as if they were in fact rows of teeth! Sky and earth often meet at around 7. The child is master of the crayon.

> Parents do their children a great service if they refrain from praising or judging their children's 'works of art'. One of the best ways of receiving a new picture is with the attitude of celebrating the *child*: 'How wonderful that you've done all that work and finished your picture!'

Lots of drawing is a good foundation for learning to write. I visited a class of 4-year-olds, where the children were asked to trace their names, and then draw a picture. Not only were most of them barely capable of following the lines except in a very hesitating fashion, but the pictures they drew were simply a few scribbles. In the afternoon, some children fell asleep at their activities. They were being stretched intellectually at the expense of physical activity and proper rest.

Moving pictures

A simple moving picture really excites the imagination, as the child moves inwardly with the characters. Fold up a flap of an inch or two at the bottom of strong paper or card, onto which a simple scene has been coloured with crayon or paint. Then cut out a figure and glue it onto a long strip. Push it to and fro inside the flap. Alternatively, cut a slit in the paper and push the strip with its figure through it, then move it from side to side. Your own inspiration can invent further creations, such as placing one or two other pieces of paper (shorter in height) inside the flap as 'scenery', with yet other figures inside them. It is nice to cut gentle curves around the sides of the paper, to soften the contours of the landscape.

Painting

The young child can find much joy and harmony in painting with water-colour on damp paper, which can bring about a lovely, quiet mood. Flowing

A simple moving picture

brush strokes suit the watery medium and fill the whole paper, the colours mixing by themselves and forming wonderful shapes of beautiful colours. The dampness disables exactness, quite a different experience from drawing. This helps children to breathe calmly and let go of impressions which may have tightened them up. Only the primary colours, red, yellow and blue are needed. For the young, choose warm and gentle tones: cerulean blue, gamboge yellow and rose madder. Squeeze a little from each tube and add a small amount of water in small glass jars. Mix thoroughly, then continue adding water, testing the colour on some scrap paper until it reaches the desired strength. A young child should use a long-handled, wide-headed watercolour brush. These are fairly expensive but they are essential for this painting and if treated kindly will last for years.

Now prepare the paper, which should preferably be a watercolour paper of about 190 grams per square metre weight, cut to A3, or A4 for children under 4 years. (This kind of painting needs a larger piece of paper compared with that used for drawing so the colours can flow better.) Gently submerge it in a sink half-full of water (or, if more than one person is painting, one piece after the other on top of each other) and allow to soak for five minutes. Lift the paper up by one corner and hold it until it stops dripping. Then take the opposite corner as well and let it down flat on to a water-resistant table or piece of hardboard. Avoid wiping the paper. Instead, lay a new J-cloth over

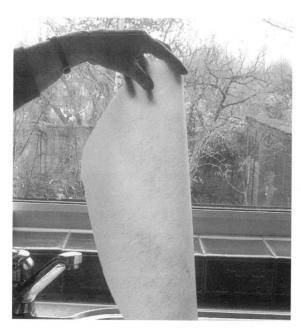

Dripping

Laying it flat

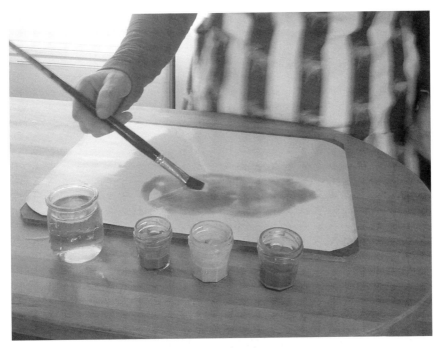

Laying on the colour

the whole paper. Pat it gently until the excess water is absorbed. Then the child is ready to dip the brush into the chosen colour and stroke it gently across the dampened paper. Allow the brush to lie fairly flat, and move it in the direction of the bristles. Avoid the metal touching the paper, or dabbing, poking or scrubbing, which damages both brush and paper. Washing the brush well in a jam jar between colours changes the water: workmanship, science and magic! It can be squeezed between two fingers or dabbed 'dry' on a cloth or sponge before each new colour. This may all sound very complicated, but actually it isn't. The children can help and then even do it themselves. When the child knows how to wash the brush before putting it into another colour, the paints will stay clean and can be kept till next time in a closed jar. A little song helps the work flow along, such as:

> Make a world of wondrous colours, paint a bridge of colours bright,
> Yellow, blue and red and green, purple, orange and brown and white,
> Let the sunshine in, let the clouds float in.
> (And whatever variations fit the weather: ... let the wind blow/ snow fly/ rain flow/ mist weave/ fog creep/ etc.)

Because children copy, they will be more free to develop their own creativity if the adult only plays with the colour rather than painting any particular thing. Following an adult's example, children will also happily paint with only one colour. In this way they gain a relationship to each one and absorb its mood, for each has its own particular character. Children can be given just one colour when they first paint, so that they get used to the medium and the washing of the brush, even with the single colour. In tinkling the brush on the side of the pots, they can hear music in the different heights of water. Children do not usually mix the paints intentionally on the paper until about 6 years old. By this time, with developing cognition, they like to experiment, to tip the paper, splash, pour paint on then blow it, and make dots. (Children sometimes paint dots when about to get a rash.) 'How do you make light blue?' asked Sophia, watching Malachi. 'Well, you just sort of, you just sort of, well, you know, just . . . put some blue on it and let it spread out.' He hadn't intended it to happen, but now in the process he realized what he had done.' How do you make orange, Ella?' 'You put red on then yellow on top.' Josie: 'How do you make purple?' I: 'Well, I wonder', then making it dreamily. Josie, copying me: 'You made purple!' Later, the same child: 'I made orange'. I: 'I see'. Josie: 'Francisca showed me'.

Children help each other; we don't need to tell them everything. Tyler, dipping into the magical world of physics, wonderingly tried to catch and hold the line of drips as I held up a pile of soaked paper by the corner.

In colouring, painting, modelling with beeswax, playing with plain cloths and nature's 'toys', children develop a real feeling for the characters of colours. There are many things around the home which can be arranged in rainbow order, as in the little bells hung along the stick which I mentioned. I have found it very satisfying for the children (and myself) to arrange objects in this harmonious way, for instance a pile of cloths, a circle of crayons, or beeswax in a basket.

Handwork and crafts

Many newborn babies seem to unfold like a butterfly, their wrinkles filling and little limbs spreading out. The hands 'unfold' too as they gradually search out their surroundings. At first the whole tiny hand explores, with the thumb slowly beginning to oppose the fingers. The baby may push food into the mouth with the whole hand, often the base of the palm. The fingers are often laid as one with the palm on to objects. As time goes by, the fingers begin to be used independently of each other. Often the index finger is used first, maybe as a kind of hoe to scrape the food. In the fingertips lie fine nerve-endings, the threads to thinking. It takes several years for the fingers and brain to co-operate well, to become our amazing servants. Sometimes I said to the kindergarten children, 'We will use our own tools in the sandpit today', by which they understood those awe-inspiring hands and fingers with which nature has endowed us, rather than the trowels, sieves, rakes, wooden spoons and saucepans we had. It is so important for children to experience, and then do, useful work which they can then increasingly do for others in later life, such as cooking, cleaning, painting, digging, building or sewing.

A friend sent one of our baby sons a beautiful, finely-knitted woollen shawl: ' I have been wanting to try my hand at one of these and I felt you might like one'. Many years ago children of even 6 or 7 years knitted fine things and stitched intricate samplers, through which they learnt co-ordination, dexterity and perseverance. How many children today would have the time to do that, let alone the ability? 'Nimble fingers make nimble minds', they say.

Nicola, 8, was knitting a hat for her doll. 'I want to knit one too', said little brother, at 4 too young to knit. I gave him a piece of felt, needle and thread, and he blissfully stitched randomly here and there. After a few minutes his (fairly crumpled) hat was 'finished', so we tied it happily somehow to his doll's head. Children of 3 years old can begin to stitch: felt is easy to use, with a crewel needle and embroidery thread. By 4 or 5, children can sew and decorate a simple bag or mat. By 5 or 6 years they should manage an array of very simple dolls' clothes. Both boys and girls can become very absorbed with doll making, and tend to identify themselves with the dolls they make. Allow them to pick out the materials they need in the colours they prefer. Dabrio loved blue, so his doll had entirely blue clothes and hair.

By 6 children can usually thread their own needle, cut out material, sew on buttons and stitch round holes. In this way, a doll can be made of flannelette about eighteen inches, or half a metre, square. A tight ball of unspun natural fleece (sheep's wool, washed and prepared, available from craft suppliers) is placed in the centre for the head, the cloth drawn together round it and tied firmly for the neck. Some fleece can hang down through the neck to make a bit of body. 'Hands' (and 'feet' if wished) are made of knots tied in the corners. You do not need to attempt to make the features of a face; this allows the child to imagine every kind of expression. Hair of woollen yarn, fur or sheep's wool can be sewn on. A standing doll without arms or legs is also satisfying to make. Children can be allowed a lot of freedom in such work, learning at their own pace and beginning to plan what they do. Ronnie, 5, asked me when lovingly sewing his doll's hair, 'Did God sew my hair on?' And Sammy, 6, possessor of

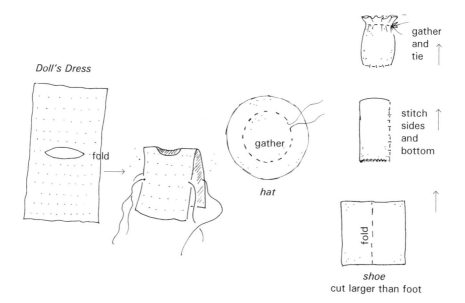

Doll's Dress

gather and tie

fold

gather

hat

stitch sides and bottom

fold

shoe
cut larger than foot

trousers

cut wider than doll

Doll's sleeping bag

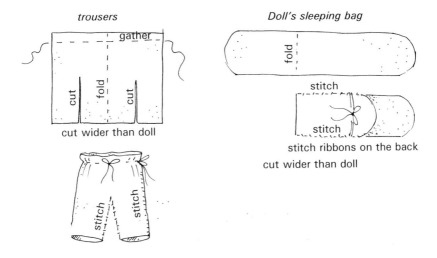

stitch ribbons on the back
cut wider than doll

Both girls . . .

and boys enjoy sewing

little concentration, did a few stitches of hair, then said he'd finished because it was his Dad (who was nearly bald). Gulliver, 6, made a coat for his teddy bear, insisting the collar be large enough to come up over the ears. He lived amongst noisy older siblings, and maybe his teddy's collar

Made by a girl of 6

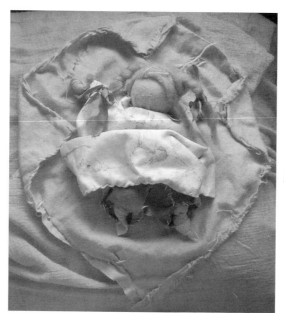

Made by a boy of 6

offered him a feeling of protection. Children enjoy stitching a soft blanket for their doll, as if it were a mantle for themselves. The edges of dolls, blankets and playcloths can be hemmed or oversewn. It is very nice to make a doll's crown of ribbon or plaited wool, which can hold a thin veil

The doll swaddled in its blanket

in place. From 6 or 7 children enjoy sewing presents in secret.

I dyed white flannelette and stockinette in a big saucepan for doll-making using onion skins, tea or turmeric spice powder with hibiscus tea. The first batch was always quite dark, the next lighter and so on, which enabled us to have dolls with every shade of skin colour. You can also use conker cases, walnut shells, or apple-tree bark. (Information on dyeing is widely available.) The wool for handwork does not have to be in long lengths and can be unravelled from an old garment. To straighten the wool, wind it tightly round a board, dip the board in water and hang it up to dry. Children enjoy standing opposite each other to twist the ends of a long piece of wool clockwise. They mustn't let go before the twist is ready! Release the tension slightly, and if the string twizzles quickly on itself, it is finished. At this point someone holds the middle with a finger, while the children meet and knot their ends together, then one of them lets go. The third person releases their finger, and the yarn twizzles itself into a rope. To make it thicker the procedure is repeated but twisting anti-clockwise. Children love their 'twizzled' strings. Finger knitting with chain-stitch makes cords too (creating a chain using the forefinger instead of a crochet hook) from which children can make hair-bands, strings for gloves (so that they can be threaded through sleeves), belts, mats, straps, edging for bags and strings for pompoms to fly through the air. Two pieces from a branch of softwood which have been whittled, sanded, and then had holes drilled through, make handles for a skipping rope. Elder wood is good for this as the centre is soft. Children of 3 years old can make pompoms: wind wool thickly round two rings of cardboard (roughly 4 in or 10 cm circumference with the holes about 1 in or 2.5 cm). Then cut through the wool at the edge, tying the centre together firmly, and remove the cardboard. They can be balls to play with, bobbles on hats, or, with two pompoms together, animals with felt ears and a tail. If wool is bought in skeins, two children can wind it up, one holding the skein and the other winding: a slow, co-operative and calming task. Boys like to do this too.

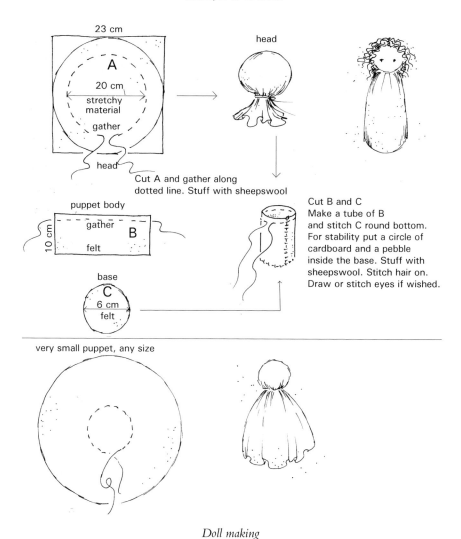

Doll making

At the age of 6 or 7, children's co-ordination is far enough advanced for boys and girls to begin knitting, which is brain gym for the child. Nowadays this is unfortunately not so common. On the train, a boy of about 12 watched me knitting with bamboo needles round the heel of a sock. 'What are you doing with them chopsticks?' 'What do you think?' 'Sewing.' 'I'm knitting.' 'What are you making?' 'Socks.' 'Cor. How long does it take you?' 'A few hours.' 'Cor. Will you make me some?' But then he had to get out, before we could exchange addresses. Nowadays most knitting is done by machine, but hand-made socks are lovely!

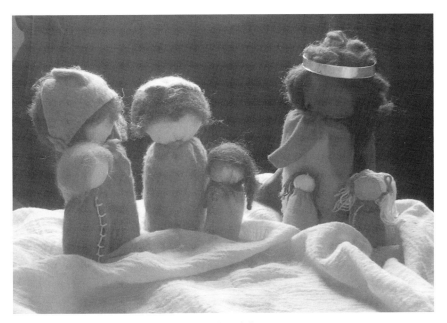

Standing dolls

Dolls of a circle of material

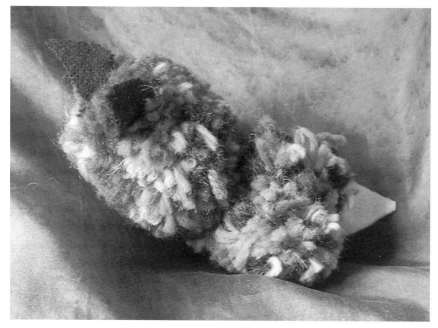

Animal of 2 pompoms

Hobby-horse

A hobby-horse can be created by pulling a large, thick, old sock over an L-shaped branch or old broom with half the broom-head cut off, then stuffing it with hay, sheep's wool, or old soft garments pulled to pieces. Buttons for eyes and felt ears are sewn on. A plaited or twizzled rope, or strips of leather, become a bridle and reins. Alternatively, a piece of cloth can also be simply wound round a broom or stick, and, hey presto, a horse is born.

With natural and coloured sheep's wool, very simple people can come to birth. A length of this wool is teased out,

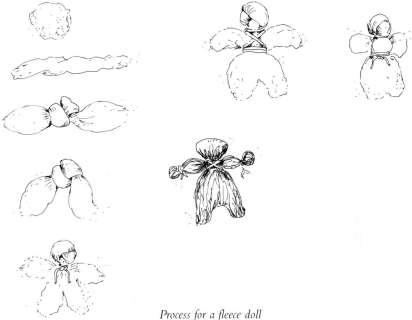

Process for a fleece doll

then stretched and tied into a knot. The knot becomes the head, and the ends the body and legs. A thin thread of the wool can be wound round where the 'waist' should be, with another piece of fleece for arms through the body, wrapping it criss-cross. Animals and birds can be created in a similar way. You can just experiment. Young children are actually perfectly happy with a piece of fleece just very carefully wound into some sort of shape by a loving adult. They will see in it what they want. My misshapen, lopsided efforts at animal-making in front of the children were greeted with such comments as 'Sally's *really* good at making sheep!' Anna, 7, made a sheep with fleece and pipe cleaners, 'But it doesn't look like a sheep because it hasn't got any ears'. A 5-year-old would happily 'see' the ears, but by 7 things have to be more real.

Embroidered felt makes pretty belts, mats, dolls' clothing, bedding, carpets, hair bands, purses, whatever. Children like to decorate it as they go along, which is more creative than following a set pattern. Woollen felt is preferable to synthetic as it is warm and the latter tends to disintegrate. There are always pieces of felt left over, too small for anything but to be cut up into 'beads' for younger children's first sewing. They can just push the needle with a silky thread through the 'beads' to make a necklace. Waste not, want not. Felt can be hand washed: rinse thoroughly, pull very gently to shape and iron

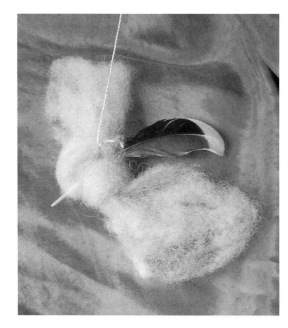

One knot for a bird

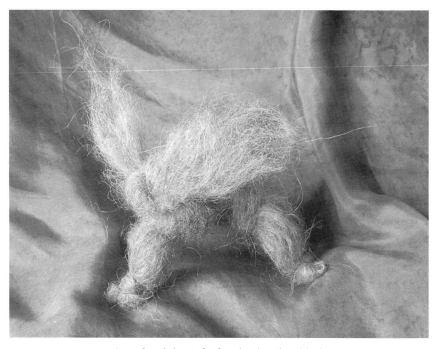

Animal with knots for feet, head, tail and body

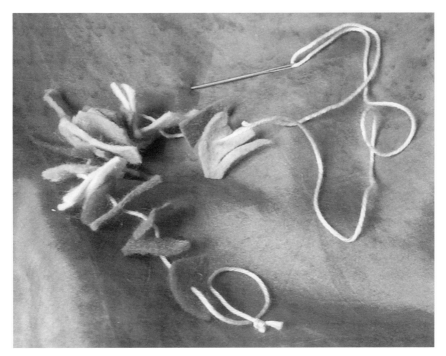

Necklace

with a cool iron when still slightly damp. There are many craft and handwork books available, including simple felt-making and candle-dipping, which I also did in my kindergarten and at home. (Be sure never to leave candles unattended, and put them on a non-combustible surface.) As with every other activity, such work has a beginning, middle and end, the end being to put everything back in the right place 'for next time', not leaving it to the parent. Baskets, drawers and decorated boxes make nice homes for everything. Having a craft corner with table, chairs and baskets or boxes of materials and tools encourages children to be creative.

Some of the parents used to come in to kindergarten and sew for fundraising activities. It was delightful for the children to watch and be involved.

Out of doors

A young woman told me she was really glad she had learned to be independently creative when young and able to play both indoors and out, which she thought had helped her gain knowledge and expertize. She said she wouldn't have understood many things, nor be able to cope with fear without the experience, for instance, of learning how to climb trees without being scared, how to chop logs and stack them so they wouldn't fall down, or build a house out of bracken. She said it wasn't easy to make such a house, for you had to form the walls, windows and doors and put the roof on, all with bendy material, without its collapsing. She had learnt not to be afraid of what's there, of what's outside: you had to work round it. This was also the case in a bracken house with adders around, you knew they were there and they knew you were there, and you learnt how to be careful. She felt that if she'd watched TV or played with computers when young instead of being creative, she would be much the poorer.

Anyone who has spent time outdoors with children will have observed what interest and joy lives in them there. Such wonders await child and adult alike. The sky is there for everyone, so are the sun, moon and stars. It is marvellous to gaze out of the window with children before going to bed, and in the early morning, whether at a clear or stormy sky. Like a great canopy, the sky is a cloak to a little child, who understands nothing of satellites, space pollution and greenhouse effects. Being outside in a natural area is therapeutic for young and old alike. In parks and in the country, children can experience huge trees and secret places. Contact with the natural world is life giving, and care for it instils a morality and respect in children. Children need to be outside for fresh air and sunlight, to feel the wind on their faces and get rosy cheeks. Babies also need fresh air and sunlight, but prefer a quiet atmosphere and the protection of a hat and hooded pram.

> We'd been gardening most of one February morning in kindergarten, with a 'tea break' for 'workmen's sandwiches' in the 'café' (sitting on logs). 'I've been outside ALL MORNING, really ALL MORNING and I haven't even been inside once!' said little Jim proudly.

What a blessing it is for the children who have a garden: here they have their own 'nature programme' to watch every day of the year. Feeding the birds helps to bring it alive. Simple hanging bird-tables can be made of a board or slice of wood with holes drilled near the edges, through which strings are threaded. Bird feeders full of seeds or peanuts can hang from a hook. (Take care to place food for the birds well away from cats.) A woodchip garden path also provides a veritable birds' larder. A delicious winter dinner awaits birds and animals in seed heads and berries if we don't rush to clear up the garden in autumn, and gives much delight to the

Bird table

watching child. Birds need water for drinking and washing, so do try to keep a little hole open in the pond ice in winter. Children enjoy threading peanuts on a string for birds' winter meals, or filling a half coconut with melted fat and seeds to hang upside down outside. Frogs, toads and other hibernating creatures need us to leave unkempt places of log-piles, rocks and stones to live in. Where there is neither garden nor balcony, the 'countryside' can grow nonetheless. Plants and treasures from nature can be cared for, hanging from windowsills and sitting on shelves. Birds will fly high to feeders in flats.

Every household can make compost, even indoors, where pot plants will be grateful for it. Enquire with your local authority whether there are any discounts on compost-bins and water-butts. It is a magical thing for children to see the kitchen and garden waste turn into sweet-smelling soil. A pond, even in an old sink, is central to the needs of a garden, for wildlife and the child's interest and joy. Of course as ponds are potentially dangerous, vigilance is essential where young children are present, along with physical protection such as a fence or strong cover where necessary. Gardening books give advice on compost and pond making. This rhyme can help children, when washing their hands, not to waste water, especially in areas where there is a shortage:

Turn the tap on and wet your hands,	(pause in the rhyme to do it, but only a brief wetting)
Turn the tap off and wash your hands,	(pause to do it carefully with soap)
Turn the tap on and rinse your hands,	(pause in the rhyme to do it, with only as much water as is needed)
Turn the tap off and dry your hands.	

This uses much less than filling the basin, and avoids 'washing' the soap. As the hands are not under the water for long they will not get cold, and the activity may make them warm. The best would be to have a mixer-tap turned to warm. Water play is to be found naturally in washing, washing up, painting and watering plants.

Being outside increases appetite, physical fatigue and happiness. I have enjoyed much time under the sky with (and without) children, playing, working, camping, biking, swimming, and hiking. A picnic can be laid out prettily with the simplest of materials and decorations. In kindergarten and family we sometimes ate up in trees and in bushes, great fun, especially when well-clad in the rain. Fires can be made for cooking, whether on tarmac or in the forest, where allowed. If possible, children should be close enough to feel the heat and feed the flames, vital life experiences. They progress in every aspect of their development and feel well in the open air, observing, listening and learning to be sociable. Outdoor 'Forest' schools and kindergartens are springing up. Children spend anything from a couple of hours there every day for a week, to the whole of every day always. It is found that their health, behaviour, play, inquisitiveness and sociability improve. They have a simple shelter and find endless opportunities for joyful learning.

> I said to my 5-year-old son, 'I can see the mast over there, can you?' 'No, you're taller than me. You can see a lot more up there, but we notice a lot more down here near the ground, like molehills for instance and tiny flowers.'

Molehill and hedge exploration, stones, sticks and puddles have high priority for children. A sandpit should adorn every garden, the bigger the better, and be surrounded with a board or slab edging which makes it easier to sweep sand back in. It needs shade from hot sun. Play equipment in it is more attractive if cleaned regularly, kept separate from mud-pie cutlery, and tidied up daily into a box or shed rather than left lying around. Rocks and logs in the sand encourage imaginative play. Logs, boards, planks, pipes and barrels offer enticing possibilities in a garden. Children really like to create houses, and they can re-build one time and again by leaning sticks and branches on to a frame of posts, then tying them up with bits of string and rope. Winding paths seem to lead to more magical places than straight ones, and a contoured landscape of holes and hills dug and heaved about by willing workers gives food for fantasy.

Proper tools and work gloves are good for children's gardening. Sowing and tending plants, drying herbs, making jam and syrups all support children's enthusiastic learning from life and the development of their senses. I really believe that whether watching water-boatmen on a pond or flying a kite, children naturally prefer to be outside. 'We haven't had very *long* outside', said Estrelle when they had to come in after an hour. It is 'wonder-full' for children to experience the elements outside: rain and fountains, fire and sun, swings and wind-socks ('for the wind to put his foot in,' said Ginny), mud and old bricks. As experiences, frost and fog are just as important for children as rippling waves and blackberry gathering. Those who can look after animals are extra lucky.

Parents had created a garden for a teacher called Susie and named it 'Susie's Garden'. Alex gazed up at the sky there one day and said, 'The whole world is Susie's Garden'.

CHAPTER 8

MEALTIMES

'This tea makes my teeth shake.'

First beginnings

Soon after birth most children are put to the breast in a mood of great relief and joy. It may not be easy at first but most mothers manage well when baby settles. A doctor said: 'Feed the baby regularly, then it will know when it's coming, and feel safe'. Whether it is two-, three- or four-hourly, whichever suits you, the rhythm gives the child a feeling of security and well-being. Recommendations tend to go in phases: the prevailing one is for feeding 'on demand'. Yet in my experience children fed at regular times are generally content, whereas many fed on demand have been grizzly and clingy. Kathy and John thought night-time was for sleeping, so they put their month-old baby down after his 6 p.m. feed, then waited till he woke up, rather than waking him at the 'classic' 10 p.m. It might be 9 p.m., midnight or 2 a.m., but she fed him, put him back to bed and waited again. He began to sleep for twelve hours at night after about six weeks, and was doing it regularly after some time. They tried the same with their next children, with the same result. It seemed that if the babies had enough milk during the day, they didn't need more at night.

Feeding the statue

There are indications that eating habits may be laid down in early life. Playing around with food later on could be attributable

to 'playing' at feeding times as a baby. Children who experience a routine may feel more satisfied than those who are continually 'topped up'.
They feel safe in a secure rhythm, and may cry less. It takes time and
patience to create a routine. A mother had no rhythm for feeding or
bedtime and wondered why her 8-month-old cried so much. A new
routine of regular feeds and fixed bedtime calmed the child. When baby
begins to stop drinking it is an indication of soon being full, so you can
draw the 'meal' to a close. Babies and children who don't feed or eat
steadily are perhaps being disturbed by radio or TV, chatter, or people
coming and going. They turn away then return for more, not having
'time' to drink or eat properly because they are too busy absorbing these
phenomena. Many children don't actually eat with adults, so they lack a
model to copy.

A child of 2 in a parent and child group was trying to cut up pieces of
paper. Her mother interrupted her for a feed she didn't appear to want.
Some mothers don't want to give up breast-feeding out of an (under-
standable) pride, or perhaps a reluctance to let the child go. Perhaps it is an
unconscious effort to replace the 'hardening' of modern times with a 'soft-
ening'. As breast-feeding is 'on tap', babies can turn to it all day and all
night. Some mothers have their babies next to or even on top of them at
night, so they can feed at will, but this is exhausting for both mother and
child as neither gets a good sleep. At his home, a child of 3 fetched himself
some cheese from the fridge. He sat next to his mother, who said, 'Do
you want a feed?' trying to put him to her breast, but he struggled off her
knee. Snacking is not good for anyone, and I sense that feeding at any odd
time amounts to snacking. It is good for everyone's stomach to rest for a
few hours between meals, to allow the digestive process time to nourish
the body. An exhausted mother said she had to feed her year-old son
hourly, also at night. I suggested giving more food regularly during the
day and resolutely putting him in his own bed. A reason given for long-
term feeding is that it helps the bonding of parent and child, but my
observation is that the bond can actually become too strong and be a dis-
advantage to the mother, the child or both. In hot countries where some
children are fed longer, the culture, background and health aspects may be
quite different. Some mothers say their child won't give up, but if gradually weaned by partially giving the breast *before* and then later on *after* the
meal, it shouldn't be a problem. Children, including babies, rely on us to
be firm with them!

A woman had her son of almost 3 with her at a talk for parents. At question time she said he could fit all the letters into a game, and knew all the numbers; then she picked him up and breast-fed him. Was she keeping him a baby while wanting him to grow up?

Mouth-watering food

Preparing food with children is half-way to their enjoyment of it. Inviting smells and colours should be so much part of a little child's life. 'I could smell this when we were cooking and it smelled yummy', said Rose. In our kindergarten the children were involved every day in the preparation of the (organic) food for mid-morning break and festivals. A child who wouldn't eat muesli at home said: 'Mummy, kindergarten muesli is the king of foods'. Mother promptly involved the child and in preparing together they put in a pinch of the ingredient called 'magic'. All was then well.

For my birthday one year, I baked several flat rounds of wholemeal and white bread, and made them into a cake with the kindergarten children. We

Making müesli

spread each one with our plain yoghurt, then piled them into a large, tall cake with treats on each pile: grated nuts and apple, raisins, naturally coloured smarties, and rose petals we'd dried the year before. Taste and 'eye' buds grew bigger as the cake grew higher. 'Mmmm', we all said. 'My tummy thinks it smells delicious', said Adeola. On the top was a final spread of cream cheese with candles, smarties and petals. 'Mmmmmm.' We held it all together with knitting needles, each with a flag made by the children. It was a good 30 cm high. We could hardly wait for our mid-morning break. We all ate so much, and there was enough for next day. Not a crumb was left, not even from the fussiest children. Our cake had the simplest ingredients, and required a good lot of chewing. Biting, licking, tasting, chewing and swallowing all require effort, help the teeth and speed the digestive process. Such a cake can be made at home, even as part of a party, perhaps with proper cake slices.

The demand for organic baby food is growing. Much food contains chemicals, but parents are becoming ever more aware and choosy, especially where babies and children are concerned. So much is processed in some way today: hardened, homogenized, heat-treated … destroying important elements. Chemicals and deficiencies in vitamins and minerals may affect behaviour. Chemical additives may disturb the natural processes of the digestive system. Of course it is all right to have convenience foods occasionally; a happy medium is the key. It is common knowledge that sugar and certain additives can make for unruly behaviour. Two girls of about 8 and 12 were playing clapping games quietly on the train. After fifteen minutes their mother gave them each a large bottle of cola; they became progressively noisier and out of control, running up and down the carriage, disturbing everyone. No amount of threats or coaxing from mother or others around made them settle. I watched a children's 6 a.m. TV programme showing how to make breakfast with toast, butter, yeast extract, cheese and ground up *crisps* on top. In my view it also contained too much salt for a child. As with all things, sugar and salt should be offered in moderation, neither too little nor too much. And again, it's all a question of balance. Many foods extol the 'virtue' of being 'fat-free' but are filled with sugar. It is very hard for over-weight children to lose weight later.

Plenty of fruit, grains, herbs, and vegetables helps children to be healthy. Preparing fresh food with the children has the advantage that they are likely to eat it. It is excellent to make babies' food from fresh ingredients. Children love to use very small biscuit cutters to make shapes in slices of cucumber, carrot, apple or any such fresh food for salads. For instance, they can grate carrots with different graters: fine, medium, coarse and sliced, to make attractive decorations on the dish, like a picture. Many fruits, vegetables and cheeses are suitable for this, even using the different ingredients at the same time. They enjoy making up their own recipes at the age of 4 or 5 years, under the guardianship of a parent where necessary.

Mark, 6, made this delicious dessert for his family and carefully wrote it down:
WIPD CREM—GRATID NUTS—CHOPD BANANA

Mennie gave her family quinoa, a nutritious grain from Peru, but they weren't keen on it. They liked couscous though, so next time she called it Peruvian couscous and they ate it up. Dora told her children what they could have for their packed lunches, and let them make their own, for then she knew they would eat them. Some children shy away from crusts. Does that come from an adult example? It is good for children to chew properly. They can be encouraged in this if an adult joins them enthusiastically in pretending to be squirrels.

> *From a letter to parents:*
> *. . . We make very simple, bland but nutritious organic food for mid-morning break in kindergarten, and the children love it; some need to get used to it but they normally do quite quickly. The children help of their own accord to set the tables and give out the food. We have napkins (a 'picture' of caring) and behave sociably through imitation and encouragement, beginning with a grace and ending with 'Thank you for our meal'. It is part of our rhythm that . . .*
>
> *On Mondays we make rice cooked with raisins,*
>
> *On Tuesdays we have muesli mixed ourselves: fresh fruit, oat flakes, grated nuts (added last in case of allergies), raisins, water and honey (milk tends to make it too rich and some children are allergic to dairy products),*
>
> *On Wednesdays we have cooked millet flakes with a little honey or jam added on serving,*
>
> *On Thursdays we have 'mousey chewing gum': rye grains cooked with carrots, onions (and maybe other vegetables in season) herbs and unsalted yeast extract (mice love grain, and it is chewy),*
>
> *On Fridays we have the bread we made earlier with nothing on it— delicious, accompanied by the yoghurt we made earlier in the week. For this, milk is heated (not boiled) and cooled to hand hot, 45°C, mixed with a spoonful of last week's yoghurt, and left in covered jam jars in a warm*

place. The arrangement of the little kitchen is such that the children can stir and watch quite safely. Of course they help with the chopping, grating and stirring. We collect all sorts of herbs as well as lime blossom, birch leaves and rose hips when they are ripe, to dry for our daily herb teas, and use them fresh in season. We have apple juice, pressed ourselves in autumn, or rose-petal tea for festivals.

It was wonderful to pick the flowers from a lime tree on a sunny early July day. As we balanced to reach the branches, our hands became sticky with nectar, and the tree higher up was filled with buzzing, humming bees: a feast for the senses of smell, touch, taste, warmth, movement, hearing, sight, balance and well-being. The whole preparation of herb teas is a bit like the layered birthday cake—the involvement is the invitation: growing the herbs and flowers in the little garden, drying and then storing them in glass jars so the children can see inside. The tea can be made in a heat-proof jug then transferred to a glass one, in which the flowers or leaves float up and down in the heat, excellent support for the child's feeling of movement. In such tea-making, children experience colour, smell, warmth and taste: light-green lemon balm, pink rosehip, gold lime blossom, mauve mallow. It is attractive served in small glasses; anything that looks nice or is put prettily on to the plate excites the appetite.

Susan, 6, saw us making tea every day but asked her mother: 'Mummy, can you ask Sally for the tea recipe? It's delicious and it's really healthy'. The 'recipe' consisted of pouring boiling water on to the herbs!

What if they don't like it?

The waiter explained the menu of the smart hotel to my friend's small niece. '*Boeuf Savoyard.*'—'I don't usually have that', she said. '*Oeufs "New York" aux Fleurs.*'—'I don't eat that.'—'*Coq au Vin avec Légumes du Jardin.*'—'No thank you. What I would *really* like is tinned tomato soup.' The waiter disappeared, to return with a tin of tomato soup (quickly bought from a corner shop?), wrapped in a brocade napkin on a silver salver, and asked if that was what madam required. Soon he kindly returned with it steaming in a pretty bowl. The foreign, completely unfamiliar words were too much for her.

'This tea makes my teeth shake', said Joey, trying the herb tea. Just a sip and then a drink of water grew into many sips and a little water after a week, and then he could forget about the water. Children may be given just a little food or drink, then something else, but not something else instead. At many parties children are given platefuls of food they can't possibly manage. It is easier and more satisfying for a child to have only one or two small things on a plate at a time. It is more likely to work well and leave little to feed the birds. When thirsty, children can be given water or herb tea. Many children are given a lot of fruit juice. Is this necessary? It can make it difficult for them to drink plain water, and increases the acidity in the mouth which harms the teeth. Giving children a bottle with juice in it, to carry around, is to my mind another form of snacking. I feel it is better to sit down and drink properly when it is needed.

How can children be encouraged to eat and finish their food? The adult's attitude to it is telling, and can be so supportive or just the opposite. My grandfather said, 'What you don't like isn't good for you', to the annoyance of my grandmother, as we struggled to swallow her boiled fish. Everyone has likes and dislikes, so parents can be sensitive to whether the child is just being fussy, or playing around, or whether it really is a problem. Eggs, fish and leeks for example can make children want to vomit. Do you encourage by saying: 'Let's try one more teeny-weeny-yummy-mummy bit, just *this* small', or give up and say: 'Oh leave it then. Do you want a banana?' You can play games of course, like: 'Maybe when I look again there won't be anything on this spoon', and there may well not be. But in the end, finishing should be from the child's own enjoyment. In a family with siblings or in a group, the other children get excited and want to help. Eddie, next to me on a picnic, didn't like the sandwiches. But when I held mine up (uneaten!) quite near his mouth and looked the other way, he took a bite and the children were delighted. I pretended nothing had happened and asked why they were laughing, holding it out again. Very soon he'd eaten the whole sandwich, by which time I'd 'realized' and offered him another, which he happily ate. You can create such little games where the child can become active rather than being spoon-fed, and certainly never forced.

Malika, 4, pointed to a bowl of very big red apples: 'Can I have an apple? That one, the red one'. 'Do you want all of it or shall we cut it?' asked mother. 'All of it!' She nibbled a bit, lost it, found it, kept it but just played with it. We know whether they really can eat all of this or that, like whether children really can push the doll's pram all the way. Their eyes may be bigger than their tummy. They are too little to know, and can have more when they've managed the first bit. I feel wasting food is not a healthy image for the future, not least because there are so many starving children.

One day during a meal in which we had to keep getting things we had forgotten, my adult daughter laughed and said, 'This is actually quite a stressful meal—we've got up and down about ten times!' How is it when children play with their food, are noisy, get up and run around, come back, eat again and play around? Is it imitation of adults getting up and down? Or a lack of routine, general restlessness caused by a noisy family, TV, radio, quarrels, toys, or even a lack of adults at the table? If children run away from the table and parents can find no good reason for it, they will be wise not to allow them back, nor give a second course if the children haven't finished the first. Although children need time to chew properly, there must be an end to the meal. It can be helpful to a child to assume that, if food is left on the plate, the meal is now finished, and avoid the temptation of offering anything in its place. I've seen 5-year-olds fed by an adult, but I think even 2 is quite old for that. It is unhappy for everyone if children don't sit quietly at the table enjoying their food with the family. Children who experience regular mealtimes in a peaceful way with quiet conversation will be able to digest properly, and make use of the food they have eaten. They like to do things properly and are pleased with themselves when they have finished all their food. If parents empty their own bowl and show a big smile, perhaps stroking their tummy, the children, out of imitation feel inclined to do the same.

> *From a letter to parents, after an evening together about discipline,*
> *including meals:*
> *. . . and about mealtimes: We should have an hour just to share thoughts on*
> *this topic alone! One can try to maintain a feeling of gratitude for all around*
> *us, including food. There are so many people with so little; everything we*
> *can do to help the child feel thankful is a bonus. Regular mealtimes are such*
> *a help, with very simple food for these little ones!*
>
> *If mealtimes can be happy, it helps the digestion as well as the social*
> *experience. The children know more or less how to set the table because they*
> *see you doing it. They need things to be the same, such as having their same*
> *place at the table, which we do at kindergarten as well. But variety is the*
> *spice of life, so we sit where we like on kindergarten birthdays and festivals.*
> *That makes it very special, at home as well!*
>
> *If a child doesn't like a food, I suggest, after giving plenty of*
> *encouragement, taking it away. You can just give something pea-sized, or*

one grain! Certainly not too much to try, and make sure you don't compensate with lots of everything else. It doesn't do any harm for a child to be a bit hungry for the next meal! The whole ambience of every meal is important. I know many of you light a candle for the meal—this makes a special focal point and is peaceful, as well as teaching the children how to take care of fire. (Make sure never to leave it unattended.) It may be difficult to keep everyone happy while the last one finishes, but there again, knowing that ending together is a real gift for the children can help one to be creative. All this actually takes no longer when a rhythm is established. Creating good habits is very important for them, and it's lovely to see when they stop breaking their food into little pieces, or can stay on their chair to the end of the meal. They feel proud if they empty their bowl!'

You can prepare for a peaceful meal by looking at what happens beforehand. Is it healthy play or other busy activity which looks forward to a rest, or a hyped-up one which can find no rest? Maybe parents are over-worked, tired and in a rush, the children uncooperative while baby screams and needs feeding. But the more children there are, the more help you can expect! Little ones can sit in a chair near a parent or older sibling and have a carrot or apple before the meal. During the meal it is wise to keep troubles out of the conversation as they may cause indigestion. Such seemingly small things as trusting children with (strong) china and glass, and giving a cotton bib rather than a plastic one can contribute to respect and calm. Patterns, habits, rhythms, boundaries—all count towards harmony. Children can begin to learn to wait for a second helping from the age of 2 or 3; it all becomes easier when rhythms and patterns are clear. Anthony, 4, asked after two helpings: 'Please may I have a third second helping?'

There are so many ways to clear a meal, and it's best if it follows some sort of pattern. Children can be involved in it: beginning—middle—end, including pushing their chairs in. It is kind to clear *others'* things away (and even to give others their food first). Children who eat their food separately from parents have no one's good behaviour to imitate, little social life, and no pattern to follow. Good habits can be encouraged out of example: having elbows off the table and not talking with a mouth full. Having toys at the table can be a distraction, although a doll or other special friend (even a little car) may like to have a chair and 'behave properly' too. Waiting to start together is easy if it is usual, even if the adults are served first. Being used to such a mealtime mood is helpful when you are visiting someone with the children or on holiday. In sharing a meal with guests, we show that we value both them and their life. Children enjoy decorating special places with pretty cloths over the chairs, cards and extra flowers, and listening to what they have to tell.

If a visitor turned up at Anne's house, before long one or more of her children would appear unprompted with tea and biscuits. Through example they had learnt when young to care for guests. Sometimes they prepared huge surprises. Once for her birthday they had baked delicious treats when she was out, and hid all the guests they had invited behind a curtain. When, unsuspecting, she came home, they all came out singing. Sometimes Anne bought fish and chips as a treat, but then the children would take over, keeping her out of the way while they laid the table with candles, flowers, special napkins and decorations, and prepared a dessert. By this time the food was often cold and needed to be reheated in the oven. But all the hearts were warm.

In my school-days, we said: 'For what we are about to receive, may we be truly thankful'. In the first years, the child is mainly a receiver. The child's moral nature develops in folding hands like the adults and bowing the head in a reverent way. Naturally children should not be made to say grace. If left free to imitate rather than be instructed, they will copy the adults. Love and giving will grow out of receiving in thankfulness. Young children who have learnt to be appreciative and grateful for things large and small will grow through trust and sharing to a feeling of responsibility in puberty.

CHAPTER 9

SLEEP, CLOTHING, ILLNESS

'I've changed my mind.'

Bedtime: happiness and relief for all?

It was sometimes planned that William, 4, would stay on after a day with his grandparents, whom he loved and saw often. However, when he felt bedtime was near, he always made it clear it wasn't such a good idea. 'I've changed my mind.' They had to take him home to his own bed, the place he was used to, with Mummy reading the story and singing the song.

Just as an attractive table and a peaceful run up to the mealtime are conducive to good eating, so are a peaceful room and quiet run up to bedtime conducive to good sleep. The stronger the rhythm in the child's life, the easier the bedtimes and nights. Children used to a rhythmical life who

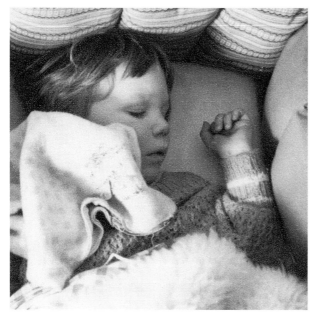

Peaceful sleep

are put to bed without TV, vacuum cleaner, radio and so on, will drop off. Sleeping in a simple and tidy room, listening to quiet talking or singing by those nearby is an example for them: they will have the chance to imitate the peacefulness and fall into sleep. The rocking of a cradle imitates the movements in the womb. You can put a warm red or pink canopy of silk or cotton over the cot of the newborn, giving a mantle, a womb-like cosy feeling to the little bed. For a restless child you can put blue over the top so a calming mauve appears. The bed and bedroom should be a haven, a loving place, never used as a punishment. Plain pastel colours are more calming than busy wallpapers. It is reassuring to have a beautiful picture near the child's bed.

Parents get to know quite quickly what needs attending to and what doesn't. When the child cries and they have checked that everything is all right, they can leave the child alone again, humming or pottering around not far away, but not over-indulging. Babies and children need their sleep, and to know when they have had enough fuss and hugs. Crying from a nightmare is obviously a different situation. Some children seem to have quite a few nightmares, so need soothing cuddles and singing. Others are mentally fatigued but can't sleep: they can't digest what they have taken in during the day—too many sense impressions along with too little physical activity.

The cooling of the room at night comes with the dwindling of the light. The heating turned down reflects the night outside whilst the child is warm and cosy in bed. It is reassuring to have a bedtime prayer, be it about the family, angels, dolls, pets or dear friends. It helps the child's feeling of being cared for. As it is natural for night to be dark, is it necessary to leave a light on? Just hearing loved ones through the open door gives reassurance. During the story and song, a soft light, perhaps with a crystal which twinkles in the light, is comforting to have until the last kiss and cuddle. Some children are afraid of the dark—perhaps from a frightening story or other trauma, or from sleeping with the light on when very little. It is calming to say 'goodnight' to the moon and stars which accompany us in the deep and dark night sky. Audrey overcame her fear of the dark in an unexpected way. At Lantern time in November (Martinmas) the entire kindergarten group loved to squeeze into a little window-less lobby. Then we lit a lantern. The rosy light made pretty patterns on the ceiling. We sang lantern songs in that cosy space, all huddled together. From then on, Audrey couldn't have her bedroom dark enough.

> Children over 6 with their new memory and sense of self may like to talk about the day gone by, especially when something went wrong. Below this age might be helpful for some, but as the consciousness and memory are barely advanced enough, it may be unnatural.

Children can be tired, pale and irritable when growing a lot, also when their second teeth are coming through. It is wise to let them rest and make sure they have good bedtimes. Bedtime can be more attractive (if not already part of a rhythm), by 'Going to see the Moon peeping in the window', or 'Watching the star children playing in the sky', or 'Flying up to bed'. It is becoming less common for children to have a nap in the day, even as young as a year old. Up to 5 or 6 they really need a rest if not a little sleep. Rubbing the 'sandy' eyes is a sure sign of needing a rest. Some settings exist which make a space for a quiet time. Without this rest many children get overtired, then can't sleep properly at night, especially if they haven't been physically active enough. A little rest after school can work wonders. Young children who are out in the evening miss the normal bedtime (if they have one) and may not sleep well afterwards. It is hard for parents to have to take sleeping little ones to fetch older children from their school, as it disturbs their rest and they can be grumpy. Disturbing the child's sleeping time disturbs every one in the end.

Sleeping in other places may upset children, but odd exceptions have to be taken in their stride. At a holiday camp, Holly, used to a strong rhythm at home, fell asleep on her father's soft cello case during the evening's festivities; covered with a scarf, she slept peacefully through all the noise. Granny Annie's 21-month-old grandson stayed with her while his house was renovated. She indulged him somewhat and when he returned home he wouldn't sleep or stay in his own room. His parents decided they had to be cruel to be kind to get him back to his routine. So they let him scream with the door shut. It didn't take long for him to give up and begin sleeping again. 'That's what happens when you move children and upset their routine. You have to be tough and establish the ground rules early', said their elderly friend. When people keep their babies in their own bed, they often can't get them out when they are older, or have them constantly coming in the night, depriving all of a good night's sleep. Parents can have the baby's cradle next to their bed for a few weeks, then move him into his own or his siblings' room. It usually works well. Just like us, the baby needs to be alone some-times, feeling safe with the family around.

Children can be very insistent. We must answer their needs but also look to our own if the insistence is unnecessary. You may have to be very firm. 'We are here, we can hear you, can you hear us? We'll leave the door open, so you can go to sleep.' Hanging up a mobile of stars and a moon, made together or as a surprise, may help. If all else fails, the child's door may be best shut. The mother of a 5-year-old was at a party but troubled by her son phoning twice to ask her to come home. 'Why don't you say you're enjoying yourself at the party and will be home later and that he has to go to bed?' responded the hostess to her anxious guilt. So she did and the babysitter said he went to sleep.

Some children find it hard to wake up and need time to come to themselves. Gently touching and stroking them may help, or washing their face and hands in warm water (in some cases cool water may be appropriate).

> The moon on the one hand, the sun on the other:
> The moon is my sister, the sun is my brother.
> The moon on my left and the sun on my right.
> My brother good morning: my sister good night.
>
> Hilaire Belloc

This lovely poem is perfect for waking up. I prefer not to change what poets have written, but could one make a sequel for bedtime by making a new last line? 'My brother goodbye, my sister good night?

Clothing the body

On giving us a cot blanket, an elderly friend wrote: 'We always found that a spare blanket was very useful indeed, knees, floors, legs, pram, shoulders, any old thing, so I hope you will'. Wrapping, in other words swaddling baby in soft clothes, shawl and cloth nappy is vital and so comforting. A health visitor said: 'Wrap baby tight, like in the womb, then he will feel safe and well'.

Everything surrounding the baby and young child should be warm, for without warmth nothing can grow, Using cold clothing uses up the baby's own warmth. Birds and animals don't come out when it is cold unless properly equipped with extra fur and feathers, and the colder the climate, the less the plants grow. Synthetic material for clothing and bedding doesn't equal natural materials, especially wool, in this respect. Hiccups may occur from wind, but also from getting cold at nappy change and bath time. The well-being and contentedness of the child are protected by warming nappies,

towel and clothing, and by laying a hand-hot water bottle at the bottom of
the cot (wrapped in a blanket against burning or leakage). Your health visitor
will show you how to check that the baby is not too hot, but you can also
check yourself by feeling feet and hands and down the back of the neck.
Several layers of bedding and clothing are better than one. I found knitted
and flannelette sleeping bags held by shoulder straps made good 'nests' for my
children, and I clamped the corners of the bedding to the bed, as wriggling
quickly moved it around. Some bedwetting occurs from being cold. Over
stimulation during the day can also cause it, particularly in easily excitable
children who need extra protection.

The disposable nappy is very convenient for the adult but not so convenient for the environment, nor so comfortable for the child as cotton.
Disposables may be especially useful for journeys. Various shaped cloth
nappies are available, which are so easily washed and dried in the machine.
There are nappy laundering services, and some councils offer special deals. A
pair of double-knit woollen pants is perfectly adequate for the infant instead
of plastic (see Resources, p. 217).

> We lived next door to a famous person who was entertaining the Queen for
> lunch. I said to him beforehand that I'd better not hang the nappies out that day,
> but he said, 'Oh, I don't know. I'd leave them out. It might be rather homely for
> her'.

A friend who sent us her children's clothes included woollen vests. She
wrote, 'Vests are always useful, I found'. They help so much to support the
developing organism, especially if of fine wool. They should reach down
over the bottom so the waist is covered. 'It is very difficult to find long vests
which cover the developing kidneys', a mother complained. 'They are all
crop-tops now, a fashion which does nothing for the child. Children have
become fashion items.' Many children have T-shirts hanging out with no
vest; the trousers slip down because there is no waist to hold a belt. It is harder
for such children to get well after colds; they may have a constant snuffle and
be miserable. Dungarees or braces on trousers are good, making the child feel
'all together'.

A child of 2 was carried by his mother in the snow. 'I can't help it if you're
cold. Stop taking it out on me. I'll put you back in the buggy if you don't
stop crying.' The exercise of walking and a few more clothes might have
been a great help. On a chilly day, a mother asked her 2-year-old, who had
little on: 'Are you cold?' She didn't answer, but Dad said, 'I shouldn't think

so, all that running'. It was good of Mum to think of it, and she could have gone a step further and *felt* her. Children only begin to know when they are cold from about the age of 6 or 7 and (this can't be said too often) need more warmth than we do. They may feel chilly but not necessarily recognize it. We can tell either by watching their body language or feeling them. Some children say they are too hot and want to strip off; yet even then we can be their guide, of course letting them take something off if they are sweating, yet remembering that they need warmth to grow, develop and feel well. Parents are able to see what they need for their own warmth, then dress their child similarly but with yet another layer. Some parents are well wrapped up in jacket, trousers and boots, while their children are barelegged and in short-sleeves without a hat. The smaller something is, the larger the surface compared with the volume. So small children need help in conserving the little amount of warmth that they can generate in order to provide them with the energy they need for their activity.

A friend of mine who had been through chemotherapy said: 'From my recent experience with hair and then no hair, I can tell you no hair is *very cold*. People don't ever think of that'. She told me that she watched a child of about 16 months old on a chilly day who had a warm coat but no hat and almost no hair. It has been shown that a very large percentage of body heat escapes through the head, so a little cap even indoors for the baby, and a hat outdoors for all children is of real benefit. The fontanelle (gap in the upper skull) closes only around 18 months, and a thick head of hair grows much later, so the little one needs special protection from cold and sun. I see many children in the sun with no hat. A surgeon told me that in their special burns unit they treat a good number of children with sunburn. In a seaside town not far from us the council pays for a lifeguard to patrol the beach and where necessary give advice, hats, sun cream and water, free to parents.

From a letter to parents:
In winter the children must have a warm hat and gloves, which don't get lost if on elastic or string through sleeves. Please no bare legs unless it's really warm, i.e. wear tights or leggings under dresses or trousers, like hot-water bottles for the kidneys. I have a game to make sure their clothes are tucked in. Being tucked in and buttoned and laced up is also of pedagogical value, especially for children who are 'all over the place', subtle but effective. Waist buttons or elastic tend to hinder the circulation, as they have to be tight round the little non-waist to stay up. It is a rule of our school that clothing

may not have writing or pictures because the images may interfere with the child's play and that of others around.

The children should have waterproof boots every day as even in summer the grass can be wet and we sometimes go in the stream. It is better for the feet to wear leather shoes or boots of course but if they are not waterproof we may have a problem, so they need both. I don't make them wear waterproof boots if they don't need to. One can use sheepskin or cork liners for warmth. Sandals are wonderful for making one feel summery, but please something else as well. In summer the children can have their own sun hat but I have plenty otherwise. I don't let them out without one, and I make sure their shoulders and necks are covered. They are so vulnerable, and have plenty of time to be outside at home as well. Please put sun cream on them if you wish, as I can't do that.

There is plenty of weatherproof, practical clothing on the market, so no one needs to fear going out in wind and rain.

'Shall I go and get my nightie on?' said Helen, 6. She had a good rhythm at home, so felt 'automatically' when to do it. Some children don't want to get dressed or undressed. This might be because they are too absorbed in what they are doing, or do not like the chill in taking clothes off. You can play games, such as hiding in a cupboard to dress, but these shouldn't be the rule. Children who are sensitive to the cold may respond to keeping the vest on for a few days. They do not get dirty. It seems a shame that young children should become fussy about clothing. So many items are made for little adults and tend to be gimmicky, with pictures and unnecessary details, emphasizing the look more than the practicality. It is lovely to have a pretty cot, yet also today's bedding often has complex decorations. The children and I wore aprons at home and in kindergarten for messy activities, but Penny, 5, said: 'I can't do baking, my top is too special'. Many little girls love pink, sparkles, bows and frills. Reserving such clothes for 'best' ensures the minimizing of an affected fashion-consciousness at such a young age. And do we really want our children to walk around with logos as free advertisers for big companies? It is not easy to find simple clothes and shoes. What's *wrong* with plain clothes? When I retire, I shall start a business called 'The Plain Clothes Company', unless someone else does it first. . . .

'Peter had a lot of lovely dreams in these pyjamas', my 5-year-old son's godmother wrote. Making simple garments is so satisfying and enables you to choose the material. Older friends used to send us a large box of their too-small garments. Squeals of delight resounded round our house as one treasure after the other was unfolded and tried on, like un-birthday presents.

Quite young children fall prey to hair fashions and change their hairstyles two or three times a day with bits and bobs and bows. It is difficult to keep young silky hair in order, but it is important to make sure the hair is kept away from the eyes so that posture is not affected. 'He won't let me comb it', said the mother of a child with matted long hair, resisting her child-minder's suggestion to cut it.

In many countries it is normal practice to remove shoes when entering a house. Some schools still have the tradition of 'outdoor' and 'indoor' shoes. This simple routine cultivates a mood of respect in the child and highlights the difference of feeling between being outside and being inside. It also keeps the house cleaner! Polishing shoes is a fun activity for children (but watch out for chemicals in shoe polish: you can put it on for them and make sure they wash their hands afterwards)—as is mending their own clothes. Even children of 5 like to sew on buttons and cobble up a hole, so they can actually help. Does it matter if it is not perfect? They have done it themselves! Putting something right creates an image of caring.

From a letter to parents:
While I'm on my chapter of thanks: the next are for your help at home time. It all seems to be working well and we are doing our best to ensure the children are buttoned up before I open the door, so they can just go straight out. It is wonderful to see so many of you letting your children do things for themselves. They feel so proud, and it is essential for them to learn independence, co-ordination and fine motor skills and to strengthen their initiative. It means waiting, I know, and leaving them time—but it's worth it in the end. Their time for being babied is past, and we need to support their effort and sense of purpose and seeing something through. There are daily events, from tidying up everything and finishing the last little bit of food, to the more occasional struggles like carrying heavy logs where not only physical strength is required but also skill and courage. Then they feel a sense of achievement. Children can be very helpful. Life becomes safer if we let them use, say, a knife, because they learn how. One can give them real responsibility they can cope with—one only has to know how and not be afraid.

Recovering from illness

'I've come to see the spot', said the doctor as he leapt upstairs to my limp and ailing daughter who was lying very still in bed, covered with the red rash of scarlet fever. When children are ill, they need quiet. It is helpful to tidy away most toys and books, for they find it exhausting to choose and may not really want anything. Flowers by the bedside and a special glass for the drink helps recovery, as does simple food made appetising and attractive. My children had a cowbell to ring if they wanted anything, as it can be exhausting to call, but any bell or rattle would do.

The baby normally sleeps with the arms up by the head like a little plant. As with the plant's leaves, when the arms droop we know they are unwell. When both parents go to work or study, some sick children are taken to school instead of staying at home. Contingency plans need to be made. It is the best thing if a parent can stay at home for their children to recover and ensure they have a proper convalescence.

> *From a letter to parents:*
> *Children who have coughs and colds are better off at home. They get well more quickly and prevent germs spreading. Sometimes it means inconvenience for the parent having to look after them, but that's life. Bed* **is** *a good and right place! It seems to be extremely difficult for some to keep their children in bed, even with a temperature. A bed on the sofa can be comforting, near to Daddy, Mummy or carer. If a child has a temperature, s/he should be* at home for at least a day without one *afterwards, two days if the temperature has been up for several days. They can seem all right again, but they may actually not be, so health or even behaviour will suffer. Children need to be allowed to be ill in order to be really well again. This also applies to childhood illnesses. We drain the children's life-forces if we don't let them be ill.*
> Please keep your child at home if s/he has:
> - *Nits which have not been treated*
> - *Been sick or had diarrhoea in the night*
> - *A cough or cold until the nose is not running and the cough is clearing up. Please put a hanky in the pocket if need be, and keep one per-manently in the child's glove pocket in the cloakroom.*
> - *An eye infection*
> - *Spots until diagnosed*

- *Had a temperature in the last 24 hours*
- *Had an infectious disease until really well. Chickenpox must wait until all the scabs are off. All childhood diseases can be strengthening to a normally healthy child but they may bring complications if not properly cared for. If your child has had antibiotics, care is still needed, for it doesn't mean they are immediately over the illness.*

  Forgive me if I am stating the obvious to you personally! I need to write these things from experience, for the sake of everyone.

When a child is hurt, we help stroke the soreness away with soothing words or a little song. One does not need always to reach for ointments, plasters and lotions—it is good not to let children expect medicine, when so much heals by itself. It can be strengthening to put up with a certain amount of pain, as it develops courage. 'Ne'mind', Ueli used to say when he'd scraped himself.

> 'You mustn't have nits because if you do and you cut yourself, no blood comes out', said Sandy, 6. 'Why?' 'Because they drink it all'.

Cleanliness

How often should one bath or shower children and change their clothes? Washing (and some bath foams) usually removes the natural protective oils from the skin. Soap and other items made with natural ingredients such as calendula are gentle for the young and are more protective of their natural oils. Baby wipes, car wipes, all sorts of wipes—are they a godsend or another environmental nightmare? They mostly contain chemicals and are generally not biodegradable. Whatever did we do before we had them? It is easy to teach children, through example, to wash properly, and it becomes an automatic habit after the toilet, after being outside or before meals. A letter from a friend: 'I sometimes wonder if time will be mine—it's the eternal trip to the loo with trail of followers that gets me some days'.

Children become dry and clean at various ages. Some children are potted quite early on, so are clean and dry before a year old, but they may go back into nappies when a sibling is born. Generally children are ready for potty training between 16 months and 2 years, but there is plenty of space for individual differences. Nappy rash has quite a lot to do with diet and what you put on the bottom. Gentle calendula oil may be helpful as a

Big brother demonstrates what is needed

daily preventative. 'I know where the toilet is, because I went there when we went to the fair', said Sylvia, 5, as we approached the centre. 'There are a lot of people going to the toilet', she surmised, looking at the row of cars outside.

CHAPTER 10

CELEBRATIONS

'She's crying for joy!'

Spring is flowery, showery, bowery.
Summer is hoppy, croppy, poppy.
Autumn is slippy, drippy, nippy.
Winter is sneezy, breezy, freezy.   Old rhyme

Winter is damp, dark and cold, but the new year makes me hopeful of the spring and summer to come, dreaming of daffodils and weeding in my sun-hat. Animals need extra care, logs are brought in to unfreeze by the fire, the ice is scraped off the car. Jack Frost paints glorious pictures on (single-glazed) windows. Many suddenly feel the urge on a sunny spring day to clean out cupboards, wash curtains and weed the garden, lovely activities in which to involve children. Finding early flowers is exciting. Summer is for pink and yellow roses, lying on the lawn, dancing and high spirits. Autumn fills the land with glorious colours of red, yellow and orange, while warm days remind us of summer as we put off getting out winter clothes. But return the winter must. Seasonal and religious festivals bring joy, and offer a potential for inner change.

'Heaven is more higher than space', mused 5-year-old Sasha.

The images conveyed to heart and mind through festive celebrations have their own moral sense. Children are naturally religious: by this I mean their totally open, receptive nature, and trust in their whole environment, their unjudgemental feelings, their belief that the whole world is good, and their love for everything that is around them. Today we live in a community of widely differing beliefs and practices. Whatever your beliefs, the celebration of festivals sustains children's natural morality, and most of them are of great benefit to the children. They drink in such celebrations through their imitative nature, and soak up the colour and music which underpin festivals

At the pond

Collecting Easter eggs

throughout the globe. Many families have a special seasonal corner in their home, decorated with coloured cloths, plants and objects of the season. Making a surprise display somewhere in the house is awe-inspiring and draws the children to hold their breath on a special day.

The whole year can be portrayed in colour through using cloths as backgrounds for seasonal scenes on table, windowsill or shelf. For instance, a dark-blue one can represent the dark, cold time of winter, decorated with shining stars, and changing to lighter blue as the days lengthen again. A white veil can show frost and snow; brown represents 'Mother Earth' caring for her 'children' of seeds and nuts. Yellow (for sunlight) 'mixes' with the blue in spring, so pale-green cloths may appear, perhaps with a warm pink. Yellow cloths will show mid-summer. The red heat of summer 'mixing' with the yellow is depicted in orange at the beginning of autumn, then the yellow dies away to leave only red at harvest time. As the cold of winter creeps in again, blue mingles with the red to make purple, until the returning blue cloths complete the circle. Such a rhythmical, repetitive wandering round the rainbow of colour is reassuring, beautiful and real for children. For a special meal, you can lay a tablecloth of whichever colour seems relevant, adding candles and flowers, and decorations made with the children according to everyone's creativity. Special foods, spices and music are part of a festival, filling the children with deep sense impressions. They can be involved in all the preparation, such as polishing apples, cutting out stars, rubbing crayons on white candles to colour them, grating nutmeg or baking special breads. They can also become very enthusiastic about the other part of the preparing, which is tidying, washing, cleaning and polishing, to prepare the 'space' for the festival.

A few suggestions for celebrating must suffice here, but there are good books available (see Crafts and Festivals, p. 215).

Celebrations

Young children cannot understand the deeper meaning of most festivals, so we present it in story form. Here are a few examples of some seasonal celebrations for children in the Northern hemisphere, born out of my experience as a mother and teacher.

Let us begin with the Christian winter festival of Christmas. This is immediate for the child because it is about the birth of a baby. Celebrating Advent, a time of expectancy before Christmas, is helpful to offset potential over-excitement and support the meaning of Christmas. *Ad + venire* in Latin means 'to come towards'. I built, over four weeks, a little landscape in a special corner of the sitting room. On dark-blue cloths there was a pebble path to a cave (or sometimes a stable); Mary and Joseph walked along, moved a step each day by the children. I secretly let a foil star 'fall' in the night on the place where Mary and Joseph were the day before. The Child Jesus also appeared in the cave at Christmas, represented by a tiny silk figure (made in the same way as the child's doll without the knots). He had been approaching down a branch, with little steps cut into it, from the cloth 'sky' above, also a step each day. (You could make a little ladder of gold card instead or anything you can dream up.) A gold foil angel 'appeared' behind Him on the step above each night. In the first week, the mineral kingdom, represented by crystals and stones, decorated the landscape. In the second week, plant life appeared: pine cones for trees, pieces of evergreen and moss, dried flowers or a winter-flowering plant or twig such as cyclamen or winter jasmine. In the third week, little animals of sheep's wool, felt, wood or beeswax arrived. I chose animals familiar to the children's natural environment. In the last week before Christmas, human figures appeared: children, shepherds, people, both from the children's doll and toy collections and our own creativity. It is a lovely and simple way to draw near to Christmas, a kind of moving Advent calendar. You can create a stable with pieces of wood from the children's toy basket, and a crib of a half-log or walnut shell. All through Advent, stars can gradually appear in the scene, pinned or stuck to the cloths. These can be attached to a wall or board behind and fall in soft folds. One year in the third week I tore little pieces off an old sheepskin which was falling apart, and set them out early in the grass for us to 'find' when we went for our walk. They looked just like sheep on a hillside, and offered the children a 'wonder-treasure' as they gently carried them home for their festival corners. How simplicity fulfils! You could do this kind of thing for any festival in which young children are involved.

A spring festival gives us the opportunity to celebrate life returning to 'Mother Earth'. Stones, pieces of dead wood, eggs and wax or fleece caterpillars can decorate the special corner. Yellow or brown chicks, black or white lambs, sprouted seeds and spring flowers can fill the scene, with butterflies flying above, made of two tissue-paper circles twisted together. A summer festival brings beautiful music, wonder-filled stories, and decorations of roses—the flower of love. Gathering the fun and high spirits of summer into one's heart can make travelling the metaphorical path through winter easier.

The harvest festivals of autumn bring opportunities to share fun and food with friends. It is nice to make a special loaf and decorate the top with little dough figures or little modelled mice. A lot of enjoyment can be had with apples: cut them crosswise and look for the star in the middle. Hang up rows of slices to dry, sieve applesauce, and make apple cake. One can fill a basket with harvest gifts and share with elderly or ailing neighbours, or join the children in making a big vegetable soup, inviting friends to share it.

Joy at the maypole

Butterfly

Celebrating a festival in late autumn by making lanterns and carrying a light out into the gathering darkness creates a memory to warm the children's hearts for the winter. After a recent hot summer, the leaves turned gorgeous colours. I pressed some and made mobiles for a presentation. One of the participants asked what I had painted them with! Children who spend much time outside and experience festivals and the seasons in an active way will not need to ask such questions.

It is important to dress up for a festival with crowns or garlands of flowers. Children feel special with a crown for a festival or birthday: a strip of card in the seasonal colour can be placed on the head, decorated with tissue-paper flowers, pressed leaves or stars. I wound some clematis and honeysuckle round my head for maypole dancing, and wore crowns and special clothes for other festivals, for children love you to be dressed up too. A simple ribbon could be tied round the head (maybe over a square of muslin) or a garland of flowers threaded into plaited string. In some cultures there are special clothes for particular occasions. If not, you can dress the children at least partially in the colour of the season as above.

Between each festival there is a lull, like a sleeping, a waiting for the next. We put everything away and savour it in our memory, until the anticipation for the next begins again. Celebrations come and go in great waves through the year, finding us breathing in with excitement and preparation, and letting go again when it is all over. Rejoicing is followed by quiet reflection and contemplation until rejoicing unfolds once more.

Making crowns

Celebrating each other

Children imitate our care and respect in celebrating each other, and love to help. It is charming to receive a little gift from a visitor and a 'bread and butter' (thank you) letter afterwards. The overnight guest can be welcomed with prettily wrapped chocolate or soap on the pillow and rose petals

My maypole crown

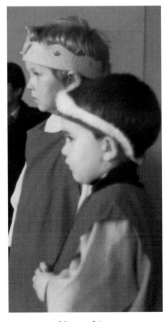

Young kings

strewn over the bed. A bowl of fruit, a bottle of water with a glass, a tin of biscuits, and/or an interesting book show our appreciation of their being with us.

Generally, over half my kindergarten group came from other countries, and we enjoyed singing songs from their nations. Special times for this were our festivals with their various themes. Parents enjoyed teaching me a song or poem in their own language for the class to learn. Families can do this, also for new friends just arrived from another part of the world. A friend learnt some basic vocabulary during a holiday in North Wales, where English is a second language for many. The bus driver looked bored as the holidaymakers asked for their tickets in English. When she in her best beginner's Welsh asked for theirs, he beamed, responding slowly and simply in Welsh.

Gifts

> A practitioner was quite overwhelmed by a wonderful gift from the parents of the class. Matthew, 6, said, 'She's crying for joy!'

Our family opens Christmas presents in turn so that each can enjoy what the other receives; we spread them out over a few days. This works well with children, lessening potential over-stimulation and allowing them to enjoy their gifts. It avoids this: 'I got 16 presents', said Jimmy, 6, who had opened them all at once but not known what to play with in the heap of paper and string. Paper which is not stuck together by sticky tape can be recycled by ironing (cool); and ribbons can be wound up for re-use, good for dexterity and a fine example.

> *From a letter to parents:*
> *How easy it is to give too much to small children! They are so easily swamped and then cannot cope because they don't know what to play with. Kind friends and relations may ask what they can give. You can suggest something which can be worked with, used up or made into something: special food, soap, beeswax for modelling, sewing materials, seeds, bulbs, wood for sawing and filing, logs to build with, a wooden spoon, a grater, a shiny polished apple . . .'*

The parent of a girl said he thought on reading this letter –'Wood? What?!' but then contemplated it. 'Yes! Good idea!'

On his 50th birthday, a well-known person asked several of his neighbours to help him open a mountain of gifts and cards. He said it was beginning to be difficult to feel grateful. How then for the child who receives a lot of presents at Christmas or birthday? Even four or five gifts can be a lot for a young child. Celebrating birthdays turns attention to another human being and brings out loving and giving in others. Celebrating festivals can bring it about towards all humankind. The peace and beauty found in wildflower, hug, sunset, poem and kind deed can be created in festivals, a prerequisite for openness to others. A moving occasion brings about a movement in the heart, new openness and tolerance. Creation is about newness. If celebrations are created with new thoughts and activities amongst the traditional, so opportunities for inner movement arise. 'Peace is a dynamic power', it is said.

Birthdays

> 'I'm 5 now; that's quite an age, isn't it?' said Gracie proudly.

To show the uniqueness of each person, one can celebrate the child's birthday by telling a story into which are woven memorable incidents from the child's life. This builds self-respect, which can become a defence against anti-social behaviour later. A circle of chairs gives a nice atmosphere, with a table with flowers, candles and cards. If each child is brought into the room separately while someone plays or sings, a quiet receptive mood can be created. Children are usually happy to wait outside the room in anticipation. If the birthday child is brought in first, he or she can receive the others, and if last, will be received by them. Children love to hear stories about each other from the age of 3 or 4. The length of the story depends on the child's age. In kindergarten, parents recalled incidents from their children's lives for me to weave into the birthday story. Typical were the following notes given to me a few days before: simple, wonderful, important.

> 11th June 1996 I was born
>
> 1996 Met my new family—grandpa, aunts, uncles and cousin Jack. Spent lots of days at the beach.
>
> 1997 Moved to a farm in Benniworth with our four cats and one dog. There was a little wild cat on the farm already and we adopted her to our new animal family.
>
> 1998 My mum, dad, and I would walk with our cats and dog from the path of our house to the lakes. The cats would wait there for us under cover whilst we walked further with the dog, Bran. Then on our return we would meet up again and return home.
>
> 1999 I met my cousin Isabella from a hot country called Malaysia. We gave her some of my jumpers, socks, and coats because she had never been cold before.
>
> 2000 One day whilst walking to the lakes with the cats and dogs we heard a loud noise. There was a helicopter flying so low we could see the pilot and crew. We waved to each other, except the animals who hid as it was so noisy.

2001   Went with my dad to a toy train shop in Lockton. When I got home I
        realized I had left Bunny in the shop. My dad phoned the shop, which
        found him and said they would put him somewhere safe. When we went
        to collect him the next day, he was sitting in the shop window by a big
        train, but he's home with me now.

'I'm 6, I'm 6, I'm 6, I'm 6, I'm 6,' said Miriam, jumping up and down all
around the visitor as she came in the door.

Birthday parties

All thirty-one 5-year-olds in Stephen's class invited each other to their parties,
which involved hiring halls for space and an entertainer. The children were over-
stimulated, overwhelmed, overtired, his mother told me, and it was expensive for
the parents.

Once I had an evening's discussion with the kindergarten parents, arising
from concerns about birthday parties. Then I drew together all the ideas and
wrote the following for everyone.

A friend accompanies the birthday child

If parents talk to each other, it is possible to break certain traditions, which may be not quite healthy. Get together! Support each other!

Some experience unnecessary feelings of inadequacy: Do I do enough? Will there be enough? With a second child it may be more relaxed. We should value the simple things such as candles on the cake. Children generally have far too much nowadays; they are little and only need little. They want Mummy and Daddy near, then other family and friends, food, clothing, a bed to sleep in, warmth, a few simple toys and dolls, a space to play and places to walk.

Some children want to invite their whole class. Do they really know what they want or are they copying another situation? It is fine for a child who doesn't want to invite many children to do just that.

What about all girls or all boys? With your guidance, children should be able to ask whom they want. It is their *special day! If there are too many children, the birthday child gets exhausted or a bit forgotten and can either play-up or cry. Parents have to worry too much about the guests instead of their special child. The children aren't peaceful and can't even share the cake properly. For whom are we celebrating? Is it also to look good in the eyes of others? Is the child absolutely the centre point? This doesn't mean the birthday child does not need to share too! But if it is peaceful this can happen quite naturally.*

Simplicity = Joy. Complicated = Being over-stimulated and wild.
No one enjoys a wild birthday party, not least whoever has to clean up afterwards!

What if the child wants something for his party seen elsewhere? If this presents a problem, one can say: 'Yes, it was nice when so and so had this at their party. And we *are going to do this'. Children trust their parents more than anyone else.*

The whole day is of course special. One does things one wouldn't do normally—balloons, special flowers etc.,—one parent described how each child in the family had their own kind of flower and even their own special cake every year. The child should enjoy everything. There is reflection (for example in the stories, the number of candles), looking forward (a candle for the coming year, hopes and wishes), and joy, games and fun.

Food is a central issue, with the cake in the middle! One should be able to let go and have smarties, chocolate etc., if the child wants. It is up to the parents to mention allergies before the party. If the cake is round, it sits easily as a symbol of community with everyone gathered around and sharing it. This sitting around the cake is the moment where everyone comes together with their thoughts centred round the child. Sometimes people make special shapes—trains, gardens, a doll's house, a space ship, letting their expertise and imagination fly! Rice paper and spaghetti make a mast and sail, Swiss roll for an engine (preferably home-made), little boats sitting on a lake of jelly (oranges cut in half with the insides scooped out, made into a jelly and returned into the skins, put on a plate of chopped jelly): the list is endless because it is full of individual creativity. Fresh or dried fruit, nuts and slices of vegetables are lovely for decorating, also flowers and leaves, especially fresh edible ones such as nasturtium, borage and other herbs. It is especially nice to have siblings as helpers in on the secret.

Many feel there is too much food at parties. Many children eat a bit of everything and waste the rest—very unpedagogical, even on a birthday! It is much easier, if, say, there are just six children round a table. They should finish one thing before being given another. At kindergarten they are used to not asking for more but waiting until being offered. It is nice to start with a simple grace and end with a 'thank you' all together, instead of children jumping up and running away, or coming back and going again. It helps to make a harmonious situation. Having no music playing during the meal helps them to be quiet. There is no need for lots of different things to eat. Children usually manage no more than two or three things anyway, and making a child choose too much is not a good thing. Some families choose to have one big cake and nothing else, because children have usually had lunch first anyway and will perhaps be having supper afterwards. In this way there is little waste. There is a lack of respect for food if there is too much of it, and it encourages greed.

It is pleasant to have a picnic party in the warmer weather or a bonfire in winter (beach/ forest/ field/ lake/ garden/ park—no sweeping up!). The children can play in a relaxed atmosphere. If the birthday falls during a holiday, one could put off the party for friends until a later time, but the birthday itself must of course be celebrated as the special day.

Particular problems are also experienced in connection with presents, prizes, things to take home, entertainment and games. Children love and need repetition, so really enjoy the same games at different parties. They may go on playing certain games afterwards for weeks! The under-7's do not actually need many games. They can get over-excited. Young children always enjoy classics like 'Hunt the slipper' and ring games, (even up to the age of 9!) such as 'Here we go round the mulberry bush', and 'I sent a letter to my love' [see Further Reading, p. 213]. One mother described to us how happy the children were just playing together while the parents chatted! The birthday child can win one game (at this age it is easy for us to direct the winning) and have the first bit of cake, but help to look after the guests too. Older children usually love to direct things.

Games where children are 'out' are best left till after 6 or 7 years of age; likewise blindfolding, as that can cause distress to younger ones in their all-at-one consciousness. A hat pulled down over the eyes as a blindfold is sometimes acceptable, as the wearer can still see the floor or even peep under the hat. So, 'the tail on the donkey' can work for 5- to 6-year-olds. There are many such games which cost nothing, need no prizes and require little or no equipment, and the children love them. If a prize is needed, it should be very small. A child full of wonder would be happy with something like a shiny stone. When we as a family played 'Pass the parcel' (and also in the kindergarten), we wrapped the little prize up in endless cloths, as children usually just rip paper off which is not very respectful. A raisin or some such tiny thing fell out of each layer. Children can be perfectly happy with this, but as always the parents' attitude and manner makes a difference.

What about music at the party? Recorded music in the background seldom creates a peaceful mood. We were all doubtful anyway about musical bumps, statues and chairs for young children, because they create tension and children get left out. It is always better to use live music for games, however simple. A few notes on a recorder, guitar or tambourine, or an adult singing, are just right for small children, and even for unsophisticated older children. We don't have to be nearly so 'grown up' as some would have us think!

What about presents to take home? Our group of parents felt this was not necessary. It can become expensive which is all right for some but not for others, and isn't the party itself a gift? We live in such a materialistic age, so we decided that if everyone got together we could break this needless habit as it can only make children expect and want more things. If nevertheless a parting gift seems to be called for, a balloon or shiny apple could fit the bill nicely. If there is an activity at the party such as bread making, every child can take a roll home, even as a gift for the whole family.

What about presents for the birthday child? I spoke of a party so big and chaotic that the children started opening the presents for the child. This is surely not what giving is about. So what could be a nice little gift which is not expensive? Something small: (homemade is nicest)—it could be food, little flowers, something stitched or a very simple toy. Other presents have to be chosen carefully according to the age, but materials for handcrafts, presented in a home-made box, are often gladly accepted.

When should the child open the presents? We felt if there were only, say, five children, they could be opened at the time of giving. It is important for the child to receive from and see the donor. At a big party this becomes more difficult.

The nicest entertainment is home-made, such as a puppet-show [see Chapter 6], the quality of which can be totally in the hands of the party-giver rather than the company or restaurant which does it all for you. Clowns are best avoided because sensitive children can be quite frightened by them. A magician could be fun for 8-year-olds upwards.

Do we really want teenage entertainment for our little ones? Is it not better for them to look forward to having a disco when they are older? Two mothers spoke of inviting a few friends to their child's birthday party and watching them having a wonderful time playing hide and seek in the cellar. It doesn't take much for children of this age to have fun!

CHAPTER 11

AT HOME

'It's handy to have a support network.'

'Heaven'

> My mother's childhood home overlooked the sea; the sitting room was upstairs, named 'Heaven' by her father, as he could recover there with his family after a day's work. They were a close-knit family, where father and mother cherished each other.

Treasuring each other's virtues in front of the children helps to counter-balance any irritations they may experience. Secure relationships cannot be overestimated, and every child needs especially one particular adult to relate to in the first years as a basis for building up stable relationships in later life.

As parenthood can be quite lonely, even with a partner, it is helpful to join friends to share difficulties (and happinesses!). When things were not going well, I myself found that putting on a nice skirt and giving myself a little treat was an invaluable pick-me-up. A forced smile can actually become a real one. When you are harassed, see if you can find a moment to sit with the children somewhere, outside or by a window, for a few minutes. They like that because it makes them feel you have time for them. Then everyone can breathe again and a problem may even suddenly be solved.

Mothers particularly but also fathers need to have strength. Taking time out for yourself refreshes your life-forces and restores inner strength: a short walk, reading a book, making music, engaging in a craft or some form of movement, or if possible joining a class at the local community learning centre. It is important to try to maintain a balance between all the demands on your energies: spouse or partner, children, friends, work. Peaceful mealtimes and rhythmical days can contribute a lot of support. Doing simple things together as a family, like going to the playground, having a walk or visiting friends is important too. Parents also need a little space to be together without the children sometimes, and a lone parent needs to have time to be with friends. Children can be so endearing: during my single-parenthood with four children, Elias, 5, asked: 'Sally, who are going to marry when you grow up?'

'Don't you have a man?' Molly asked me with the tenderness a 6-year-old can feel. Sometimes it was hard to be a mother without a partner, but I felt glad to be near family and friends who had strong relationships. One cannot underestimate the gift to a child of living in a stable, happy home. Nonetheless, single parents can give their family a stable home too and build up secure relationships with their children, which support them for their adult life. I once said to my grown-up children, 'I'm so glad you help each other'. One of them replied, 'Yes, it's handy having a support network'.

Jealousy

Any new arrival, baby, new partner or step-sibling in a family may cause jealousy at *any* age. Melanie, 3 was very jealous of her new brother and had lots of tantrums. After a while she settled down and said, 'Mummy, go to hospital and fetch another baby'. A friend wrote: 'Philip (6 months) can crawl, and makes himself more and more noticeable. Christopher (2) finds his presence difficult and defends himself in his own way from his brother upsetting his games. Luckily peace and happiness seem to return nevertheless, even when I've dealt with it the wrong way'. One can try to prepare a sibling but one can never predict a child's reaction. Presents don't replace the fear of not being important any more. Wise visitors make a fuss of the older child/ren, allowing them to show the way and introduce the baby. Special soap or oil for only the older child to use for the baby (and of course for the child too), new nappies for dolly or even a new doll: such gifts find a good home. It is especially lovely to make a simple doll with the child (see Chapter 8). Most children adore their baby sibling but for some parents tricky times lie ahead which need patience. Helping the child to dispense with the stroller and to stop breast-feeding well before the baby arrives is constructive, as are lots of hugs for reassurance, appreciatively trusting the child to help care for the little one.

The wonders of sex

'When the baby is born, you'll know whether it's a boy or a girl, because when it's about 5, if it has a deep voice like me it will be a boy', said a 5-year-old boy.

'How do you tell the difference between girls and boys when they are born?' asked a 6-year-old. Yet most children know about genital differences, having seen other children and/or their parents. They find each other fascinating, and investigations in toilet or garden bush are natural. One's reaction to this is important. To children giggling unhealthily in the toilet I might say: 'There isn't room for both of you. One of you can wait out here till the other has finished'. Of course there are children who experience their parents making love, and some who are subjected to disrespectful and dirty language and even wrong actions regarding sex. How can we guide children in the best way in this most vital area of life?

'We watched a video at Nanna's', said a 4-year-old to her teacher, 'but it was ok, it wasn't sexy'. From time to time sexual talk came up at kindergarten. At breaktime one day there was a silly conversation about willies, descending into what I felt was unhelpful to all and really uncomfortable for some. I managed to lift it onto a different level by taking advantage of the right moment, saying: 'Some little boys have long, thin penises, that's the grown-up word, you know, and some have short fat ones, and some a penis with a little bend in the middle, so they are all *different*. Just like some of us have straight, long hair and some short and very curly, and some like to wear baseball caps and some wear bobble hats. We like to be different from each other'. The children were silent at first, then they began to offer more suggestions of differences. The fact that I talked about sexual differences quite openly brought the conversation out of the realm of the 'naughty'. I could see all the children were actually relieved. In many settings there are dolls with genitals, and I wonder whether this is really necessary. I've often seen children making rag dolls 'pee' as boys or girls, all in their fantasy world without any need of defined genitals. Sometimes this whole subject was a theme for a parents' evening.

My younger children attended our village school with a small outdoor pool. Even 9-year-old boys and girls changed naturally together by the poolside without hiding anything. Fear of sexual abuse has got in the way of such common sense today. Wendy, 6, watched a bull mounting a cow. 'They are going to have a baby. They're having sex.' Watching two flies on top of each other must have stretched Avril's imagination: 'They're going to have a child'. Concepts may become confused: 'Once upon a time there was an old woman called Mr Herrots. He lived in a house and she grew carrots'. Young children cannot grasp any concept of gynaecology, so questions are better answered in a very simple story-like way and

no more than is asked, always keeping the beauty and dignity of the
human being in mind.

> We three were in the bath, asking where babies come from. 'What I should really
> like to know', said my 6-year-old brother (putting my mother in a momentary
> quandary as to how to explain in front of two small girls), 'is how they fit door
> handles onto doors'.

Pocket-money

Grandpa told his small grandson how Robin Hood took money from the
rich and gave it to the poor. 'I hope he won't come near me then. I've got
some pennies!' Mathematically-gifted Allie learnt to barter in Thailand at 5
years old, but young children don't usually understand the value of money.
Older children understand it better when rewarded with a little payment for
extra jobs that aren't part of the daily round. An attitude of gratitude and
value, separate from the monetary, can be developed while the child is quite
young, for example receiving a pretty leaf with warm interest.

Some children had decorated their Daddy's birthday-breakfast table with
carefully collected leaves, seeds and twigs, but at the end of the meal he swept
them into the bin. Had they been displayed in a basket or on a shelf afterwards, that would have demonstrated more appreciation for their efforts. At
the end of the Christmas term, Jenny, 3 and a half, asked me: 'Where's my
present?' Consumerism is a potent force in our society for both adults and
children. Sometimes one needs to get it into perspective. Pocket money can
be decided in a different way by every family, but some parents see no need
for pocket money before 10 years old or so. Instead, they like to give their
children treats when they go out somewhere. A mum said as they were going
on holiday, 'You can have an ice-cream *every* day!' which made her children
perfectly happy. The important thing is to give the children love and
appreciation: no amount of money will make up for that. A young man said
to me, 'Materialism has become too important today, having to have designer
labels and keep up with the fashions. Some people live for the material. Some
people live for the spiritual. We need both'.

'Wrap-around' care

By the age of 3, children do need to be brought into connection with other
children, even though true playing together doesn't occur till a year or two

later. However, for the first three years at least, it is better not to remove the child from familiar surroundings and to keep one stable, primary relationship. Research is showing that it has a beneficial effect on the child's whole, especially emotional, development, and strengthens the ability to form good relationships. Unless the child has an abusive parent, there is no question that being at home with the parent is by far the best for the child.

Many children today have to be put into a care situation when very young to enable parents to have jobs, but otherwise friends getting together and having their children around them is all that is needed. It can be traumatic for a little child to be left away from home. 'I have to go to after-school care because it's booked and paid for', explained 5-year-old Stephen plaintively to his friend. I rejoice at any government which enables parents to care for their own child/ren, should they wish to do so, with grants, part-time work and help to re-enter a career where needed and wanted. The results of a parental survey in my county showed that a large number of mothers wished to stay at home but did not have the means to do so. Some fathers as well as mothers have told me how they are at their wits' end trying to juggle a job and family, thinking that much of their earnings go on childcare. Many parents are more than happy to stay at home, but other young parents are lonely and frustrated and simply don't feel fulfilled. One way of getting round this is by getting together with friends. For some, a part-time job two days a week is enough to make the other days bearable. Caring for the young is exhausting, refreshing, worrying, rewarding, joyful, life-giving, but never worthless. This is the priceless contribution of the parent left at home with the child. Often I've wondered what I've been doing all day, yet the hours have been filled with living, a complicated jungle of the demands of life.

Dialogue between home and school

A new assistant in my sister's store in the United States took my call, telling her: 'There's someone on the telephone for you. She talks—you know—that language she speaks?' For this lady, English was obviously not a mutual language. Even if you speak the same language you don't necessarily understand each other.

Parents have hopes and wishes for their children as well as for themselves. By the time they leave them for the first time in the care of a teacher, they have already played a large part in their growing up. It can happen that the demands and wishes of the setting don't entirely coincide with those of the parents. Trying to see the other's point of view involves listening, patience and quiet within oneself. Dialogue is essential for the well-being of child, parent and teacher. I found that if parents knew a lot about our kindergarten from the outset, this knowledge gave them a security which ultimately filtered through to the child. In the first days, if the parent delayed separating from the child it was not usually helpful. Sometimes it was my observation that parents were unable to let go rather than the other way round. Parents who showed the child they were 'going now' and *coming back later* seemed to have got it right. Children who cried when left by mother often didn't do so if father or someone else brought them. Tillen was an exception. She screamed for Daddy for three weeks, but suddenly said, 'Go on Daddy, go now'. Aya, who even had no English yet, also told her worried father to go after a few days when she started non-verbal play with others.

It was calming to describe the morning to a child who wouldn't settle: 'First we play.' 'And then?' 'Then we make bread.' 'And then?' 'Then we tidy up.' 'And then?' 'Then we sing our songs.' 'And then?' 'And then we eat.' And so on until, 'And then Mummy [or whoever] comes!' The beginning, the middle and the *end*. Children like that to be repeated two or three times. A little girl said, 'I need to cry a little'. 'Yes', I said, giving her a hug. Soon she was all right. For young children, practitioners are stand-in parents, helping to bridge the gap and smooth the way for future schooling. Frances, 6, was describing her practitioner to her mother after she had left pre-school: 'She's like a' . . . (thinking) . . . 'mother!'

Truth and respect

Sometimes children secretly took something home from kindergarten. I would ask the group if anyone knew where such and such was, or whether it had gone 'on holiday' to someone. Often this brought a positive response.

> *From a letter to parents:*
> Pockets*: a few kindergarten things haven 'fallen into' the children's*
> *pockets recently. If anything comes home which you are not sure about,*
> *please check with me! The children are happy to have a look when I ask if*
> *anything has fallen in when they weren't looking. It is surprising what*
> *reappears!*

I always thanked the child and asked whether whatever it was had a nice time in their house. Tolerance and gratitude, rather than punishment, bear fruit.

As a teacher, one strives to respect parents. When a child swore and I said, 'Your Mummy and Daddy don't say that', he responded gleefully, 'Yes, they do!' Bethly came in to the teacher I was mentoring and said to her, 'I tapped your bum'. 'I like you to say "good morning",' said her teacher. 'My Daddy taps my bum.' 'Well, Daddy may do it and I like you to say "good morning".'

A mother said, 'You're getting just like your father'. This kind of speaking disparagingly of the children in their presence is just as disrespectful and damaging as speaking badly of one's partner or the teacher before the children. They cannot cope with it and it destroys their trust. If an argument seems likely to arise between adults, not blaming each other and waiting for a moment to work it through without children present can only strengthen family relationships. We all make mistakes, which can be difficult to acknowledge, but finding the courage to apologise creates a warmth between all.

> *From a letter to all new parents:*
> *A good and open relationship between teacher and parents is of great benefit to the child. In this light, I hope we can build up mutual trust and understanding. I am always grateful for whatever parents say to me. I hope you will feel able to come to me if you don't understand what I'm doing or why, or if you have a concern. Then we can hope for a happy and fruitful time together.*

Occasionally a child would tell me that the family was going on holiday in term time, and that the parent had said, 'Don't tell Sally'. Children should not be expected to keep such things to themselves: it simply presents confusion and a conflict of morals. Taking children on holiday in school time does make certain things difficult. In almost every case I have experienced, it has been hard for the child to settle again, especially if jetlagged. Handling this comes down to a matter of respect between parent and teacher and parent and child.

Listening

> *From a letter to all new parents:*
> *About once each term, more if requested, I invite all parents of the class to come to my house for an informal evening to talk about whatever you like—usually unprepared. It is optional. These evenings give an opportunity for*

discussion in a smaller circle than at parents' evenings. Please ask me if you
would also like me to visit you either with or without the children around.

I was told of a challenging child now at his fourth pre-school at age 5, because
'no one handled him properly'. A home visit and a 'listening' to the
environment there might have revealed that over-stimulation and lack of
play were part of the problem. I enjoyed my home visits. It was a great
privilege to be invited round, and extremely helpful for teacher, parent and
child.

Sometimes we hear things but don't take them in. Allan, whose son had
left us for school in July, came running up to kindergarten after our session
the following January. 'Have you seen Toby?' I: 'No'. Allan: 'Is he not here
anymore?' I: 'No, was he here with his class?' It took a few more questions on
either side for us to realize he'd forgotten Toby wasn't in kindergarten
anymore!

CHAPTER 12

PRACTICAL TIPS FOR BEHAVIOUR

'It's all right now.'

Everyone is different

Our nature is coloured by so many things. On the one hand people all over the planet have the *same* needs: food, water, shelter, love and so on; on the other hand, our *differences* are fascinating: hot-tempered and strong, cooler and more withdrawn, comfortable and conscientious, light-hearted and easy-going. Added to this there are the external influences which come from our racial and cultural background, and whether we are first-born, second, third or more, or an only child. Within the same family, with the same background and upbringing, the children are so often very different from each other. All this is part of our personal biography, having a profound effect on how we react to our environment. The younger we are, the more we are affected by outside influences.

Happiness versus stress

It is natural for our young children to be full of the joys of spring, unfettered by troubles of the world beyond their comprehension. This bubbly liveliness becomes the basis of healthy behaviour in maturity. So it is normal for children to be happy to go to school or nursery. This is a most precious time of life, not one for being stressed. Yet many teachers speak of children under stress and even burnt-out. A teacher in the USA told me that in their State children don't have to go to school till they are 8, but that most parents say: 'Whoa! Let's get them in as early as possible or they will be lost later'. I wondered in what way they might be lost—intellectually? socially? physically? emotionally? In my experience, many pre-schools, nurseries and kindergartens today are actually, unfortunately, a watered-down version of school.

In my kindergarten I endeavoured to create a real 'home from home', having for instance a little kitchen where we cooked or baked every day and washed up. We sang and played, dusted, helped each other and listened to stories: in fact every activity I have mentioned in this book and more. We ran around in the fields and got muddy, worked in the garden, sewed, did woodwork and had a daily rest. The children learnt many songs and poems by heart. Dressed appropriately, they especially loved our big outdoor sandpit in all weathers, and often went for long walks and picnics with my assistants and myself all year round. Celebrating festivals was an especially important part of our life. My colleagues and I were able to demonstrate to Ofsted inspectors that the children were happy, active, dextrous, enthusiastic and sociable, besides having the pre-skills necessary for numeracy and literacy. And all this came about mainly through imitation of us adults and having freedom in their play. Many of our visitors went home saying they (the visitors) felt calm and peaceful, and a couple of inspectors who just came out of interest said they were going to think about using less interaction and authority. Such a homely life really suits the young child, and is a rich ground for learning.

At a pre-school of 4-year-olds, several children said, 'I'm tired'. Some yawned or had a thumb in the mouth. They were occupied with intellectual stimulation, and their 'play' was actually games mostly involving thinking. What I would call real play was confined to seven or eight minutes with building bricks and soft animals. Their teacher tested them: 'Faster, faster— you are all so clever!' Most children couldn't keep up with this cleverness, but were exhorted to: 'Put on your brainwaves!' and 'Put on your thinking caps! Zizz, zizz, zizz!' I wondered what the children made of this as she waggled her fingers up by her head, but she was obviously under pressure to get them 'on' quickly.

In my work I have met wonderful teachers from all streams of education. Many are concerned about too early and too pressurised formal learning. 'We know they can't do it, but we still have to try because of the targets, although we know most won't reach them', said one. People are finding that, like the synthetic felt which as I mentioned earlier tends to fall apart, over-contrived intellectual and social activity won't hold together as well as that of the 'woollen felt' of naturally occurring and repetitive activity from daily life. Research soon to be published shows a severely dwindling number of *minutes,* not hours, that children have to play freely every day. Added to the fact that millions of young children watch several hours of television every day and even have a set in their bedrooms, one could be forgiven for thinking, 'What on earth are we are doing to childhood?' Unprescribed play in children today has less and less chance of being a foundation for their development.

Separation

There are aspects of life today seeking to alienate us from each other. I commented to a swimming-pool instructor how happy the children looked around her in the water, and wondered why the other two instructors stood on the edge. 'I'm a bit old-fashioned', she said, 'I like a bit of "hands-on".' You can give directions to the children till you're blue in the face but they still won't understand until you *show* them how. Of course we've been advised to teach from the edge so there is no possibility of touching the children.' We agreed that the world had gone mad. How can we protect the child's *right* to be close to an adult where the circumstances are normal and proper? Fear of abuse has muddied the waters of what for generations we have considered to be a right level of physical closeness, such as the stroking of a child's head. Surely we want to avoid the sort of situation where children suffer because teachers are not allowed to examine their hair for head lice. If children themselves are inhibited from touching adults, how does this affect behaviour? A little boy put his teacher in a quandary when he wanted to kiss her goodbye (as so many children do), as to whether she should let this happen. How does it feel from the child's point of view? What image does it give? What about the abused child who sorely needs a warm and innocent embrace? In my view, this kind of separation between children and adults is encouraging society to condone alienation, and has a profound effect on behaviour.

Actions speak louder than words

Horace rapidly made himself known in the class, with his loud and obstinate behaviour. Every morning he stomped up to the door and I greeted him warmly: 'GOOD MORNING, HORACE!' He would stop, taken aback, greet me and quieten down. This I called my 'homeopathic' treatment: meeting children with a little of the same. For children who had a finger with an invisible wound I might look anxiously as well. 'It's all right now', they would say, responding to my anxiety. 'Education' comes from the Latin *educere*: to lead out. I also found that one could lead the children out of wild behaviour into calm, simply through entering their world, first imitating *them* and then leading them out as they copied *me*. So I might join them in a brief roll on the floor on a bundle of cloths. (After initial laughter, they became uneasy because they were not used to my behaving in this manner.) Then I would stand up and take two corners of a cloth to fold it, and they usually began to copy me.

Imitation becomes awe-inspiring when one realizes how powerful it is.

From a letter to parents:

In response to some recent questions:

If you feel your children aren't responding when you ask them to do something, you could try dispensing with words and using gestures instead! Discussions with young children may lead to arguments and frustration for both, because it is difficult to reach the young child through the intellect. It is only possible to have meaningful discussions after the age of 6 or 7 years. Children can be battered by too much talk, and may suffer from what we call 'verbal diarrhoea', their words spilling out in imitation. Sometimes this even affects their concentration and develops into restlessness. Anyone seeing me with the 24 children may be surprised how much my mouth is closed, considering all the wants and needs! (My husband says I compensate at home.) I often find an answer with a gesture: 'Where do I put this?' a child might ask, and I would respond with a smile, a gesture towards a cupboard and 'thank you'. To 'I've hurt my knee', I might respond with, 'Come!', a look, then a little rub (body language) and all would be well again.

Young children can be busy for a long time in silence. As little ones copy what we do, we can make them really noisy if we talk a lot. Of course children must learn to talk and express themselves! But daily life, stories and songs can give them a rich language experience. A constant stream of orders, for example: 'Go and put your shoes on', may not work, or even stir up defiance. Putting your own on, and/or making playful walking steps with theirs may bear fruit. Often you can make a picture with your words. Instead of 'Pull your chair in', which might not get a response, try: 'Let's make a sandwich', i.e. pull your chair in, so you're the jam squashed inside the 'bread slices' (table and chair). Do remember that the speed and the tone of your speaking influence the behaviour of the child.

At the beginning of the term I needed to be strong with the group as we were a bit all over the place! But the calming was often through gestures (body language) and not explanations; any words were often repeated, and we did the same things every day. When the children know where they are—exactly how far they can go—what to do—hear the repetition of familiar words—then they feel secure and can unfold and blossom. Over-stimulation is very much a part of today's world, but young children need some protection from it. 'Education is so simple' is my motto. Give the children space and opportunity: they take it up through their own way of learning.

A mother arranged to talk with her child's teacher about her unco-operative, sulky 5-year-old. She brought him with her and the child wouldn't leave her side to play. 'He won't stay without me', she said, as Alfie screamed. 'You have to go, Alfie' ... (hesitating pause) ... 'He'll have to come ... Do you want to be with me, Alfie?' The teacher said, 'Come, Alfie, you may play with these bricks while Mummy and I talk grown-ups' things. We'll leave the door open so you can come if you want us.' Mother's jaw dropped as Alfie started to play. 'How did you get him to do that?' she exclaimed. 'I expect him to do it!' the teacher said. He knew where he was with her and therefore felt no fear.

Limits

Eleanor, 2 and a half, had appropriated the picnic punnet of strawberries, but the lid came off. 'Stobbelies, stobbelies!' she said excitedly, running around showing them to everyone as they threatened to fall out. But when her grandfather rescued them she sobbed piteously. Even being given a straw-berry immediately didn't pacify her. Where do you draw the line? Shop-keepers often have to be diplomatic with people who let their children behave as if their shop were a playroom. Once a couple let their two large dogs lick us, despite our protests. The woman called them, 'Come on, sillies! Come on! They just want to be friends'. Parents can be wonderfully diplomatic though: Jamie wanted to take his very long icicle to bed. 'It will have to have a bath if it's going to bed with you', said his mother.

Mollie and her husband had been brought up very strictly and had decided to let their own children grow up freely. However, they often drove Mollie to distraction, wouldn't clear up, come when called, nor co-operate. In discussing it later, she saw the connection between not giving them limits and their being unco-operative. Behaviour has a great deal to do with setting limits. We have to learn that we cannot do everything we like, but learn to live in sociable way. This requires discipline, will-power and conscious effort. Too few boundaries create poor discipline and antisocial behaviour. Young children feel lost without them. A mother of two children, one wild and strong and the other flighty, said she felt it was right to let them go their own way as that was their natural character, although she found them difficult. She was surprised when I suggested the opposite, that maybe it was just such children who needed 'four walls'. They needed to know exactly where they were to help them calm down and be sociable.

Another mother on a housing estate, with a rather wild 3-year-old who was allowed to do much as he liked, asked me if I thought it was ok for him to play out alone with the other children (all older). I thought it wiser for him to be out only with an adult or specific children. 'Oh, but he really wants to go and really likes it. Don't you think it's all right?'—'Your little one is incapable of judging the situation at 3 years old. He only sees the fun on the bikes and tearing around', I said. 'It's up to you to make that decision.' She followed my advice for two months, then let him out again. When he then exhibited a lot of very rough play and became even more unmanageable, they had to seek a psychiatrist's advice. How easy it would have been to give him boundaries in the first place.

In all my years of teaching, I found that over-stimulation and not setting limits was the major reason for difficulties in behaviour. This seems to be increasing today at a time when we value our 'freedom' more, often at the other's expense. 'They always win, don't they', said the elderly milkman when we talked of the battles someone was having with her 2-year-old. Saying 'No' is a natural stage of development for a 2-year-old, and we must welcome it because it is the first hint of the confidence and independence which will grow in future years. However, if this is met with authoritarian commands, nagging and other 'No's' from the adult, this usually only results in creating distance and animosity between adult and child. It closes doors, and not only between adult and child but between the child and the wonderful world that they are exploring. Understanding the power of imitation, the sensitivity of the little child and the importance of rhythm can be so helpful in this situation. Children under the age of 6 have little awareness for their so-called misbehaviour and therefore can't be held responsible: I hold that misbehaving is not yet the child's 'fault'. If one studies this, one sees that the actions and words are often straightforward imitation, which is what the child actually needs to be doing. Dealing with 'No!' means the adult working to give the child helpful examples to imitate, developing diversion techniques, and discriminating between the behaviour which must be changed and that which one could turn a blind eye to, with no harm done. Jennifer was slowly pulling petals off a flower stalk, watching her parents but not responding to their authoritative commands. 'How does one get her to stop?' I was asked. I suggested going to her and saying, 'Aren't they pretty? We'll leave the rest now and you may have these'. I observed the child actually challenging the adults to set limits for her.

'Daddy, can we have ice cream?' 'Did Mummy say ok?' 'Oh yes.' So Daddy started setting it out slowly, but not fast enough for his 5-year-old. 'Quickly Daddy, before Mummy comes back!' Playing one parent off against the other is a classic, but children can try to wheedle all kinds of wishes out of us if we are not consistent. Children who are over-indulged can also become a bit manipulative if we don't create boundaries. Some parents experience their children as little tyrants and have such a struggle, unhappy for all. Decisive, firm and warm handling can work miracles quite quickly.

Freedom?

I spoke earlier about how boundaries relate to the sense of touch, and, with reference to the secure wrapping of the infant, to security, stability and a feeling of well-being. Increasingly many children are missing these today because of a mistaken understanding of freedom and a fear of being too restrictive. A couple had difficulties in making their children use seat-belts because they made so much fuss. Using one's creativity, one could say, 'Is the belt too stiff? Let's put something soft under it, this cosy blanket', to avoid becoming impatient. I watched a young woman in the supermarket coping admirably with her screaming, foot-stamping 3-year-old. She continued packing the trolley, talking quietly to the child, who continued shouting. She said calmly, 'I'm not putting those yoghurts back. I like those yoghurts and those are the ones we are having'. Eventually her daughter stopped and took her mother's hand.

One can challenge children over about 4 with this kind of thing: 'Are you helping me or are you chatting (or playing about/ pushing etc.)?' One can appeal to the children's 'grown-up ness': 'Tomorrow you will stand (or sit/ eat etc.,) like a 7-year-old.' 'Now you are 5 and a half you know how to push your chair in (fold your clothes/ help me etc.,).' If a young child is at a loose end, one can think: can my child help with what I am doing? Offering something 'really difficult (heavy/ grown up etc.)' will usually find willing recipients. 'I can't manage this on my own. Please could you help?' Such an appeal may well encourage children to help. 'I need someone strong to take all these things to the kitchen (clean up this shelf/ tidy this cupboard/ carry this box etc.).' If your children are ready for their meal or some other activity and you aren't, you can try this game, just sung on two notes. Pause between each line to let them do it (and probably giggle), while you get on with what you are doing and make up the next line!

Everyone who's ready may touch their toes now.
Everyone who's ready may nibble their knee now.
Everyone who's ready may wink their eye now.
Everyone who's ready may sit on the floor now.
Everyone who's ready may do a somersault now.
Everyone who's ready may tickle their ankle now.   etc., . . . then:
Everyone who's ready may come to the meal now.

It is possible to break unwanted habits quite quickly if one is determined enough. For example, in a setting I visited, snack-time was chaotic. The children were helping themselves, taking too much and leaving food on their plates in an antisocial, noisy atmosphere. I suggested they prepare less food and that for the time being the teacher herself pass it round, until the children, in imitation, learnt how to do it. She was afraid they would complain and it wouldn't work but next day she tried it. The children looked enquiringly at her. 'Are you always going to do it this way?' 'Yes', she answered with a sigh of relief as the meal progressed happily and quietly. Children are grateful when we show them the way. Education is so simple, once one has found the key.

Spoiling

'Can't *you* carry some of this?' said the Dad to his three children as he struggled down the High Street with three large bags of their new beach toys, 'I'm tired of carrying it all'. They grumbled but did eventually. How many parents carry their children's clothes, bags, dolls, boots, toys, scooters . . . ?

A common frustration amongst single parents is that the other parent, with whom the children don't live, spoils them, takes them on expensive holidays, gives them lavish presents, and doesn't make them do things the other one thinks necessary. Some fathers often away for work bring special gifts home to try to make up for their absence, whilst mothers do all the ordinary things. 'Daddy says he's going to bring me something *amazing* when he gets back.'

Some parents find it hard to make decisions, so their children take over, as *someone* has to decide what is going to happen: I feel parents should decide on things large and small, from where to go on holiday to quantity of sweets. A grandmother working amongst children told me she was amazed how many parents let their small children decide where to eat, and that often only McDonald's will do! Letting children rule the roost overburdens and spoils them. As their powers of judgement are still unripe, they feel more secure when they are led in the right way.

'It's bedtime.' 'But I want to watch another programme.' 'Well you ought to go to bed.' 'Oh, *please!*' 'Well, it's late, you ought to be in bed now.' 'But I *really* want to watch, it's really good.' 'Well, you ought to go to bed, but all right, you can.'

Or, in the shop, mother said to her child: 'You can't have that chocolate.' 'But I want it.' 'Haven't you had enough?' 'No, I want it. I'm going to have it.' 'Oh, go on, then.'

Another mother responded differently. 'Can I have some more chocolate?' said her small child. 'No, you've had enough chocolate today.' 'But I just had a likl bit.' 'No.' The child was perfectly happy with this decision.

Consequences

Giving children consequences, rather than shouting or being angry, creates stability. These are not punishments, but merely reasonable followings-on from certain behaviour. Jason was swinging sharp scissors around. A worried adult friend asked whether he knew how to carry them. 'He's been told a hundred times', said his Mum, 'but he just goes on doing it.' A challenging but firm and reasonable consequence would be to take them away, saying: 'You may have them back when you remember how to hold them the grown up way'. One can even make up effective games. For example: for children who repeatedly throw things, one can let them 'practise throw-ing'—'I can see you are learning how to throw. Come, let's see if we can get these balls (or pieces of paper, feathers, stones or other suitable things) into this big basket.' Repeat it a few times until the child tires of it. Children who throw things may not be healthy in their sense of touch, and therefore are looking for ways to establish a periphery, constantly seeking to find the edge of themselves. Climbing, walking barefoot, rolling bread dough, playing with fleece: all such activities can be good 'consequences' for children whose sense of touch is underdeveloped. Antisocial behaviour may arise in imitation of aggressive treatment, or any number of other phenomena, but I found it helpful to use such games as therapy.

Children hurting others

> Max, a feisty 4 and-a-half-year-old, had a reputation for punching, biting and kicking. On his first morning five minutes elapsed before the first punch. I led him to a table, saying, 'You may sit here, because we look after our friends'. He was surprised and affronted. 'When can I get up?' 'Soon.' After a few minutes I said, 'You may get up now'. After another few minutes there was a kick. I repeated the table episode with exactly the same firm but loving gestures and words. I repeated the sequence many times that morning every time he used his body to express himself inappropriately.
>
> Next day, Max and I needed to repeat it five times, and on the following one only three, when I also found him sitting at the table unasked. 'Why are you sitting at the table?' 'Because I hurt someone.' I was moved almost to tears. On the fourth day he bumped into someone by mistake. 'It was an accident', he said, anxiously. 'I know', I said warmly. Intentional hurting had ceased. He had found his limits in this simple, repetitive and firm way.

Little children, not yet adept with words, use their body to express them-selves. 'Judy was a very easy baby, I could put her down and anyone could pick her up', said her mother. At 2, things began to get difficult. She bit, kicked and hit. 'Why is she doing this to me?' mother asked. The parents were gentle so I suspected Judy wasn't actually retaliating, but expressing her frustration at a rather too busy, unrhythmical life.

Natalie, 2 years old, screamed and hit her mother's face as she picked her up from the pond edge. This was not aggression, but frustration at having been thwarted in her curiosity. Another child was kicking his mother, but she just removed herself from him and didn't react, so he stopped. It is important to remember that when children hurt others it may be a sense of injustice, which won't go on forever. Sometimes children just need to be noticed, recognized, appreciated, which one does best in moments when they are not demanding it. Gary, 4 and a half, had been in the same day-care setting since the age of 2 months, and often saw the practitioner who had cared for him as a baby. One day when he was screaming and kicking because he had not wanted his mother to go, this practitioner happened to be there. Trying to avoid his kicks, she said: 'Why are you kicking me? I've never kicked you and I've had you since you were a baby. All I've ever done is cuddled you'. Gary stopped, looked, and they had a cuddle. (And what a blessing it is for both children and their parents to have that kind of unbroken continuity in a setting.)

'An eye for an eye makes the whole world blind.' Ghandi

Fighting may result from reacting through imitation, or from being told to retaliate. Having punched David back, Jeff said to me, 'My Dad says I have to hit back'. I said, 'Then David will punch you and you punch him back and he you and you him and you and he him and you them and what a muddle!' We all laughed, Dad was not disrespected, and the child was not so quick to hit back after that.

How much aggression is caused by imitating what is on a screen? 'You must not fight because there's no fighting in the kindergarten', said Sandy, 4, who had done much of it in his first months there after being brought up with TV. To create an image of no fighting, one can demonstrate calm, warm and unjudgemental words and gestures when reacting to a tricky situation. Ensuring there is plenty of work and physical activity to do diverts potential aggression into something positive. Many boys like a rough and tumble, which needs space to avoid hurting others and damaging things. Recognizing it as a natural part of boyhood, one can say, 'Please can you put your play-fighting in your pocket' (meanwhile demonstrating putting something invisible into your own pocket) 'and wait till you are outside where there is more room'.

One could call anti-social behaviour 'unhappy' behaviour. Poor behaviour is to me a cry for help, from the endlessly crying baby, to the grumpy child, to the aggressive teenager, like saying: 'Look at me! Do something for me!' Problems may be caused by reactions to traumas, fear, poor examples to follow, jealousy, unsatisfactory diet, lack of routine or a difficult or over-stimulating environment. Everything that causes unhappy behaviour surely has some kind of rejection at its root. We can't prevent everything unhelpful in children's lives, but we can strive to shield them to a certain degree. It is also possible to overprotect them, creating fear or unsociability.

It seems increasingly difficult for some parents to spend quality time with their children, so essential for happiness and inner harmony. A health visitor told me she finds many parents have no opportunity to spend time with them at the 'prime time' between 5 and 7 p.m. She asked a parent who had hurt her leg whether she could get down from the meal-table all right, to which she responded that they had no meal-table. I have seen parents out walking with their children, concentrating on a mobile phone conversation rather than them. How can parents devote themselves wholly to the family at some point during the day? What inessential thing can one leave undone?

Positivity or negativity

If a child behaves unwisely, such as licking a knife, one can ask, 'Are you going to do that again?' with a slight sternness to one's voice which is also a challenge, and the child will probably answer in the negative. This is more effective than, 'Don't do that, you'll cut yourself'. If a child is playing with a spoon, saying 'Let's leave that on the table,' rather than 'Put that down!' will bring better results. Removing it can also be effective, as long as the child knows she can have it back when sitting properly. To inappropriate behaviour one can say, 'Did you forget? I believe you forgot, didn't you? You need to remember next time'. One can even have a special place in which to sit and remember. We had a particular step on the stairs in our house.

> *From a letter to parents:*
> *. . . responding to your requests for examples of when I say 'yes' rather than 'no' . . . Since our evening together I have been trying to think, but our mornings seem so full of them I hardly know where to start! I firmly believe that little ones don't want to be 'naughty'; some of them have more apparent 'naughtiness' than others—but this may either be a part of their character which they will have to cope with during life, or a result of their environment, or both. Challenging children may be protesting against their surroundings, physical and emotional. Many children are not challenging, but it is on the increase. In remembering that the key to the young child is in example and imitation, we are a long way along the path to providing the right environment. We can try saying 'and' instead of 'but', in our striving to find the positive. 'The table is nearly ready but you aren't', or: 'The table is nearly ready and you are nearly ready too'. The child knocks his glass over either because he is unconscious of what he's doing, is clumsy, or through some protest. 'Let's get a cloth', is the best 'punishment' possible! Children love things to be in order—visible and invisible, and putting*

something right that is broken, untidy or unhappy is healing. Children are relieved and sparkle when all is well again—be it a tidy basket or tears dried up. Children enjoy being 'good', feeling well and joyful.

'Mmmmmmm,' and a little rubbing of the tummy speaks more to the young child than, 'Don't you like it?' (Though that isn't wrong!) A child who is disturbing is helped more quickly by being told quietly: 'I like it better when you are quiet and friendly again,' rather than 'Stop it!'. Then one can smile from ear to ear. Or the child can be distracted in some way, for example, you do a little dance with a ladle while cooking, or sing a familiar song (music is the greatest healer) or give a big laughing bear-hug. Children respond well to something funny! For an older child, if nothing improves one can try, 'I don't feel happy when you are like that so I'm going upstairs and hope you will come up soon when you feel better'. One needs to use endless imagination, while at the same time trying to see the reason why the child is rebelling. If one remembers that especially at around 3 years it is natural for children to rebel, it can help one to be patient. This is a wonderful, exciting, awe-inspiring time for children: most of them have by now achieved walking, talking and the beginnings of thinking, whilst also being able to say 'I' to themselves as they enter the world of self-awareness.

If I was to hear one child say to another: 'You can't come in our playhouse', I would wait to see how it develops, simply observing instead of trying to sort it out. Waiting is helpful as children often help each other in the end and sort themselves out. If it is still not too good I may knock at their 'house' and say, 'Pedro needs somewhere to live'. The children's trust in me, as in you parents, usually soothes everyone. It is not difficult to work in a positive way rather than judging. If they hear 'yes' rather than 'no', and see our friendly body language, they will be responsive and therefore easier to deal with. Children may be disturbed by things we don't particularly notice as adults, for they soak up their surroundings like sponges. It is common knowledge that if it's windy the children may be restless. So drop the broom and duster, go out in it, get excited, come back fulfilled and peaceful! Pretend the broom is a horse and ride around the house on it!

Children don't need many toys; they find their own with the healthy creativity of childhood. How many times have your children taken your things instead of their toys to play with? They are using their imagination to create their play world. A sharp kitchen-knife may seem an excellent sword! You can say, 'I'm going to need that—you may use this instead', giving a wooden spoon or bottle brush to relieve matters. If not, one can try taking a 'sword' oneself (wooden spoon etc.), saying another spoon-sword is for the child. How children love sticks and all sorts of potentially dangerous things! Should we need to say they are dangerous? You could say, 'When you are older, you may use a knife like this too. Just now you may cut the pastry with this other one'. When they play with sticks, you can show them how to use them properly so they won't hurt anyone. If adults are irritable, the children imitate and make the situation worse. (If they are in love, the children will be in love too!). That is also why we as teachers strive to 'hang' our private troubles on a peg outside the classroom door. Adults do well to argue in private. If background noise is kept to a minimum or removed altogether, e.g. radio, news etc., the child copies the quietness. If children see and hear caricatures in toys, books, magazines or voices, they will want to imitate them. If they see images of the dignity of a human being in toys and illustrations they experience a different basis for life.

Children want to struggle and achieve—the first feeding of oneself, the first button, the first lace-tying. They imitate your goodness and love for them too, so they need your fairness and constancy. They need the positivity and security of knowing that the same old things will happen again and again: the same songs, the meals and bed which come at the same times, the baby's milk which appears at the same regular intervals (the stomach is also grateful for the rhythm). One of today's problems for adults as well as children is 'too': too soon, too often, too fast, too loud. We become frenzied through 'too much'. Sometimes I feel I haven't handled a situation well or have done something not good, and apologise to the child/ children. A wonderful glow comes over them, 'That's all right!' How they love it if I forget things: they preen themselves on being able to help. We help children to develop their will by remembering they need space for healthy activity. Even high-rise flats are no obstruction to this. Stirring the sauce, walking up and down the mountain (stairs), brushing the mat, running in the park—very important activities not requiring much thought.

How does one get them to do it?

'Calm down!' Often I've heard this phrase spoken to children. It generally has little effect because the child is unaware what the words mean in relation to the behaviour. It is really only the environment, including people, which can make the child calm down. After the age of 5, the words begin to make sense, but actually fitting behaviour to the words is yet another step. 'Now we're quiet', is more helpful; meaning we are all quiet together, even just you and one child.

For shouting children you can say, 'That's an outside noise which we can make when we go out'. 'You're not to say that word', may make the word even more interesting for rude children. 'We'll keep our rudeness for when we are at the bottom of the garden (in the park/ alone) and no one else needs to hear it', I found works better. 'We' instead of 'you' suits the young child's consciousness, one of being an integral part of their environment rather than being separated from it: *'We do it all together'*. I was in the habit of saying: 'You may...' rather than, 'You can/ have to/ must/ I want you to...'. Somehow it feels more respectful. 'The person who made all the mess in the bathroom may go and tidy it up. I'm not saying who it was', can help older children as well, keeping blame and guilt at bay and giving the child a chance to put things right. Imagination can be used as a disciplinary tool. If your children don't want to get in the car/ come to breakfast or any such thing, you can try getting there in an imaginative way: 'Let's go on our motor bikes to the car' (with appropriate noises)/ 'Let's swim to breakfast'. If a rhythm has been established there won't be a problem anyway, as they will do it without thinking, on 'automatic pilot'. If one knows boots or coats are lying about: 'Shall we see who is making all that noise by the front door? It might be the boots chattering', or 'The coats are crying because they are too young to hang themselves up'. In imagining that everything in the world is alive we can travel a long way with children. Using different terminology creates a new scene, conjuring up curiosity and interest, such as going for an 'expedition' instead of a 'walk'. (This is what I called our regular morning-long outings in kindergarten.) Such imaginations are useful for children who need encouragement—this word contains the word 'heart' (*coeur*). There are exciting things to be seen everywhere—a spider on a wall, a big red van, a funny-shaped cloud, if only we have the eyes to see them. Many parents know that getting your child to pee or pass a stool may be made easier by your doing it (or pretending) yourself, or using a favourite doll or animal, with appropriate noises!

The distraction of little games can be very helpful for children with challenging behaviour: at the bus-stop, chemist or at home. 'Baby Small' (little finger) helped me out of scrapes with restless children. He can be introduced through this rhyme. Sing in a heavy but friendly voice:

> Tommy Thumb, Tommy Thumb, where are you?
> Here I am, here I am, and how do you do?'   Old rhyme

First one, then the other thumb appears from behind the back and they bow to each other. Hands hide again, and Peter Pointer appears, (index fingers), repeating the rhyme in a quick voice, then Toby Tall (middle fingers) in an important one, Ruby Ring in a quiet one, and Baby Small (little fingers) in a squeaky one. However, Baby Small didn't always 'want to come out', or when he did, he often 'messed about', going up to my ear to whisper something, or pulling the other Baby Small. Something in my ear was imaginarily 'audible' to myself, but also to the children, although they weren't sure what it was until I told them. How they love all that, not least because they identify with and imitate the characters which are all 'alive'.

A great favourite:

'Exercises, exercises, watch me do my exercises.' This must be spoken very rhythmically. Holding your forearms upright and still, palms facing, let the fingers move in turn as they each do their 'exercises'. Pointing them straight up at 'ex-', bend them down at '-er-', point them towards each other at '-ci-', bend them back at '-ses', 'watch' straight up, 'me' bent down, 'do' towards each other, 'my' bent back etc. . . . You can do Peter Pointers first, then Toby Talls, or whatever order you like, but end up with Baby Small, who inevitably gets 'muddled up' and does the movements 'wrong' to the child's delight. He can 'try to do it' when it is 'not his turn', getting in the way of the other fingers and causing great merriment, especially when you pretend you don't notice. You can let him do the movements of another rhyme such as the following, while you are saying 'Exercises', which causes many giggles.

'Roly, poly, ever so slowly, Roly, poly, ever so slowly', (wind your forearms slowly round each other).
'Whirly, whirly, whirly, gig' (wind your forearms fast round each other and hide them behind your back at 'gig').   (Old rhyme)

The children enjoy playing it fast when it should be slow and vice versa.

These fingers are real characters that children imitate because they identify with them, and are such fun.

Addressing the child

Much annoyance can be spared and confrontation avoided by taking a moment to think carefully about what we are doing or saying in the light of a child's stage of development. When children are squabbling we can say: 'Oh, what happened?... Oh, I see (in response to their account). Did you?... did she?... Well, I'll come back in a minute and see if you're both all right', and it most likely will be, as one has helped the children to help themselves without putting our adult judgement in their way. Children want to be good. It is their nature, and they are disillusioned if we don't respond well. Henry, who found it difficult to be quiet, said to me one morning: 'Mummy said I must be good today'. I asked, 'What did you say?' 'I said I would be.' He was. Later I asked his mother about it, but she knew nothing of it, and we looked at each other in wonder at this child's self-help.

The mother who told her two small children to 'shut the door', 'put that down', 'sit at the table', 'put that away', wondered why the children were so unco-operative. Speaking to children like this is really an affront to their dignity. Remembering that they are only smaller versions of their adult selves, one can ask whether *we* should like to be spoken to thus. 'Let's shut the door', 'We can put that down here', 'We may sit at the table now', 'Let's put that away', might have helped the children. 'I'm giving you one more chance ... I'm giving you one last chance ... This is your last chance ...', a 5-year-old was murmuring to himself at play. Such expressions tell a tale.

A father, desperate with his over-active 4-year-old and finding that shouting and angry body-language were to no avail, would resort to putting him in front of a video to quieten him. This proved to be a measure with only temporary effect, for when the video had finished his behaviour worsened. Understanding the power of imitation and the effects of over-stimulation helped him to deal more wisely with his child.

'He's been a naughty boy today', said a young mother of her son of 2. 'Has he? What's he done?' asked her friend. The child was smiling and squirming in his pushchair. 'Yes, he's been very naughty', said his mother, planting a large kiss on his forehead, 'He got me up at 7 a.m.!' Conclusion: to get a big kiss, you get Mum up at 7 a.m., and be naughty! Everything we do and say and the manner in which we do them will become part of the child's own response to their environment and the people in it.

Disruptive children may have low self-esteem, so there is a need to feel important and wanted. To meet this we can offer 'important' jobs for them for instance. They may be particularly sensitive and seek attention when they are feeling uncomfortable. They may feel cold, or have unhelpful things in their tummy. Often such children are crying out for boundaries. Sometimes it is quite easy to see where the problem lies, and sometimes it is not at all straightforward. Often I have needed to seek the help of parents, carers and colleagues, to find a way forward. For some parents it has been difficult to see that their child actually has a problem. Challenging behaviour is not only on the increase but is *often seen as acceptable or even normal.*

And to sum up

May I recapitulate on some ideas I have presented.

The social, physical, moral and cultural environment has a considerable impact on behaviour. Children's imitative, absorbent, wide-open nature reproduces what they experience. Whether we tell children what to do, or conversely let them act out of their own interest and enthusiasm, it changes the way they develop their strength of purpose. The way they learn best is through *activity*. Giving them challenges which are age-appropriate, such as struggling with buttons or going out in a rainstorm, prepares them to exercise self-control, an essential ingredient of socially acceptable behaviour. Setting reasonable limits, giving a pattern to the day and night, making 'consequences' rather than giving threats or treats, meaning what we say—all this is not difficult to achieve.

How the child feels within him or herself may also be influenced by allergies as well as diet. If we don't feel well, we react accordingly. A friend's son often showed uncontrollable behaviour for the first three years until she discovered that he was allergic to gluten. As with learning differences, recognition and help at an early age is paramount. Much is said about 'yob culture': does it come from a failure to meet these young people's specific needs in their earlier years? Drugs such as Ritalin are given for hyper-activity, but do they help the child in the long run? The need for behavioural therapy is on the increase today, and yet from my experience I know how much can be solved so simply.

Let us seek to understand a child's inner 'mystery kingdom' through sustained observation and flexible thinking, rather than judgement and over- or quick reaction. It will be well worth our while to try to discover in all challenging children what is upsetting them. Those who are really challenging are often particularly interesting. An example: of two children who kept me and subsequent teachers on our toes, one became a fine professional musician and the other a deep-sea diver.

Control or trust?

'How do you find a balance between control and trust?' asked a young mother. I think one may find an element of control in simple things: joy and laughter, a good diet, enough sleep and fresh air, freedom to move and play and to be active. We give positivity and simplicity, along with the 'again-ness' every child craves. Children's trust is developed out of the security of a daily round against the background of tolerant, warm and loving hearts in the home. This will be a potent counterweight to the fear and anger pedalled by the media.

Parents are always questioning themselves, but they also need to trust in themselves to develop confidence and courage. 'How can we trust our children are going to be ok?', asked the same young mother. Can one trust that one's child will be ok? The realistic answer is 'no', as we cannot *know* whether it will be so: we have to have some trust in life itself. If we eliminate all risk from our children's lives, we deny them an essential part of living. Although children under about five need a certain protection, over-'cottonwooling' children generally is doing them a great disservice. The clear and firm guidelines laid down in early childhood will need to be loosened gradually as the child grows up into the teens. I have observed many children growing up into adulthood, and seen their particular characteristics remain as they develop, which is their individuality shining through, even though they can give us great surprises later in going down a quite unexpected path. In view of all this, parents and teachers can only rely on their own common sense and good judgement to trust in a child's own sense for what is safe, sensible and sociable behaviour.

It's early days yet

The little girl who gazed rapturously at the harp player in the town square was uplifted by the beautiful experience. She lived in every extraordinary, wonderful movement and sound: food for the soul. To the little child, growing up from babyhood, each new thing is a mysterious new acquaintance. Little Lars gazed long and wonderingly at the 'giant' man before him in the shop and said loudly, 'Mummy, who *is* that fat man?' By realizing that it is of supreme importance to allow the child time to stand and stare, we leave

Well, I wonder

room for the development of future individual thought and creation. Allowing the child a rich yet simple childhood gives time and space for the spirit to mature. If we adults were to see someone walking upside down in the sky, we would probably be awestruck with fear, yet a little child might find it as interesting as every other new experience and be filled with awe-struck rapture.

'Don't overdo it, it's early days yet', we say if the convalescent patient tries to do too much. After the birth of a child, for mother too it's early days. Baby also needs time to become accustomed to this earthly world, growing, exploring, watching, listening and wondering. Wonder inspires all creativity, all unique, philosophical thought.

What I have written in this book will leave many questions unanswered. 'Who cut the moon in half, Grandma?'—'Well, I wonder.' How good it is for children to live with their questions. How good it is for *us* also to live with ours. Will my book make any difference to our children? Well, I wonder.

Let's let children be children with a true childhood. It's early days yet.

GLOSSARY

Organic/Biodynamic:	Grown without chemical fertilisers, pesticides or herbicides, in harmony with the environment and to protect the welfare of animals.
Practitioner:	Someone who works with young children
Setting:	Any place of care and education for young children

For readers in USA:

Biscuit:	Cookie
Buggy:	Stroller
Conker:	Nut of horse chestnut tree
Dummy:	Pacifier
Fringe:	Bangs
Icing:	Frosting
Jelly:	Jello
Letter box:	Mail box
Morris dancers:	Traditional English dance
Mobile phone:	Cell phone
Nappies:	Diapers
Pants:	Underpants
Ofsted:	(Government) Office For Standards in Education
Rucksack:	Backpack
Stockinette:	Fine knitted material, e.g. as in T-shirts
Supply teacher:	Substitute teacher
Sweets:	Candy
Trousers:	Pants
Water Boatmen:	Water striders

FURTHER READING

There are many books available on the subjects contained in this book. The following are some of those I like. For publishers' websites please see further below.

Wilhelm Zur Linden, *A Child is Born* (Sophia Books, 2004).

Glöckler, M. and Goebel, W., *A Guide to Child Health* (Floris Books, 1990).

Michel Odent, *Birth and Breastfeeding* (Clairview Books, 2003).

Lucinda Neall, *Bringing the Best out in Boys* (Hawthorn Press, 2003).

Karl König, *Brothers and Sisters* (Floris Books, 2000).

Heidi Britz-Crecelius, *Children at Play: Preparation for Life* (Floris Books, 1972).

Frans Carlgren, *Education Towards Freedom* (Lanthorn Press, 1996).

Eric Schlosser, *Fast Food Nation* (Penguin Books, 2002).

Richard Mabey, *Food for Free* (Fontana Collins, 1975).

Lynne Oldfield, *Free to Learn* (Hawthorn Press, 2001).

Wendy E. Cook, *Foodwise* (Clairview Books, 2003).

Martyn Rawson, *Free Your Child's Own True Potential* (Hodder and Stoughton, 2001).

Angus Jenkinson, *From Stress to Serenity* (Sophia Books, 1995).

Russell Evans, *Helping Children to Overcome Fear* (Hawthorn Press, 2000).

Sevak Edward Gulbekian, *In the Belly of the Beast, Holding Your Own in Mass Culture* (Hampton Roads Publishing, 2004).

Gudrun Davy and Bons Voors (eds.), *Lifeways* [A parents' anthology] (Hawthorn Press, 1983).

Michel Odent, *Primal Health* (Clairview Books, 2002).

Aric Sigman, *Remotely Controlled* (Random House, 2005).

Martin Large, *Set Free Childhood* [A parents' survival guide to coping with computers and TV]; (Hawthorn Press, 2003).

Wendy E. Cook, *The Biodynamic Food and Cookbook* (Clairview Books, 2006).

Willi Aeppli, *The Care and Development of the Senses* (Steiner Waldorf Schools Fellowship, 1955).

Neil Postman, *The Disappearance of Childhood* (Vintage Books, 1994).

Rudolf Steiner, *The Education of the Child* (Rudolf Steiner Press, 1995).

Rudolf Steiner, *The Essentials of Education* (Rudolf Steiner Press, 1997).

Rudolf Steiner, *The Foundations of Human Experience* (Anthroposophic Press, 1966).

Sally Jenkinson, *The Genius of Play* (Hawthorn Press, 2001).

Rudolf Steiner, *The Kingdom of Childhood* (Rudolf Steiner Press, 1982).

Thom Hartmann, *The Last Hours of Ancient Sunlight* (Hodder and Stoughton, 1998).

Sally Goddard-Blythe, *The Well Balanced Child* (Hawthorn Press, 2004).

Freya Jaffke, *Work and Play in Early Childhood* (Floris Books, 2000).

About Teenagers:

Betty Staley, *Between Form and Freedom, A Practical Guide to the Teenage Years* (Hawthorn Press, 2004).

Julian Sleigh, *Thirteen to Nineteen, Discovering the Light* (Floris Books, 1998).

Felicitas Vogt, *Addiction's Many Faces* (Hawthorn Press, 2002).

Stories

Picture Books:

Astrid Lindgren, *The Fox and the Tomten* (Floris Books, 1992).

Astrid Lindgren, *The Tomten* (Floris Books, 1975).

Other picture books from Floris Books, Myriad, libraries and bookshops.

Other stories:

Estelle Bryer and Janni Nicol, *Christmas Stories Together* (Hawthorn Press, 2002).

Joseph Jacobs, *English Fairy Tales* (Everyman's Library, 1995).

Grimms Fairy Tales, [complete]; (Routledge and Kegan Paul, 1975). [The illustrations are not for young children, but you can read them without showing the pictures.]

Grimms Fairy Tales, [a large selection]; (Puffin Classic, 1994). [The illustrations are not for young children, but you can read them without showing the pictures.]

Dan Lindholm, *How the Stars were Born* (Henry Goulden, 1975).

Joyce Lancaster Brisley, *Milly Molly Mandy* [and others in the same series], (Kingfisher Books).

Andrew Lang (collection), *The Green Fairy Book* [and other colours], (Dover Publications, and various other publishers).

Isabel Wyatt, *The Seven-Year-Old Wonder Book* (Floris Books, 1975).

On the Meaning of Fairy Tales:

Norbert Glas, *Once upon a Fairy Tale* (Wynstones Press, 1976).

Rudolf Meyer, *The Meaning of Fairy Tales* (Floris Books, 1981).

Bruno Bettelheim, *The Meaning and Importance of Fairy Tales* (Penguin Books, 1991).

Poems, rhymes and songs

Compiled by Eleanor Graham, *A Puffin Book of Verse* (Puffin Books, 1953).

'Spring', 'Summer', 'Autumn', 'Winter', 'Spindrift', 'Gateways': a series of seasonal songs, poems and stories (Wynstones Press, 1978).

The Book of a Thousand Poems (Evans Brothers, 1942).

Wiseman and Northcote, *The Clarendon Books of Singing Games* (Oxford University Press, 1957).

Edited by Iona and Peter Opie, *The Oxford Book of Children's Verse* (Oxford University Press, 1973).

Edited by Iona and Peter Opie, *The Oxford Dictionary of Nursery Rhymes* (Oxford University Press, 1951).

Edited by Iona and Peter Opie, *The Puffin Book of Nursery Rhymes* (Puffin Books, 1963).

A collection of poems compiled by Matthew Barton, *The Winding Road* (Hawthorn Press, 2004).

Compiled by Elizabeth Matterson, *This Little Puffin* (Puffin Books, 1991).

Crafts and festivals

Ann Druitt, Christine Fynes-Clinton, Marije Rowling, *All Year Round* (Hawthorn Press, 1998).

Sue Fitzjohn, Judy Large and Minda Weston, *Celebrating Festivals Together* (a guide to multicultural celebrations) (Hawthorn Press, 1993).

Ruth Marshall, *Celebrating Irish Festivals* (Hawthorn Press, 2003).

Estelle Bryer and Janni Nicol, *Christmas Together* (Hawthorn Press, 2001).

Thomas and Petra Berger, *Crafts through the Year* (Floris Books, 2000).

Diana Carey and Judy Large, *Families, Festivals and Food* (Hawthorn Press, 1982).

Petra Berger, *Feltcraft* (Floris Books, 1994).

Angelika Wolk-Gerche, *Making Fairy-tale Wool Animals* (Wynstones Press, 2000).

Christel Dhom, *Making Magical Fairy-tale Puppets* (Wynstones Press, 2001).

Maricristin Sealey, *Making Waldorf Dolls* (Hawthorn Press, 2001).

Ann Druitt, Christine Fynes-Clinton, Marije Rowling, *The Birthday Book* (Hawthorn Press, 2004).

Stephanie Cooper, Christine Fynes-Clinton, Marije Rowling, *The Children's Year* (Hawthorn Press, 1986).

Thomas Berger, *The Christmas Craft Book* (Floris Books, 1990).

Thomas Berger, *The Easter Craft Book* (Floris Books, 1993).

Noorah Al-Gailani and Chris Smith, *The Islamic Year* (Hawthorn Press, 2003).

Freya Jaffke, *Toy Making with Children* (Floris Books, 1998).

Various books on crafts: George Weil and Sons Ltd. and Myriad

Publishers

Clairview Books: www.clairviewbooks.com
Evans Brothers: www.evansbrothers.co.uk
Floris Books: www.florisbooks.co.uk
Hawthorn Press: www.hawthornpress.com
Hampton Roads Publishing: www.hrpub.com
On Line Waldorf Library (OWL): www.waldorflibrary.org
Penguin Books: www.penguin.com
Puffin Books: www.puffin.co.uk
Rudolf Steiner Press and Sophia Books: www.rudolfsteinerpress.com
Steiner Waldorf Schools Fellowship Publications: www.steinerwaldorf.org.uk
Wynstones Press: www.wynstonespress.com

And of course bookshops and libraries!

RESOURCES

Art and craft materials, various

George Weil and Sons Ltd; www.fibrecrafts.com
Mercurius; www.art-makes-sense.com
Muladula; www.muladula.com
Myriad; www.myriadonline.co.uk
Texere Yarns; www.texere.co.uk

Beeswax crayons

Mercurius
Myriad

Children's lyres

Mercurius
Myriad

Children's Clothing, Nappies and Bedding

Apart from various shops:
BORN: organic and fair trade cotton nappies; prams; www.borndirect.com
Fogarty Ltd.: wool duvets; www.fogarty.co.uk
Greenfibres: organic/bio-dynamic cotton/wool clothes, nappies, woollen nappy
    overpants, bedding; natural babies' cosmetics; www. greenfibres.com
Muladula, also for organic cotton nappies, woollen nappy overpants, woollen socks
    and felt slippers
Natural Clothing Ltd.: organic clothing, bedding and nappies;
    www.naturalclothing.co.uk

Natural Collection: organic cotton nappies; www.naturalcollection.com
Patra: silk underclothing for babies and children, silk and cotton bedding;
    www.patra.com
Raindrops: children's outdoor clothing; www.raindrops.co.uk
Smilechild; www.smilechild.co.uk, for felt slippers and hip sling seat
The Baby Gift Place: organic nappies and children's clothing;
    www.thebabygiftplace.co.uk
TOGZ: children's outdoor clothing; www.togz.uk.com

Dye

Natural dyes: books are available from craft and bookshops
Chemical: from hardware stores and craft shops; cherry red, gold and royal blue are
    particularly suitable for young children; they also mix well to make other beautiful
    colours.

Fabrics

Whaleys (Bradford) Ltd; www.whaleys-bradford.ltd.uk, plain cotton, silk and
    muslin, white and coloured
Myriad: (dyed silk and muslin)
Thai Silks; www.thaisilks.com

Fruit presses and crushers

Vigo Limited.; www.vigoltd.com

Grain mills and grinders

Hehlis Holistics; www.hehlis-holistics.com

Natural, organic health products and toiletries

Muladula
Weleda U.K. Ltd; www.weleda.co.uk
Spiezia; www.spieziaorganics.co.uk

Natural paints for house decoration

Auro; www.auro.co.uk
Ecos organic paints; www.ecos.me.uk
Ieko; www.ieko.co.uk

Sheepswool and woollen yarn

Garthenor Organic Pure Wool; www.organicpurewool.co.uk
Local sheep farmers
Mercurius
Myriad
Texere Yarns
Wingham Wool Work; www.winghamwoolwork.co.uk

Toys

Bramblecorner.com for 'household' toys e.g. brooms, seeds, doll's prams and cots

Water-colour paints and large brushes

Art and Craft Shops
Mercurius
Myriad

Water-colour paper

Art and Craft Shops
Mercurius
Saunders Waterford Series
Stationers

Film on Video

Time to Learn, produced by Jonathan Steddall, 110 minutes; 1992; available from the Steiner Waldorf Schools Fellowship in PAL or VHS. A survey of Steiner Waldorf Education, in which my kindergarten also plays a part.

Other useful websites for further information

A few relate solely to Britain but most have international links.

Alliance for Childhood: an international forum working to fight poverty and neglect, promote better health, strengthen family life, protect children from commercial pressure and counter children's dependence on electronic media; www.allianceforchildhood.org

Bio-Dynamic Agricultural Association; www.biodynamic.org.uk

County Wildlife Trusts: (for interest, walks and adventures); www.wildlifetrusts.org.uk. Each county has its own trust and website; see main website for further information.

Disabled Children: Advice and Information for Families with Children with Special Needs; www.cafamily.org.uk/helpline.html

Forest Stewardship Council (for sustainably resourced wood, also furniture); www.fsc-uk.info

Friends of the Earth (for supporting the future); www.foe.co.uk

Mailing Preference Service (for stopping unwanted junk mail); www.mpsonline.org.uk

National Trust (for interest, walks and adventures); www.nationaltrust.org.uk

Pipedown International: 'formed to counter one of the under-recognized scourges of contemporary life, piped music . . . muzak/ acoustic wallpaper'; www.pipe-down. info

RSPB: Royal Society for the Protection of Birds (for interest, walks and adventures); www.rspb.org.uk

Soil Association (for healthy soil and food); www.soilassociation.org

Steiner Waldorf Schools Fellowship; www.steinerwaldorf.org

Steiner Waldorf Teacher Training; www.steiner-teacher.org

Sustain: The Alliance for better Food and Farming; wwwsustainweb.org

Telephone Preference Service (for stopping unwanted sales calls); www.tpsonline.org.uk

The Children's Food Bill: this seeks to protect children from unhealthy food marketing; www.childrensfoodbill.org.uk

INDEX

Songs and Poetry	Source	Page
A master I have	*Oxford Dictionary of Nursery Rhymes*	74
Anna Maria	*Puffin Book of Nursery Rhymes*	79
Babies' shoes	source unknown	37
Everyone who's ready	by the author	198
Exercises	source unknown	206
Father and mother and Uncle John	*Puffin Book of Nursery Rhymes*	79
Five little peas	*This Little Puffin*	77
Here we go round the mulberry bush	*The Clarendon Book of Singing Games, Book 1*	181
I know a little man	source unknown	10
In a tiny little house	source unknown	78
I sent a letter to my love	*The Clarendon Book of Singing Games, Book 2*	80
Make a world of wondrous colours	by the author	132
Roly poly, ever so slowly	*This Little Puffin*	206
Round and round	by the author	77
Sing a song of washing up	Elizabeth Gould; *The Book of a Thousand Poems*	120
The lightning and thunder	George McDonald; *On the Back of the North Wind*	51
The moon on the one hand	Hilaire Belloc; *Book of a Thousand Poems*	161
To market	*Puffin Book of Nursery Rhymes*	79
Tommy Thumb	*Puffin Book of Nursery Rhymes*	206
Turn the tap on	by the author	145
Twas on a Monday morning	source unknown	123
We are woodmen	*This Little Puffin*	126
Yesterday upon the stair	source unknown	10